ADVANCE PRAISE FOR *THE MODERN WEB*

"This is a useful book, and it's an important book. If you follow Peter Gasston's advice, then test your sites across all browsers and on a variety of devices, you'll impress your bosses and please your users. You'll also be making the Web better and keeping it open."
—BRUCE LAWSON, AUTHOR OF *INTRODUCING HTML5*

"Peter Gasston has now done for the modern web platform what he already did for CSS: write a consult-it-first compendium of information for web developers of practically any skill level."
—STEPHEN HAY, AUTHOR OF *RESPONSIVE DESIGN WORKFLOW*

"Peter Gasston strikes a great balance between producing fantastic real-world code and staying right on top of the latest developments in web technology. He has a considerable gift for explaining difficult technical topics in a lucid and entertaining manner."
—CHRIS MILLS, DEVELOPER RELATIONS MANAGER, OPERA SOFTWARE AND AUTHOR OF *PRACTICAL CSS3*

PRAISE FOR PETER GASSTON'S *THE BOOK OF CSS3*

"I can honestly say I will never need another book on this subject, and I doubt anyone else will either. *The Book of CSS3* covers it all and covers it well."
—DEVON YOUNG, CSS3.INFO

"One of the best technology books I've read."
—CRAIG BUCKLER, OPTIMALWORKS WEB DESIGN

"This book deserves a place within easy reach of the developer's keyboard and is a must have for anyone looking to join the visual revolution that CSS3 is bringing to the Web."
—C.W. GROTOPHORST, CHOICE MAGAZINE

"There are a lot of neat things that you can do in CSS3, and this book is a great introduction to these features."
—STEVEN MANDEL, .NET DEVELOPER'S JOURNAL

"An easy-to-read, easy-to-implement handbook of the newest additions to the Cascading Style Sheet specification."
—MIKE RILEY, DR. DOBB'S JOURNAL

THE MODERN WEB

Multi-Device Web Development with HTML5, CSS3, and JavaScript

by Peter Gasston

no starch
press

San Francisco

THE MODERN WEB. Copyright © 2013 by Peter Gasston.

Printed in USA

First printing

17 16 15 14 13   1 2 3 4 5 6 7 8 9

ISBN-10: 1-59327-487-4
ISBN-13: 978-1-59327-487-0

Publisher: William Pollock
Production Editor: Serena Yang
Cover Ilustration: Charlie Wylie
Developmental Editors: Keith Fancher and William Pollock
Technical Reviewer: David Storey
Copyeditor: LeeAnn Pickrell
Compositor: Susan Glinert Stevens
Proofreader: Ward Webber
Indexer: Nancy Guenther

For information on book distributors or translations, please contact No Starch Press, Inc. directly:

No Starch Press, Inc.
38 Ringold Street, San Francisco, CA 94103
phone: 415.863.9900; fax: 415.863.9950; info@nostarch.com; www.nostarch.com

Library of Congress Cataloging-in-Publication Data
A catalog record of this book is available from the Library of Congress.

For Dave, Jim, Morena, Nick, Rupert, Steve,
and all of the other organizers of the
London Web Standards group, who help to
keep the London scene active and gave me
my first opportunity in public speaking.

About the Author

Peter Gasston has been a web developer for over 12 years in both agency and corporate settings. He was one of the original contributors to CSS3.info, the leading online destination for CSS3. Gasston is the author of *The Book of CSS3* (No Starch Press) and has been published in *Smashing Magazine*, *A List Apart*, and *.net magazine*. He gives talks about technologies at developer conferences and runs the web development blog *Broken Links* (*http://broken-links.com/*). Gasston lives in London, England.

About the Technical Reviewer

David Storey is an HTML5 evangelist at Plain Concepts, a founding member of the IE userAgents program, and a CSS Working Group member. Prior to this, he was the developer advocate manager on a top-secret skunk works project at Motorola. He also founded the developer relations team at Opera, product managed Opera Dragonfly, and worked at CERN, home of the World Wide Web. His passion is keeping the Web open for all.

BRIEF CONTENTS

CONTENTS IN DETAIL

3
DEVICE-RESPONSIVE CSS 39

4
NEW APPROACHES TO CSS LAYOUTS 65

5
MODERN JAVASCRIPT
89

6
DEVICE APIS
107

7
IMAGES AND GRAPHICS
125

8
NEW FORMS   141

9
MULTIMEDIA   161

10
WEB APPS
177

11
THE FUTURE
191

A
BROWSER SUPPORT AS OF MARCH 2013
211

B
FURTHER READING   217

INDEX   227

ACKNOWLEDGMENTS

Huge thanks are due to David Storey, the technical reviewer for this book; his deep knowledge of the field meant his feedback was invaluable to me. Although he corrected and guided me many times, if there are any errors in this book they're entirely my responsibility.

Keith Fancher, Serena Yang, Bill Pollock, and the rest of the No Starch Press team provided fantastic support and guidance throughout the writing of this book. Their collective contribution is beyond measure.

Dimitri Glazkov helpfully answered a few questions on web components, and Bruce Lawson gave extra feedback on the new HTML5 elements in Chapter 2. His work as well as that of his fellow HTML5 Doctors was a constant reference during the writing of this book.

Although I've never met him, I'd like to thank David Walsh for maintaining an excellent website that I have used a lot.

Stephen Hay and Chris Mills have been generally useful in helping me to consolidate ideas, as well as incredibly nice people to know.

Great thanks to my friends and occasional colleagues Giles McCartney, Richard Locke, and Tom Shirley. Thanks also to all my other colleagues at Preloaded, Poke, Top10, Believe.in, and rehabstudio.

As always the biggest thanks must go to my wife, Ana, for her patience and support during the time I spent writing this book.

INTRODUCTION

We are in a time of unprecedented innovation on the Web. Not too long ago, one company, Microsoft, dominated the web landscape; in 2003, Internet Explorer was used on some 95 percent of computers worldwide. This domination brought the advantage of a stable market for developers, but there was also a serious drawback: Microsoft chose to end nonessential work on IE, and innovation on the Web stagnated—a consequence of a lack of competition and a closed environment.

Things could not be more different now. There are some four or five key browser vendors, about the same number of major operating systems, and more parties are getting involved all the time. Adobe has switched its focus from Flash and apps to the open web, and technology companies like Samsung and Nintendo are joining key players such as Google, Apple, and Microsoft in shaping the future of the Web and the way we build for it.

And the way we access the Web has changed enormously too—think devices. No longer are we limited to browsing the Web with a desktop or laptop. So many categories of devices exist now—including smartphones, tablets, and games consoles—that I'm running out of fingers to count them on.

This book is about front-end web development in this new web-everywhere era. It's about learning methods to make first-class websites, apps, or anything built on open web technologies, with the multi-device world aforethought. This is not a book about how to make mobile websites or smart TV apps; it's about learning the latest developments in current and near-future web technologies so you'll be better able to build sites capable of offering the best experience everywhere.

I'll return to what you'll learn from this book in more detail at the end of the introduction, but first I want to talk about the bewildering array of today's web-enabled devices.

The Device Landscape

The year 2008 was a landmark year and not only because of the theatrical release of *Indiana Jones and the Kingdom of the Crystal Skull*, which introduced the phrase "nuking the fridge" into our vernacular. This was the year that saw the number of Internet-connected devices exceed the number of people using them. This super-connectivity between devices is commonly known as the *Internet of Things (IoT)*, and this book is aimed at an already substantial and fast-growing subset of those things, namely things with web browsers.

The range of web-enabled devices is enormous and getting broader by the day. As I write this, I'm the owner of the following devices that have a web browser: a desktop, a laptop, a tablet, a smartphone, an ebook reader, and a games console. I suspect that's not an uncommon scenario to more affluent members of society; many people could add a smart TV and a portable games console to that list.

Of course, with this incredible range of web-enabled devices comes incredible opportunity for web developers, and this book is here to help you make the most of that. But first, let's look at some of the core device categories and define some key terms so you'll better understand what you're dealing with.

Desktop/Laptop

The Web as we've known it until recently has primarily targeted the larger screens and more powerful processors of desktop or laptop computers (shorthand: desktops), where the operator is usually seated and using a fast Ethernet or Wi-Fi broadband connection. This mode is still the default for people at work in offices, so many *business-to-business (B2B)* sites are built to suit this configuration.

But desktop computer use is on the wane as many people nowadays, especially home users, tend toward mobile or tablet devices (which I'll come to shortly). In the last quarter of 2012, global PC shipments were down almost 5 percent from the previous year. That said, research shows that people still tend to use desktops when performing tasks that involve significant amounts of text, multitasking across different tabs of a browser, or using programs that require close control of the content, such as image editing. Desktops are also used when security is a major concern, such as for Internet banking.

But even within this venerable and mostly stable group variation abounds. The 1024×768 screen resolution is slowly dying away but still prominent, while newer versions of Apple's MacBook Pro sport a resolution of 2880×1800. Sites optimized for the former will look quite small and be somewhat lost on the latter.

The desktop browser world includes five major players: Chrome, Safari, and Opera, which share the WebKit engine (Opera had its own engine, Presto, which is now being phased out); Firefox; and Internet Explorer (version 9 can be considered semimodern and 10 fully modern). Thankfully they all tend to implement features in a standard way, and they all have a frequent or semifrequent update cycle (or are moving toward it), so users tend to get new features fairly quickly. Of course, a sizable percentage of users are still running older, less capable browsers, so you should always build with that in mind. (Much of the innovation in web standards comes to desktop browsers first because they're the ones that developers tend to use on a daily basis. Therefore much of this book is written with desktop browsers in mind, although what you'll learn can be applied anywhere.)

Mobile

When I say *mobile*, I generally mean phones. The range is wide: from older, cheaper hardware running rudimentary web browsers to mid-range feature phones with browsers optimized for speed over power to high-powered expensive smartphones with browsers on par with those on your main computer, as well as a series of apps that often use an embedded browser to view content.

In many countries, a majority of Internet users are on a mobile device; in India, for example, some 55 percent of web visits are made on mobile devices, and in Egypt nearly 70 percent of people rely on phones as their sole access to the Web. Worldwide estimates are that the number of mobile web users will exceed that of desktop computer users sometime between 2014 and 2015.

Across the developing world, the dominant mobile device is the *feature phone*, which has functions beyond basic phoning and texting but often lacks full web access. The rise of low-cost and secondhand smartphone sales, however, is already changing that market drastically. Within the next few years, we can expect to see smartphones dominate the mobile landscape. In 2011, smartphone sales were estimated to account for 27 percent of the global market; at the end of 2012, estimates were that 1 billion smartphones were in use, with that number predicted to double by 2015.

The sheer variety of mobiles and mobile browsers in the global market means that I'm selective about the coverage in this book, so for future-proofing I target phones with fully capable web browsers, that is, features on par with their desktop equivalents.

The WebKit engine dominates the smartphone browser market because it's used on iPhone, Android, Blackberry, and more, powering many different browsers. Each OS uses a slightly different version of WebKit, but general interoperability is good.

Windows Phone OS from version 7.5 and up uses a mostly desktop-equivalent Internet Explorer as its browser; older models have IE9, and more recent models, IE10. Firefox is also available as an option for Android, and Firefox OS, a full operating system based around the browser, is set to launch in 2013. That launch may well impact the market in the long term.

Opera has a significant share in the global mobile browser market thanks to Opera Mini, a proxy browser that compresses requested pages and returns the data as a kind of image with very limited interactivity. Opera Mini is lightweight and fast, which makes it popular in countries with limited Internet connectivity, but its lack of full interactivity means I won't give it much attention. As I write this, Opera has announced that it'll be releasing new mobile browsers based on WebKit, although no details are available.

Today's smartphones, although getting more powerful all the time, tend to have less available memory and storage, and lower potential connection speeds, than desktop or laptop computers. On the surface, this would seem to make them the poor cousin of web-enabled devices, but as Jonathan Stark says in "The 10 Principles of Mobile Interface Design":

> Smartphones are actually more powerful than desktops in many ways. They are highly personal, always on, always with us, usually connected, and directly addressable. Plus, they are crawling with powerful sensors that can detect location, movement, acceleration, orientation, proximity, environmental conditions, and more.

Obviously the advantage of mobile is just that: its mobility—the ability to find things around you, get directions, and look up information fast when out of the house or office. But increasingly, mobile devices are being used at home while watching TV or on the morning commute or when bored standing in line. Mobile is really less about being on the move and more about always being available.

The mobile space is changing faster than any sector of the market, as many users change devices on 12- to 18-month update cycles and hundreds (if not thousands) of new models are introduced every year.

Tablet

Tablet computers have been around for years, but it wasn't until Apple came along with the iPad in 2010 that they became more of a leisure item than a desktop accessory. Many other devices have followed the iPad, with Android-based tablets doing especially well in the mid-sized 7" range and Microsoft pushing forward with the heavily tablet-focused Windows 8. From a market that was negligible at best in 2009, estimates are some 390 million tablets will be in use worldwide by 2015. That's an incredible figure, and the growth is exponential.

Their larger size and reliance on Wi-Fi (in many cases) makes tablets portable rather than truly mobile; they exist in a space more akin to a laptop than a mobile device. Most people use them at home, and although they are carried around, they're usually taken out and used only when the user is stationary, rather than walking down the street. That said, it's not uncommon to see them used as somewhat awkward and ungainly cameras in public places!

Like smartphones, tablets are tactile, relying on touch input in most cases (although some also accept stylus input). Research shows they tend to be used for entertainment and browsing when time is less of an issue. The core browsers on tablets are essentially the same as those on mobile devices.

TV

The TV is still the most-used screen in the home, though mostly for passive viewing rather than interactivity. That's changing as the new breed of web (or smart) TVs and media boxes begin to get a foot in the door. Although global figures are hard to come by, predictions are that there will be 100 million web-enabled TVs in Europe and North America by 2016.

Although many web TVs use applications rather than websites, they're often built using web technologies and sometimes contain an embedded browser view. After all, if you're making a Twitter app, you want your users to be able to open links.

The biggest drawback with web TV is that navigating with a TV remote is a horrible experience, made worse by some of the multibutton monstrosities that have been built to provide the level of interactivity required for Internet use—notably, a keyboard. Some manufacturers are making gesture- and voice-controlled TVs or remote controls that incorporate a trackpad, but the best solution seems to be to pair a mobile or tablet with the TV and use that as an interactive control.

Another obstacle to web browsing on the TV is that the television is inherently a communal device, viewed by many people at the same time—an experience that is fundamentally opposite to the personal Internet experience. Would you like to have your Facebook account broadcast on a big screen for everyone to see? Probably not.

The emerging common behavior is for web TVs to be used for video and interactive services, with a real-time social aspect happening concurrently on the user's mobile or tablet. Recent research shows that 77 percent of people use another screen while watching (if that's the right word) TV, and of that figure, only 5 percent or so are performing an activity that's relevant or complementary to what's on screen.

The Others

These four broad categories—desktop/laptop, mobile, tablet, and TV—cover the majority of the web-enabled device market, but they're by no means exclusive. Many other devices have web browsers, even if they aren't always used with great frequency.

Each of the current generation of home games consoles has a browser: The PlayStation 3 uses the WebKit-based NetFront, Microsoft's Xbox 360 has Internet Explorer 9, and Nintendo's Wii U has a custom build of WebKit. Likewise, portable games consoles have browsers: The PlayStation Vita uses NetFront, as do newer versions of the Nintendo 3DS (older versions use Opera). Bear in mind that each uses a slightly different control system. (For more on the topic, see Anna Debenham's amazing work in the field as listed in "Further Reading" on page 10.)

And let's not forget ebook readers, such as Amazon's Kindle, the Kobo, Barnes & Noble's Nook, and a series from Sony. (When I use the term *ebook readers*, I'm referring specifically to "e-ink" readers, as each company also has a full-color screen version that is more like a tablet.) The ebook browsers tend to be WebKit based, and their challenges come from low-powered processors, little memory, and very slow refresh rates. They wouldn't be the first-choice browser of many, but as ebooks become more interactive, they may become more popular.

The In Betweeners

The iPhone 4 has a screen size of 3.5" diagonally, and the iPhone 5, 4". Samsung's Galaxy S III has a diagonal length of 4.8"; LG's Optimus Vu, 5"; and Samsung's Galaxy Note II, 5.5". Google's Nexus 7 is 7" diagonally, and Amazon's Kindle Fire HD comes in 7" and 8.9" formats. The iPad mini is 7.9" diagonally and the iPad, 9.7".

In other words, the great variety of screen sizes makes the distinction between mobile and tablet quite hard to pin down. The only criteria I can think of to separate them are based on whether they have native telecom ability, can fit comfortably in a pocket, and can be used comfortably with one or two hands.

In fact, computing is experiencing a general convergence. Microsoft's Surface is a tablet with an optional keyboard in the cover. When keyboard and tablet are attached, the Surface looks and behaves like a laptop. The Ubuntu Phone runs Android, except that when you dock it to a screen, it runs a full version of the Linux desktop. The PadFone by Asus is a phone that turns into a tablet when docked with a larger touchscreen. Your TV becomes a media center when you plug Apple TV or Roku into it.

This change is set to outdate all of our existing terminology. In the foreseeable future, the word *tablet* will be as meaningful as the floppy disk icon currently used to mean *save* in many software applications. One day, everything will be screens.

The Multi-screen World

The idea of a user being a "mobile user" or "tablet user" is somewhat misguided because people are much more likely to use many devices, often at the same time. Research conducted for Google in 2012 indicated that 81 percent of participants used their smartphone while watching TV, and 66 percent had it available while using a desktop. This use of multiple devices concurrently is known as *simultaneous screening*.

Meanwhile, 90 percent of participants started a task on one device and finished it on another; for example, they browsed shopping websites on a smartphone and then moved to a laptop at the time of purchase. This movement between consecutive devices depending on the task being performed is labeled *subsequent screening*.

In other words, visitors to your website will visit from two or three different devices, and although they'll have slightly different aims each time, they'll still want access to the same information.

Context: What We Don't Know

The most important thing to bear in mind is how much we don't know about the people using our sites. We don't know where they are—I don't mean geographically, as we can use GPS to locate them. I mean whether they're at home, at work, on the bus, and so on. In essence, we have no idea of the context in which someone is using our site.

The common presumption is that people using mobile are on the move and in a hurry, often using low-bandwidth 3G connections, but that's not always the case: Mobile is often used at home with a good fast Wi-Fi connection. But even the connection doesn't tell the whole story; the signal may be poor or the bandwidth reduced because of congestion in the neighborhood. In fact, the 3G (or 4G in many countries) networks might actually provide a much better connection in many cases.

We also presume that mobiles are less powerful than desktops, but even that may not be true for much longer. Twin- or even quad-core phones with fast processors are making their way to the market, and within a year or two, who knows how much power they'll have. And tablet/laptop hybrids like many Windows 8 devices are now more capable than laptops just a few years old.

There's also the issue of size. The presumption is that for a large-screen device like a TV, viewers want a richer graphical environment, but a large screen doesn't equal a powerful processor or a fast connection. Many web-enabled TVs have processors no more powerful than a smartphone, and the connection speed is open to the same vagaries as any other device. And with size comes the question of portability. The more portable the device, the less certain we can be of the context in which it's being used.

Really, the cardinal rule is this: We cannot make presumptions. And having said that, I'm going to break my own rule.

Some Context Stereotypes

To avoid repetition in this book, I rely on a few shorthand contexts based on common scenarios. These won't necessarily be the *most* common scenarios, but ones that I think are common enough to serve a useful purpose. One example: Mobile users don't have a super-fast Internet connection. Often mobile users are using their devices from home with a mega-fast fiber-optic connection broadcast over clear Wi-Fi from 2 feet away, but the opposite is often just as true: They're away from home and relying on a very weak 3G signal (as happens to me too often). Many smartphones are built with scenarios like this in mind; they limit the number of connections that can be made at any time in order to not gobble precious data from the user's limited tariff.

Likewise, a user with a desktop computer will likely have a direct broadband connection, providing fast data transfer rates. That's not always true, of course—many people in rural areas have extremely low broadband speeds or still use dial-up—but the first scenario is common enough that I can use it as a shorthand.

I use shorthands like these throughout the book simply to avoid constant clarification and repetition, but I can't drum home enough the idea that these presumptions can't, and shouldn't, be foremost in your mind when building and planning websites or applications.

"Fast" Is the Only Context That Matters

You have a challenge. You don't know who your users are, where they are, what they are doing, or which device they are doing it with. You can find out some (although not all) of that information, but their full context is completely unknowable and varies for each individual. The only thing you can reasonably know for certain is that either they want access to what you're offering or they want to find out it's not what they want. Either way, they want the answer quickly.

Performance is the only criterion that matters. Whether users are on a smartphone during rush hour and looking for information about the next train home or browsing through a shopping site while curled up on the sofa at home, they have a task that they want to complete as soon as possible, and completing this task using the nearest device will make them feel more efficient (this is known as *found time*).

Your site needs to be fast—and feel fast—regardless of the device it's being displayed on. And fast means not only technical performance (which is incredibly important) but also the responsiveness of the interface and how easily users can navigate the site and find what they need to complete the task that brought them to you in the first place.

What You'll Learn

I'll be up-front and start by telling you what I won't be teaching in this book: designing to the strengths of each platform. I can't do that because I can't teach what I don't know. I became a developer rather than a designer for a reason, and that's because when I use Photoshop, the result looks as if I were using the mouse while wearing boxing gloves.

What I will teach is modern coding methods and techniques that you can use to build websites that work across multiple devices or that are tailored to the single device class you're targeting. (The technologies themselves are all explained in Chapter 1, so I won't go into detail here.)

As you read this book, keep in mind these two very important points:

- The pool of technologies is so vast that I can't cover it all. I'll teach you what I consider to be the core techniques and technologies that you need to know to build web projects across the range of devices.

- Not everything in this book will end up having widespread adoption—at least not in the form I show in this book. The Web is constantly evolving, and book publishing means taking just a single snapshot of a moment. Some things will change; some will wither and be removed. I've tried to mitigate this by covering only technologies that are based on open standards rather than vendor-specific ones and that already have some level of implementation in browsers.

As a web developer, you should do this: Stay informed. Keep up-to-date with the developments in web standards, be curious, be playful, keep on top of it all. You're lucky enough to work in an industry based on sharing knowledge, so follow some of the people and websites I mention in this book, find your own sources, get on Twitter, go to local web development community meetups. Stay involved and be active. There's never been a more exciting time to work in web development, but you'll need to put in an extra shift to really take advantage of it.

Above all, think of what you build in the greater scheme of things. If you're building a website, don't think of "building a site for web *and* mobile," think of building a site that works everywhere. Think of how people will use it, what they'll want from it, and what you as a developer can do to aid them in achieving their goals—not just now but in the future. We've seen such a major transformation of the Web in the past five years—who can say where it will be another five years from now.

Further Reading

Statistics used in this chapter were taken from many sources, notably Vision Mobile's "The Mobile Industry in Numbers" at *http://www.visionmobile.com/blog/2012/10/infographic-the-mobile-industry-in-numbers/* and Cisco's "The Internet of Things" at *http://blogs.cisco.com/news/the-internet-of-things-infographic/*.

You can find a good primer on the IoT in The Next Web's article "Why 2013 Will Be the Year of the Internet of Things": *http://thenextweb.com/insider/2012/12/09/the-future-of-the-internet-of-things/*.

David Storey wrote a great post about the non-smartphone mobile web, "See your site like the rest of the world does. On the Nokia X2-01," at *http://generatedcontent.org/post/31441135779/mobileweb-row/*.

The best article I've read on designing for mobile devices, and from which I quote in this chapter, is Jonathan Stark's "The 10 Principles of Mobile Interface Design": *http://www.netmagazine.com/features/10-principles-mobile-interface-design/*. Jason Grigsby's excellent article "Responsive Design for Apps" is a good primer for designing for multiple screen dimensions and capabilities: *http://blog.cloudfour.com/responsive-design-for-apps-part-1/*.

UX Magazine's article by Brennen Brown, "Five Lessons from a Year of Tablet UX Research," has some great findings on how people use tablets: *http://uxmag.com/articles/five-lessons-from-a-year-of-tablet-ux-research/*.

A good starting point for Anna Debenham's research on games console browsers is an *A List Apart* article "Testing Websites in Game Console Browsers": *http://www.alistapart.com/articles/testing-websites-in-game-console-browsers/*.

Jason Grigsby (again) gave an excellent talk, "The Immobile Web," on developing for TV. The video is at *http://vimeo.com/44444464/*, and the accompanying slides are at *http://www.slideshare.net/grigs/the-immobile-web/*.

For the full research on multi-device usage, see Google's blog post "Navigating the New Multi-screen World" at *http://googlemobileads.blogspot.co.uk/2012/08/navigating-new-multi-screen-world.html*.

Making your websites Future Friendly is always good: See *http://futurefriend.ly/*.

1

THE WEB PLATFORM

In this chapter, I'm going to talk about the web technologies that you'll learn in this book, the knowledge you'll need to get the most from reading it, and the demands and requirements of working on the multi-device Web. This chapter is about making sure we're on the same page, figuratively speaking—I know we're literally on the same page because you're reading this now—before we get into the really technical things in the next chapters.

If you're keen to get on with the learning you're probably considering skipping straight to Chapter 2, but I urge you not to as Chapter 1 contains some quite interesting and useful background information, and the less technical subject matter allows me to show off the best examples of my wonderful sense of humor.

A Quick Note About Terminology

Throughout the book, I refer quite often to building websites or sites, but this terminology is just convenient shorthand to avoid repetition. The features you'll learn from this book are relevant to websites, web applications, packaged HTML hybrid applications—in short, anything that can use HTML, CSS, and JavaScript. But that's a mouthful, so I mostly just say "websites," except when I need to be more specific.

I also use "browsers" and "user agents" interchangeably when what I mean is any instance of software that renders web pages or applications. Again, I'm just trying to avoid repetition. Once more, I'm trying to avoid repetition.

Who You Are and What You Need to Know

Before I begin, I'll explain some of the presumptions I'm making about you and tell you what you need to know to get the most out of this book. First, let's talk about you. Whether you're a professional, you'd like to be, or you're just someone who enjoys playing around with the Web, you have a working knowledge of HTML, CSS, and JavaScript—not to any deep, intimate level, but enough that you don't need me to teach you what they are or how to write them.

Perhaps you learned to build websites a while ago and need to bring your skills up to date; maybe you're learning web development at school and want extra lessons; or perhaps you're a working developer but don't get the opportunity to keep up with developments in coding for the Web. Whether any of those descriptions fit, I assume you want to get involved in building websites in a modern way, which work across multiple devices and are sympathetic to the dimensions and capabilities of each device—that's doubtless why you picked up a book with this title.

This book builds on your knowledge of web development. It's not a beginner's guide, but it's not an advanced book either. Rather, this book is a snapshot of current, new, and near-future features in HTML, CSS, JavaScript, and related technologies, with a bias toward those that are best for building sites in the multi-device world.

As well as that basic knowledge, you need to know your way around the developer tools in your browser, although not in any power-user kind of way. In some of the JavaScript examples, I log results into a tool's developer console; this is a standardized method of working and is the same if you use the native tools in Chrome, Firefox, IE9+, Opera, Safari, or third-party tools like Firebug. I might, for example, use a line of code like this:

```
console.log('Hello World');
```

And the result will be shown in the console; Figure 1-1 shows how this is displayed in Firebug. As I said, I won't use the console or developer tools much, but if you don't know how to use them, you should really take the time to learn now.

```
console.log('Hello World!');
Hello World!
```

Figure 1-1: A Hello World message logged in the console in Firebug

If you're still reading this, either you have all the knowledge required to proceed, or you're getting ready to try to bluff your way through. Regardless, let's move on to talk about technology.

Getting Our Terms Straight

There's some confusion over what HTML5 actually is. There's what the general public (and, for many of us, our clients) believe, and what it actually is. HTML5 is not a brand new platform that we use to build websites; it's not a rich multimedia environment; it's not a thing you enable to make your websites work across multiple devices. HTML5 is basically an attempt to evolve the Web to meet the demands of the way we use it today, which has mutated dramatically from its earliest iteration as a simple network of linked documents.

To the public at large, HTML5 has become a shorthand term for a series of related and complementary technologies, including CSS3, SVG, JavaScript APIs, and more. Although some developers are happy to use this broader meaning, I don't really like this conflation of all the technologies, so I'm happier with calling HTML5 the *web platform*. I actually prefer Bruce Lawson's proposed term, *New Exciting Web Technologies (NEWT)*, which is both a cool acronym and has a cute logo, but I have to admit that I've lost this battle, so the web platform it is.

The web platform is vast. To see how vast, take a look at *http://platform.html5.org/*, which lists all of the technologies that are considered part of the platform; the list is really quite impressively long and contains far more than I could ever hope to cover in one book.

Instead, I'll concentrate on the core, the technologies I feel are sufficient and useful for authoring websites that work across multiple devices: HTML5, CSS3, SVG, Canvas, and some device APIs. I'll explain each of these as I get to them throughout the course of the book, but first I want to clarify in more detail what is meant by HTML5 and CSS3.

The Real HTML5

HTML5 is an iteration of HTML4.01 with some new features, a few deprecated or removed features, and some modified behaviors of existing features. Its aim is to standardize the many common hacks and design patterns that developers have used throughout the years and to expand in order to meet the demands of the modern Web, which is as much (if not more) about applications as it is about documents; indeed, the original proposal for what became HTML5 was called Web Applications 1.0.

New features in HTML5 include ways to structure documents for providing meaning and accessibility; I cover this in Chapter 2. HTML5 also has a whole range of new form functionality and UI controls that make it easier to build applications, which we'll look at in Chapter 8. And HTML5 includes what many people still associate with it—native (without plug-ins) video, which is covered in Chapter 9.

Two main groups are working on HTML5, and their roles and responsibilities are broadly this: The WHATWG (you don't need to know what that acronym means), a consortium of browser makers and "interested parties," through the main spec editor Ian Hickson, creates a "living spec" of HTML— basically a versionless specification that constantly incorporates new features and updates existing ones; and the W3C (World Wide Web Consortium), the Web's standards body, takes snapshots of this spec to create numbered versions, ensuring compatibility of implementation by the browser vendors.

The situation is, in fact, a bit more complex than that and plenty of political wrangling is going on, but that's of interest only to standards wonks and shouldn't make any practical difference to you.

The W3C has proposed, although not confirmed as I write this, that HTML5 (the W3C snapshot) be brought to Recommendation status—that is, "done"—by 2014, with HTML5.1 to follow in 2016. HTML5 would also be broken into separate modules rather than a single monolithic spec, so work can progress on different aspects without delaying the whole. These dates don't really matter to you, however; all you need to know is when HTML5 is in browsers and ready to use.

The HTML5 Template

As someone with basic working knowledge of HTML, you're familiar with fundamental page markup. But things have changed a little bit in HTML5— not much, but enough to mention. The following code block shows the basic template that I'll use for all of the examples in this book (you can also see this in the example file *template.html*):

```
<!DOCTYPE html>
<html lang="en">
<head>
  <meta charset="utf-8">
<title></title>
</head>
<body></body>
</html>
```

Most of it should be familiar to you, but I will discuss two points of interest. First is the *Doctype*. This is a remnant from the days when you had to tell the browser which type of document you were writing: strict HTML, transitional HTML, XHTML1.1, and so on. In HTML5, that's no longer necessary—there is only one flavor of HTML—so the Doctype declaration really isn't needed any more. In theory, that is.

Modern browsers tend to have three rendering modes: *quirks mode* emulates the nonstandard rendering of Internet Explorer 5, which is required for compatibility with legacy pages on the Web; *standards mode* is for modern, standards-compliant behavior; and *almost standards mode* is standards mode with a few quirks.

To know which mode to use, the browser looks to the Doctype. You always want to use standards mode, so the Doctype in HTML5 is the shortest possible that triggers standards mode:

```
<!DOCTYPE html>
```

The second point of interest, and the only other change to the standard HTML5 template, is the meta tag, which declares the range of Unicode characters used to render the text on the page—UTF-8 is the default used across the Web, so this is what you'll use in most cases. The meta tag uses the charset attribute:

```
<meta charset="utf-8">
```

That's really it. If a client ever asks you to "make their website HTML5," you can update those two tags and charge them a fortune for it. (Please don't; that was just a joke.)

I could have included plenty of other options, which I've left out for the sake of clarity and simplicity. The popular *HTML5 Boilerplate* website provides a comprehensive template, so look through the documentation to see what the template does—but please keep in mind it should be a starting point, not used verbatim.

New Best Practices

In addition to the changes to the core template, HTML5 has one or two new best practices that you should consider implementing. HTML5 has been written to take advantage of the many different ways developers write code, so these shouldn't be considered hard-and-fast rules, but in my opinion, they'll make your code easier to write and maintain.

The first best practice is that you are no longer required to use the type attribute when calling the most common external resources. Using HTML 4.01 or XHTML, you had to declare a type for each link, script, or style tag:

```
<link href="foo.css" rel="stylesheet" type="text/css">
<script src="foo.js" type="text/javascript"></script>
```

But when working on the Web, CSS and JavaScript are the de facto default resource types used with these tags, so writing them out every time is a little redundant. Therefore, you can now drop them, making your code a little cleaner while still being understood perfectly well by the browser:

```
<link href="foo.css" rel="stylesheet">
<script src="foo.js"></script>
```

The only time you need to use the tags is when you're not using default CSS or JavaScript; for example, some releases of Firefox have experimental implementations of recent versions of JavaScript, and for safety's sake they require that you include a flag on the type attribute if you want to use it:

```
<script src="foo.js" type="application/javascript;version=1.8"></script>
```

HTML5 is also very forgiving of syntax. Whether your preference is to use all lowercase characters, quote your attribute values, or close empty elements, HTML5 is happy to parse and understand them. That being the case, all of these are equal:

```
<img src=foo.png>
<img src=foo.png />
<IMG SRC="foo.png"/>
```

NOTE *Attribute values require quotation marks when they have multiple values, such as a list of class names, or if they contain certain special characters.*

Some attributes, known as *Boolean attributes,* have only true or false values; their presence is presumed to mean true unless otherwise specified, so you don't need to supply a value—unless you're using an XML-like syntax where values are required, in which case you use the name of the attribute itself. This means both of these are the same:

```
<input type="checkbox" checked>
<input type="checkbox" checked="checked">
```

My own preference is to use all lowercase, all quoted, but not to close empty elements:

```
<img src="foo.png">
```

This is the style I use throughout the book, as I find it neater and easier to work with, and the text editor I use has syntax highlighting, which makes looking through the code nice and clear. You can use whichever system you want, but be consistent to help with maintainability.

CSS3 and Beyond

As HTML5 is to HTML4.01, so CSS3 is to CSS2.1: an evolutionary iteration that standardizes some existing features that are implemented slightly differently across browsers, and introduces a whole new set of features to make CSS fit for purpose in a world where web browsers can be embedded anywhere.

The first CSS3 features to make it into browsers were largely presentational and based on hacks that developers had been using for years: using fonts from any source, rounded corners, and drop shadows on text and boxes. Next to land were a range of new selectors that made document traversal for styling much easier, and more dynamic effects such as two- and three-dimensional transitions and transitional animations (you can read more about these in *The Book of CSS3*, by this author, from this publisher).

But beyond the many glittery visual effects, the real revolution of CSS3 has come through media queries, a syntax that allows you to provide styles to browsers based on their dimensions and capabilities, the first step toward true multi-device styling. I cover media queries in Chapter 3, along with a range of other CSS properties that are useful for building responsive and adaptive websites.

The next big challenge for CSS to solve is the issue of layout—that is, to enable layouts that are truly sympathetic to the capabilities of the user agent viewing them. These include properties for dynamic user interfaces and CSS-controlled grid systems, which you'll read more about in Chapter 4.

CSS3 is not a single spec as CSS2.1 was, where everything is described in the same document; it's far too big and complex for that. Instead CSS3 is modular—a series of shorter, more specific specs that can be implemented by browsers in a modular way. As with HTML5, the idea of waiting until CSS3 is "ready" before using it is pretty foolish, as some modules will be ready and implemented long before others.

CSS modules are given level numbers to show how many iterations they've been through; some are already at level 4, and they could well be implemented before others that are at level 3. This doesn't mean, however, that one day we'll have a CSS4; there won't be. CSS3 is a shorthand term for "everything more recent than CSS2.1," and one day that distinction will be dropped and everything will be just CSS.

Vendor-Specific Prefixes

When browsers implement features in an experimental or prestandard way, they try to make them safe by using vendor-specific prefixes to avoid compatibility problems with standardized property names. Consider, for example, that a CSS Apes module proposes a new property called gorilla, and both Firefox and WebKit implement it experimentally but slightly differently. If both used the same property name, the effect would be different in each browser; instead, they avoid those potential conflicts by using a vendor prefix:

```
-moz-gorilla: foo;
-webkit-gorilla: foo;
```

In principle, the system is great, but in reality, things have gotten somewhat confused. Among other problems, some prefixed properties became so widely used by developers that other browser makers felt the need to implement their rivals' vendor prefixes too, which is justifiable but kind of makes the whole thing nonsensical.

Browser makers are trying to bring this system under control, but on occasion using vendor-prefixed properties will be close to unavoidable. In most cases, I use only unprefixed properties in my code examples and make a note in Appendix A of where vendor prefixes need to be used.

CSS Frameworks and Preprocessors

Nowadays using a helping hand with CSS development is pretty de rigueur, especially when working on large development teams and/or on large projects. Usually these helpers come in the form of frameworks or preprocessors and quite often both.

A framework is a set of predefined CSS rules that you can use for rapid development; they usually cover typography, forms, and, quite often, layout patterns. *Blueprint.css* is one of the more venerable frameworks, used on many well-known websites, but the popular current framework is *Bootstrap* by Twitter, which offers many preformatted layout, typography, and form options, a range of reusable components, and even JavaScript extensibility.

Preprocessors are programs that work on the server-side, offering extensions and shorthand syntax in a CSS-like language that is transformed into correctly formatted stylesheets at build time. These extensions include time-saving features like variables and nested rules, and custom functions that provide incredible power to the user. The two key rivals in the preprocessor arena are *LESS* and *Sass*, with the latter being the most popular.

While both have their role in modern web development, I won't discuss or use either in this book, as what I'm teaching is the more fundamental language that both depend on.

Browser Support

You should understand by now that the multi-device web is unknowably vast and varied, that the range of browsers running on those devices is immense, and that even within those browsers there is a variety of versions and implementations (I hope you understand that, as most of the introduction was dedicated to trying to get that point across). That being the case, some of the features in this book may well not be implemented or may be implemented slightly differently.

Rather than covering the levels of implementation in the text, I treat every new feature as if it's fully implemented and make a note of real-world implementation oddities and curiosities in Appendix A.

Also, cutting-edge standard proposals are subject to change, even when experimental implementations have already shipped in some browsers (the Grid Layout module featured in Chapter 4 was updated while I wrote this book), so by the time you read this, some of the syntax in the book may already be out-of-date. This is an unfortunate risk when working with evolving standards in dead tree publishing, but I try to mitigate it by noting features that may be at risk of changing and by keeping a list of errata and updates on the companion website, *http://modernwebbook.com/*.

You'll probably want to follow a few online resources to learn about levels of implementation, although most tend to be focused on desktop and mobile browsers. *Can I Use...* shows levels of support for a wide range of technologies in recent past, current, and future versions of popular browsers, whereas *HTML5 Please* shows how safe it is in general to use cutting-edge features, mostly CSS3 and JavaScript (which is why the name annoys me a little).

The HTML5 Test is a site that tells you how many features from the HTML5 spec your browser supports, but also very usefully keeps records of implementation levels across many different browsers and devices, including TV and games console browsers, and also allows you to do side-by-side comparisons of up to three different browsers. The site is limited to only HTML5 support, however.

Test and Test and Test Some More

With the device landscape the way it is, the only way to be sure that the sites you build work across multiple devices is to test. Test at the start of the project, test at the end, and test at every opportunity all the way through. If you're planning a multi-device project, factor in testing to take up to 40 to 50 percent of build time. Seriously.

You can't find a substitute for testing on actual devices, so start building a library of as many devices as you can. If you work near other agencies, consider pooling resources so you can get a broader range. In many cities, open device labs are being assembled, with a range of devices donated by local developers and companies that are available for anyone to use. Search online for your nearest lab, or consider getting involved with creating one at your company or place of work.

And don't stick to only mobile and tablet testing; think about games console browsers if you're targeting your sites at a younger audience (research suggests that some one in four teens in the US use their games console browser to go online) or TV devices if your sites are aimed at a leisure market.

If you can't get access to actual devices, some dedicated tools are available, and most (if not all) OS creators and/or device manufacturers have free-to-download software development kits (SDKs) with device emulators. In the mobile and tablet space, Android, Windows Phone, and Blackberry all have SDKs, and doubtless many more besides. Apple's Xcode, available through the App Store, features an iOS Simulator that lets you switch between device and OS versions for testing.

Once set up, many of these SDKs also allow you to connect physical devices via USB to do debugging via a paired browser, but an easier way to do this is with Opera's Mobile Emulator; once opened and connected to an Opera desktop version, you can use the developer tools on the desktop to debug the page on the mobile. If you need to use WebKit—and as it's the dominant multi-device engine, why wouldn't you?—software called weinre lets you connect a version of Chrome or Safari on the desktop with Android, iOS, or Blackberry emulators/simulators.

Adobe has a tool called Edge Inspect, which synchronizes the Chrome browser with any device running the Edge Inspect app (currently available on iOS and Android), allowing you to preview your site on many different devices simultaneously and use the Web Inspector for remote debugging.

Summary

This chapter provided you with all the information you need to get started in modern web development. I disambiguated the common meaning of HTML5 and introduced you to the web platform. You learned what HTML5 is useful for and how to start writing it, and you also had a brief introduction to CSS3.

The chapter's key messages are in the latter parts: First, always keep up-to-date about the levels of implementation of web platform features across common browsers; and second, test, and then test, test, test some more, and when you think you have no more testing to do, test again. Then once more for good luck.

With all of that explained, let's roll our sleeves up and get to work.

Further Reading

In case you missed it, the list of technologies that make the web platform is at *http://platform.html5.org/*. Bruce Lawson proposed NEWT on his blog: *http://www.brucelawson.co.uk/2010/meet-newt-new-exciting-web-technologies/*.

The W3C's HTML5 spec is at *http://www.w3.org/TR/html5/*, and the WHATWG's living spec is at *http://whatwg.org/html*. More usefully, they also have an *Edition for Web Developers*, which leaves out some of the more arcane language and is, therefore, more readable: *http://developers.whatwg.org/*.

The complete HTML5 Boilerplate is at *http://html5boilerplate.com/*. Remember, just use the bits you need; don't copy the whole thing verbatim.

For finding out about feature implementation levels, I recommend Alexis Deveria's site Can I Use... at *http://caniuse.com/*, the community site HTML5 Please at *http://html5please.com/*, and The HTML5 Test at *http://html5test.com/*.

The LabUp! website is a resource for finding or getting involved with open device testing labs: *http://lab-up.org/*. The chief tester at the BBC, David Blooman, wrote a long and detailed article, "Testing for Dummies," about how a global organization performs multi-device testing: *http://mobiletestingfordummies.tumblr.com/post/20056227958/testing*.

Patrick Meenan's slides for his talk "Taming the Mobile Beast" contain a wealth of links and information on testing mobile devices: *http://www.slideshare.net/patrickmeenan/velocity-2012-taming-the-mobile-beast/*, and Anna Debenham's article for *A List Apart*, "Testing Websites in Game Console Browsers," is about . . . well, the title's quite self-explanatory: *http://www.alistapart.com/articles/testing-websites-in-game-console-browsers/*.

Opera has written detailed instructions about remote debugging at *http://www.opera.com/dragonfly/documentation/remote/*. weinre is available to download from *http://people.apache.org/~pmuellr/weinre/docs/latest/*. You can get more information on Adobe Edge Inspect at *http://html.adobe.com/edge/inspect/*.

2

STRUCTURE AND SEMANTICS

Remember the parable about the man who built his house on sand? Or the pigs who made their houses out of straw and sticks? Losers. They lost because they didn't put enough value on the importance of structure.

To make good sites you need good structure, and on the Web that starts with HTML. How you mark up your pages gives them a solid structure both now and in the future. Whatever the context, whether you're building a heavily interactive web app, a hybrid mobile app, or a one-page brochure site, putting a sound structure in place is a top priority. A solid structure makes your pages more accessible and easier to author and maintain, and helps browsers and other user agents make sense of your pages. A well-structured DOM can also give a performance boost, making parsing easier for the browser and requiring less memory.

Beyond simple structure is semantic richness. Giving the content on your pages this extra meaning provides an immediate benefit: It's easier for search engines to crawl and understand your data. And longer-term benefits that haven't even been invented yet may arise.

HTML5 and related technologies make all of this easy. Using existing and well-implemented methods, you can create pages that are solid, meaningful, high performing, and rich in data.

New Elements in HTML5

One of the major new features in HTML5 is a range of new semantic elements, extending the suite far beyond its roots in marking up scientific documents with headings, lists, and paragraphs. Most of the new elements are aimed at giving a page better structure and developers more options for marking up areas of content than just using a div with an associated id or classes.

Here's one example. In the past, developers might have used this:

```
<div class="article">...</div>
```

In HTML5, they have the option of using this:

```
<article>...</article>
```

The W3C's HTML5 spec lists ten structural elements. Of these, three already existed in HTML4: body, h1–h6 (if we cheat a little and count them as a single entity), and address. Of the seven new elements, four are what are known as *sectioning content*; I'll get to what this means in a little while, but for now here's the list:

article   An independent part of a document or site, such as a forum post, blog entry, or user-submitted comment

aside   An area of a page that is tangentially connected to the content around it, but which could be considered separate, like a sidebar in a magazine article

nav   The navigation area of a document, an area that contains links to other documents or other areas of the same document

section   A thematic grouping of content, such as a chapter of a book, a page in a tabbed dialog box, or the introduction on a website home page

The other three structural elements define areas within the sectioned content:

footer   The footer of a document or of an area of a document, typically containing metadata about the section it's within, such as author details

header   Possibly the header of a document, but could also be the header of an area of a document, generally containing heading (h1–h6) elements to mark up titles

hgroup   Used to group a set of multiple-level heading elements, such as a subheading or a tagline

HTML5 has other new elements that don't affect the basic structure of a page; I'll cover them where necessary throughout the rest of this book. For now, let's look further into the reason these new elements were created in the first place.

What's the Point?

The stated aim of these new elements is to provide clear document outlines for better parsing by the browser and other machines, notably assistive technology like screen readers. Consider these outlines to be like document maps, showing the hierarchy of the content within, which headings are most important, the parent-child relationships between content areas, and so on.

In HTML4, this task was mostly done using the header elements, h1 through h6: The h1 would be unique or the most important heading on the page, h2 elements were usually the direct children of h1, and so on. Seeing something like this was fairly common:

```
<h1>Great Apes</h1>
  <h2>Gorilla</h2>
    <h3>Eastern Gorilla</h3>
    ...
    <h3>Western Gorilla</h3>
    ...
  <h2>Orangutan</h2>
  ...
```

Nesting headings in this way creates this document outline:

1. Great Apes
   a. Gorilla
      i.   Eastern Gorilla
      ii. Western Gorilla
   b. Orangutan

NOTE   *Great ape fans will notice that I've left out the bonobo and the chimpanzee. That's for reasons of space and clarity, not because of any bias.*

The structure I've created makes visual sense, and using headings in this way to create a document outline is known as *implicit sectioning*.

In HTML5, the sectioning content elements introduced earlier in this chapter create the sections in the outline, not the headers within those sections. This is *explicit sectioning*. So to get the same structure with our Great Apes markup in HTML5, we'd go for something like this:

```
<h1>Great Apes</h1>
<section>
  <h1>Gorilla</h1>
```

```
<article>
  <h1>Eastern Gorilla</h1>
  ...
</article>
<article>
  <h1>Western Gorilla</h1>
  ...
</article>
</section>
<section>
  <h1>Orangutan</h1>
  ...
</section>
```

The resulting outline would be the same as in the HTML4 example because each section or article element creates a new section in the outline. These are the sectioning content elements I mentioned earlier, along with aside and nav.

Each outline section should have a heading—any heading will do. In my example, I've used all h1 headings, but the heading level used doesn't really matter because the sectioning content is what creates new sections. I could have rolled a die and used that number for each heading level for all the difference it makes.

NOTE *I'm being a little glib here. You can (and should) still use h1 to h6 in a hierarchical way, as it aids in backward compatibility and makes styling easier.*

As well as the heading (or headings, and possibly an hgroup element to wrap them in), each section can contain a distinct header and footer, plus further sections and *sectioning roots*. These roots are elements such as blockquote and figure, which can have their own outlines but don't contribute to the overall document outline.

If this discussion isn't making a lot of sense to you, you're in good company. The confusion over what each of the sectioning content elements does is so common that the good HTML5 Doctor has created a flowchart (Figure 2-1) to help you choose the right element for the task at hand.

A flowchart. To help you choose an element. If you're a good judge of tone, you might have started to get the impression that I'm not a fan of the new HTML5 structural elements. If so, you're right.

The Downside of HTML5 Sectioning Elements

As implied through my perceivable mounting sense of frustration in the previous section, coming to grips with some of these new elements can be quite challenging, especially understanding the difference between article and section. To recap: A section can contain articles and sections, and an article can contain sections and articles, and both make sections in the outline. There is a difference between the two, but no one—not even the writer of the spec—has yet managed a definition so clear and succinct that developers remember it easily.

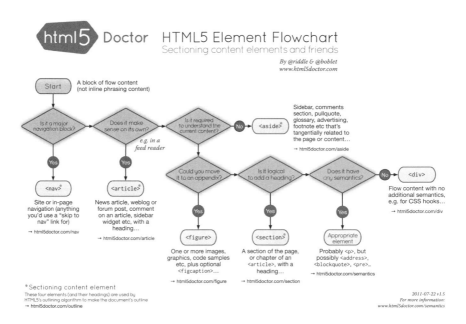

Figure 2-1: *If you're confused about which sectioning element is the correct one to use, the HTML5 Doctor has the answer.*

In his book *The Truth About HTML5* (CreateSpace, 2012), Luke Stevens says this about the vague description of article:

> Specifications fail when they leave things up to you to work out. The whole point of a specification is to *specify* exactly what you should do. But here it's open to interpretation, has no clear benefit, and repeats existing functionality. . . .

I can't disagree. My prediction is that these elements will be badly misused by many people unless clearer definitions can be found.

For technical reasons, I suggest not using the new elements on the open Web: For one, they're simply not supported in older versions of Internet Explorer (8 and below). To make those browsers recognize the new elements, you have to create them in JavaScript. You can do this fairly easily; just implement the popular HTML5Shiv using conditional comments:

```
<!--[if lt IE 9]>
<script src="html5shiv.js"></script>
<![endif]-->
```

But doing this creates a dependency on JavaScript for your visitors; anyone using old IE with JavaScript disabled doesn't see any of the content contained inside the new elements. Although that may be only a small percentage of users, accessibility should mean that *everyone* gets to see your content.

On top of that, no currently available browsers support the new outlining algorithm (the JAWS screen reader does, albeit with bugs), so all your hard work doesn't really have much benefit—this is likely to change in the future, of course.

In the end, the decision to use the new structural elements is, of course, up to you. They're not mandatory—you can still use div elements as you do currently. I find it hard to recommend using them, however, unless you're prepared to read the HTML5 spec and fully understand exactly how the new elements work on the outline of a document—and you're working in an environment where legacy browsers aren't an issue. As things are at the time of writing, I would look for an alternative way to show page structure. Luckily, one is available, in the shape of WAI-ARIA.

WAI-ARIA

The Web Accessibility Initiative's *Accessible Rich Internet Applications* suite (*WAI-ARIA* to its friends) was created to address the shortfall in accessibility that was created as the Web moved beyond simple document markup and into an era of applications and interactivity.

WAI-ARIA does this by creating a number of HTML extensions (or, in fact, extensions for any DOM-based languages, such as SVG and XML), allowing developers to make browsers and assistive technology aware of interactive content. For example, if you have a link that uses JavaScript to create an on-screen dialog overlay when clicked, you have no way to make the browser aware of it; the markup just looks like a standard link:

```
<a href="http://example.com">Launch popup</a>
```

Because the event is attached to the link using script, the screen reading device has no information about what happens here and can't give any context to the user, who remains unaware of the functionality. WAI-ARIA introduces a new attribute, aria-haspopup, for just this situation, giving information to the user about what's going on:

```
<a href="http://example.com" aria-haspopup="true">Launch popup</a>
```

A whole range of new attributes is available, among them what are known as *landmark roles*; these attributes make screen readers and other accessible navigation devices aware of your page's structure, so the user can easily find their way around your document. This solution goes some way toward fulfilling the structural obligations that the new HTML5 elements were created to fulfill.

NOTE *As mentioned, at the time of writing, some user agents and assistive technologies don't parse the new HTML5 document outlines correctly, so the use of landmark roles may help with backward compatibility.*

Landmark roles are applied using the role attribute with a series of predefined values. These values do not directly correspond to the HTML5 structural elements, but they mostly match very well. For example, if you want to define the document area that contains general information about the site, such as the logo and strap line, you add the *banner* role:

```
<div role="banner">...</div>
```

This role is broadly analogous to the header element and, in most cases, will be used in its place.

Some landmark roles don't have an HTML5 equivalent: Believe it or not, no suitable element exists for indicating where the main content of a page is, so to let the screen reader know the location of key content, we have the *main* role:

```
<div role="main">...</div>
```

Eight landmark roles are defined in the WAI-ARIA spec:

application   Shows an area of a page that's an interactive application rather than a document

banner   As mentioned, indicates general site content, probably contained in the page header; in this specific context, analogous to the header element

complementary   Shows content that's related, but not integral, to the main content, like a sidebar; analogous to the aside element

contentinfo   Gives you information about the document, such as legal instructions. Often located in the footer, so in this context, is analogous to the footer element

form   Indicates any form except search, for example, a contact form

main   Indicates the core content of a document

navigation   Contains groups of links for navigating this or related documents, analogous to nav

search   Indicates forms specifically used to search this site or others

As well as being useful for navigating and providing some semantic value, the landmark roles make convenient styling hooks for CSS. Using the Exact Attribute Value Selector, you can easily apply rules to, for example, the page header:

```
div[role='contentinfo'] { background-color: blue; }
```

This selector has been implemented in pretty much every browser made in the last 10 years (that I'm aware of), so unless you're using a very old or basic one, this technique is useful—be aware that complex selectors can have an adverse effect on page-loading times, however.

The Importance of Semantic Markup

Before moving on to look at different ways of adding deeper rich meaning to your pages, let's pause to ask the question, "Why bother with semantics at all?" I mean, is something intrinsically wrong with marking up a page using mostly div elements (as in the following code block)?

```
<div class="first">This is the heading.</div>
<div class="main"><b>This is the first sentence.</b><br>This is the second sentence.</div>
```

Divya Manian addressed this in a polemical article, "Our Pointless Pursuit of Semantic Value," in which she argues that putting too much emphasis on semantic markup is a waste of time for most people:

> Mark-up structures content, but your choice of tags matters a lot less than we've been taught. . . .

I would say, however, that there are two good reasons for using correct semantic elements. The first and most prosaic is that you're working to a de facto standard and writing code with good maintainability. You know if you use semantic elements, your colleagues or eventual successor will be able to work on your code without having to learn your naming scheme. And the reverse is also true: If you take over someone else's code, you'll know exactly what's going on in the code if he or she has coded to standards.

A more recondite reason is that using semantic elements gives your content increased *aboutness*. Simply put, aboutness is a measure of the quality of meaning; what something is about is described by its aboutness.

As a simple illustration of that principle, imagine you have a web page that contains W.H. Auden's poem "Funeral Blues":

> He was my North, my South, my East and West,
> My working week and my Sunday rest,
> My noon, my midnight, my talk, my song;
> I thought that love would last forever: I was wrong.

Although *we* know that the poem is about death, the word itself doesn't appear in the poem. How could a search engine that indexed the page know what it was about, and return it in the search results for that topic? The search engine looks at the text of the links to that page, so a link with the text "read more" provides no context, whereas a link with the text "W.H. Auden's poem about death" provides some aboutness.

Using correct semantic elements provides the same benefit. If all of the content on your page is marked up with divs, the content has no context; if you mark up your page semantically, you give the content context:

```
<h1>This is the heading.</h1>
<p>This is the first sentence.</p>
<p>This is the second sentence.</p>
```

Now you clearly know which header is important and what the main body content is. You've given the content some aboutness.

As well as using semantic elements correctly to mark up your content, you can increase the meaning of your documents for machines rather than users (commonly known as *structured data*) in a number of ways. You can use existing attributes and elements in defined patterns (*microformats*) or extend HTML with new attributes (*RDFa* and *microdata*), and I'll introduce them all briefly right now.

Microformats

Created by a grassroots coalition of developers, microformats add extra meaning to content through standardized markup patterns using existing attributes. Their main attraction is that they work with current development methods; rather than being an extension to HTML, they are a design principle or a set of standard usage patterns.

Microformats range from the fairly complex to the extremely simple. Here's an example of probably the most simple of all:

```
<a href="http://flickr.com/photos/tags/gorilla/" rel="tag">About Gorillas</a>
```

That's called the *Rel-Tag microformat*. The keyword *tag* in the rel attribute lets other machines know that the URL linked to in the a element is a page that is described by a tag, the name of which is the last path component of the URL—in this case, *gorilla*. At this point, I should probably point out—in case you hadn't noticed—that I really like gorillas.

A more complex, although just as straightforward and useful, example is the *hCard microformat*, which marks up common user details with a standardized "business card" syntax. Consider, for example, this markup, which I might use to link to someone's contact details online:

```
<div class="details">
<p><a href="http://about.me/petergasston">Peter Gasston</a> writes for <a href="http://broken-links.com">Broken Links</a>.</p>
</div>
```

The markup is fine, but the data doesn't have a lot of aboutness; the reader would understand that this is my name and where I write, but a search engine crawler would probably not be able to make the same cognitive leap. Using the hCard pattern, I can add attribute values to that markup that provide more semantic richness:

```
<div class="vcard">
<p><a href="http://about.me/petergasston" class="url fn">Peter Gasston</a>
writes for <a href="http://broken-links.com" class="url org">Broken Links</a>.</p>
</div>
```

Those few standardized class names have given much more meaning to this content for machines that are programmed to find it; a crawler that recognizes the hCard pattern will see the *vcard* class and know that the content inside contains the information it's looking for: It knows the first link contains the full name (*fn*) of the contact, and the second link contains the organization (*org*) the contact works for.

There's more to microformats than this; there are patterns for events, reviews, geographic coordinates, even recipes, and plenty more besides. Search engines like Google use them to improve their search results, so using microformats in your pages is not (only) an exercise in developer esotericism.

RDFa

The *Resource Description Format in Attributes* (*RDFa*) is an extension of HTML that provides context to content using a whole new set of bespoke attributes. The main syntax is known as RDFa Core, and a simple subset called RDFa Lite is also available. Both rely on predefined *schema* (descriptions of data) to describe content.

Better than telling you what that means, I'll show you (those years at screenwriting school didn't go to waste!). One common item of data across the Web, especially on blogs and news sites, is a date. Quite often you'll see a date marked up something like this:

```
<p class="date">2013-04-01</p>
```

The markup is functional and uncomplicated, but the only semantic context is provided by the class name. With RDFa Lite, you can make this more meaningful and let other machines know this is a date by using the new property attribute:

```
<p property="http://purl.org/dc/elements/1.1/date">2013-04-01</p>
```

The value of the attribute is the URL of the relevant description of the term "date" from a schema that is part of a standardized vocabulary known as the *Dublin Core*.

You probably noticed that the date I've used isn't in a very reader-friendly format. This is a drawback of RDFa Lite: All the content must be formatted in a strictly machine-readable way. To provide content better suited for humans, you must use RDFa Core. With RDFa Core, I can give one set of information to machines and another to people, using the content attribute:

```
<p property="http://purl.org/dc/elements/1.1/date" content="2013-04-01">April 1</p>
```

What the reader sees is the content of the element; what the machine sees is the value of the attribute. It means extra markup, but everybody's happy.

As with microformats, some search engines look for common RDFa patterns to improve their search results. I'll go into this in more detail in "Rich Snippets" on page 34.

Microdata

HTML5 has addressed the semantic issue with the creation of a simple syntax called microdata. This is essentially a series of name-value pairs that provide meaningful machine-readable data. As always, before trying to explain it, showing you how it works is easier:

```
<p itemscope>I live in <span itemprop="city">London</span></p>
```

This markup creates a single *item*. The attribute itemscope is used on the containing element to mark the limits, or *scope*, of this particular item. Inside we have the name-value pair, known as a *property*: The value of the itemprop attribute is the name—which, in this example, is *city*—and the element's content is the value—in this case, *London*. The result is an item with a single property:

```
city: 'London'
```

But you're not limited to a single property per item; you can have as many as you like:

```
<p itemscope>Hello, my name is <span itemprop="given-name">Peter</
span> and I'm <span itemprop="role">a developer</span> from <span
itemprop="city">London</span>.</p>
```

In this case, the item's property list looks like this:

```
given-name: 'Peter'
role: 'a developer'
city: 'London'
```

As you can see, this markup is somewhat similar to RDFa, and just like that format, you can give different values to machines and humans. Look at this example where I use the datetime attribute:

```
<p itemscope>My birthday this year is on <span itemprop="birthday"
datetime="2013-12-14">December 14</span>.</p>
```

And, as with RDFa, you can describe content with predefined schema by linking to it with the `itemtype` attribute:

```
<p itemscope itemtype="http://example.org/birthday">My birthday this year is
on <span itemprop="birthday" datetime="2013-12-14">December 14</span>.</p>
```

You can use schema such as the previously mentioned Dublin Core, or even one of your own invention, as I just showed in the previous code block.

The Microdata API

Microdata has a companion DOM API, which is useful for extracting the data from the page and is already fairly broadly implemented in modern browsers. The key to the API is the `getItems()` method, which returns a `NodeList` containing all of the items on the page:

```
var items = document.getItems();
```

From there, you can choose a single item and, for example, see how many properties it contains using the `properties` object:

```
var firstItemLen = items[0].properties.length;
```

Or you can discover the value of one of those properties:

```
var itemVal = items[0].properties['name'][0].itemValue;
```

You can see these demonstrated in the example file *microdata-api.html*. I've logged the results in the console, so open up your favorite browser and take a look. I encourage you to play around with it yourself. For anyone who doesn't have a browser handy, Figure 2-2 shows how the results are logged in Firebug.

```
Items NodeList[p]                                    microd...pi.html (line 12)
1 Properties HTMLPropertiesCollection[span]          microd...pi.html (line 13)
Value Peter                                          microd...pi.html (line 14)
```

Figure 2-2: The results of some simple explorations of the microdata API, shown in the console

Microdata, Microformats, and RDFa

If you've decided that adding machine-readable semantic data to your pages is the right way to go, which format should you use? The answer, of course, is it depends. Evaluate your content, read about the strengths and weaknesses of each of the data types, and decide which one's best for you.

My personal feeling is that in the future we'll mostly see a mixture of microdata with simple microformats. One of the interesting things about microdata is that it's capable of accommodating both of its contemporaries within its own flexible syntax. For example, here's how to mark up hCard using microdata:

```
<div itemscope itemtype="http://microformats.org/profile/hcard">
<p><a href="http://about.me/petergasston" itemprop="url fn">Peter Gasston</a>
writes for <a href="http://broken-links.com" itemprop="url org">Broken Links</a>.</p>
</div>
```

Likewise, you can easily use RDFa data schema:

```
<p itemscope itemtype="http://purl.org/dc/elements/1.1/date" datetime="2013-04-01">April 1</p>
```

In my opinion, microdata's flexibility will lead to it being used more and more. That said, it's not perfect for everything; some microformats, such as Rel-Tag, are so concise and easy to use that's there's little point in trying to replace them.

Schema.org

One good reason for using microdata, and another reason I think it's set to conquer microformats and RDFa, is that you might receive a nice advantage and get your content noticed and promoted by search engines and portals. In 2011 four big Web giants—Google, Microsoft, Yahoo!, and Yandex—launched a new website, Schema.org, which introduced a set of shared vocabularies for marking up common patterns using microdata.

Those patterns include reviews, events, places, items, and objects, things that get discussed frequently across the Web. To illustrate, say you're writing a book review on your website (I've chosen a book at random and given it an unbiased review):

```
<div class="review">
  <h1>The Book of CSS3, by Peter Gasston</h1>
  <p>What an amazing book! 5 stars!</p>
</div>
```

This review actually contains two items: the details of the book and a review of it. Schema.org has two vocabularies that you can use to mark this up semantically: they are *Book* and *Review*. A visit to the relevant sections shows me which microdata patterns I should use. With that done, I can update my markup:

```
<div class="review" itemscope itemtype="http://schema.org/Review">
  <h1><span itemprop="itemReviewed">The Book of CSS3</span>, by <span
itemprop="creator">Peter Gasston</span></h1>
  <p><span itemprop="reviewBody">What an amazing book!</span> <span
itemprop="reviewRating">5</span> stars!</p>
</div>
```

Although my markup has gotten more complex, it means more now. Each of the vocabularies I've used is defined with a link to the relevant schema in the `itemtype` attribute, and the items are marked up with preset `itemprop` values.

What's interesting about Schema.org is the way that specific schema inherit properties from broader ones; *Book*, for example, has properties from its own schema, the broader *CreativeWork* vocabulary, and the top-level *Thing* (great name!), which has the most generic properties.

By marking up my content using Schema.org patterns, all of the crawlers that reach my page will know the author and title of this book, the fact that I'm reviewing it, and that I gave it a five-star rating. If someone searches for that book, my review could appear in the search results or be aggregated with others to provide a decent overview to the reader.

Rich Snippets

The method of giving extra information in search results, which is used by many search engines, is known by Google as *rich snippets*. Rich snippets give a user's search query more context, allowing the user to better evaluate the relevance of the result without having to click through to the page. You can see an example of a rich snippet in Figure 2-3.

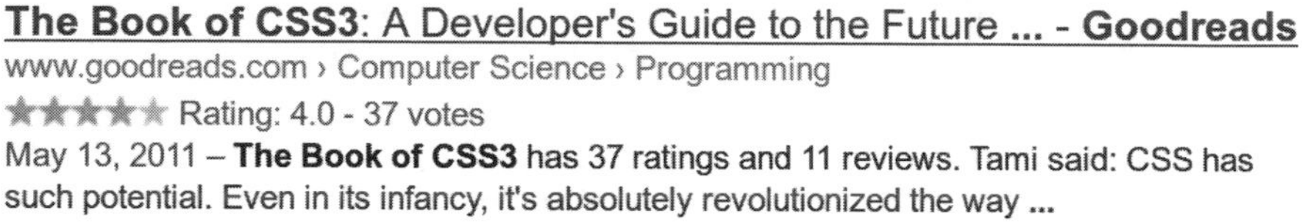

The Book of CSS3: A Developer's Guide to the Future ... - **Goodreads**
www.goodreads.com › Computer Science › Programming
★★★★☆ Rating: 4.0 - 37 votes
May 13, 2011 – **The Book of CSS3** has 37 ratings and 11 reviews. Tami said: CSS has such potential. Even in its infancy, it's absolutely revolutionized the way ...

Figure 2-3: Example of a rich snippet giving extra information on Google search results

Rich snippets work with microformats and RDFa, but its preferred syntax is microdata. Plenty of information and documentation is available for developers on Google's Webmaster pages, including a useful tool to test if your microdata is formatted correctly. In Figure 2-4, you can see the data this tool has extracted from the book review created in the previous section.

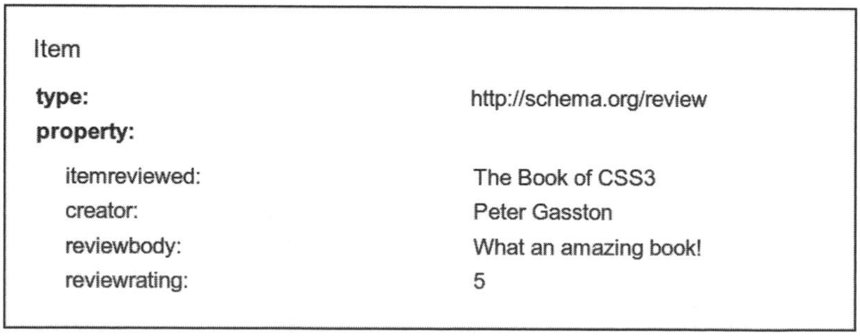

```
Item

type:                        http://schema.org/review
property:

    itemreviewed:            The Book of CSS3
    creator:                 Peter Gasston
    reviewbody:              What an amazing book!
    reviewrating:            5
```

Figure 2-4: Data extracted from the marked-up book review by the rich snippet testing tool

Data Attributes

A further way that HTML5 extends the meaning that elements have is through the use of data attributes. These are user-defined attributes, the values of which are intended to provide information related to an element but without giving any extra semantic meaning to either machines or humans. Let me explain that in a little more detail.

Say you want to output a set of data, each item of which has two values—a name and a number (a unique database ID, for example). You want the name to be shown in the document, but you also want to make the number available for running scripts on. As it stands, no relevant attribute is available to store that information; you'd probably have to use a class:

```
<p class="id-123">Peter</p>
```

Data attributes were created for just this reason: associating data. They let you store that extra information without implying any extra meaning, as a class does. Each data attribute starts with the word data- and then a user-defined unique key; for our example, we could use this:

```
<p data-id="123">Peter</p>
```

The data attribute *id* is now associated with the value *Peter*. Although it gives no extra semantic meaning to the element, the attribute is available to provide context to other processes: perhaps information about this data is in an associated JSON file, so you can use JavaScript to look it up.

The Data Attributes API

So scripts can get at this data more easily, a simple DOM API is available that uses the dataset property. To get the value of a data attribute, use this property with the key of the attribute you're querying:

```
var el = document.querySelector('p');
var id = el.dataset['id'];
```

Applied to this example markup, the returned result would be *123*. You can also update attribute values with dataset:

```
el.dataset['id'] = 100;
```

Here's an example that shows this at work:

```
var el = document.querySelector('p');
console.log('The ID is',el.dataset['id']);
el.dataset['id'] = 100;
console.log('Now the ID is',el.dataset['id']);
```

In this example, I perform three operations: first getting the *id* data, then setting it to 100, then getting it again, and each time logging the results into the console. The resulting output is shown in Figure 2-5.

```
The ID is 123          data-a...es.html (line 11)
Now the ID is 100      data-a...es.html (line 13)
```

Figure 2-5: Showing the results of data attribute manipulation with the API in the console

jQuery and Data Attributes

If you use jQuery, interacting with data attributes is even easier (if you don't know what jQuery is, I'll explain it in Chapter 5; you can come back to this section after you've read it). Use the data() method for getting and setting data values:

```
var id = $(el).data('id');
```

This code is analogous to that shown in the previous section and would return the same value, 123.

One big advantage, however, is that, unlike dataset where all results are returned as a string, the data() method also parses the value of the attribute and converts it into the correct type; using the previous example, the type would be a number. But if you change the markup:

```
<p data-name="Peter">123</p>
```

And use the data() method again:

```
var name = $(el).data('name');
```

The value of the variable *name* is *Peter*, and its type is a string.

To see this in action, take a look at the example file *data-attributes-jquery .html*. In it, I've combined the two different data attributes in the same markup:

```
<p data-id="123" data-name="Peter">Gasston</p>
```

Using jQuery, I've logged each data attribute's type into the console using JavaScript's typeof operator:

```
var el = $('p');
console.log('ID:',typeof el.data('id'));
console.log('Name:',typeof el.data('name'));
```

The resulting output is shown in Figure 2-6.

| ID: number | **data-a...ry.html (line 13)** |
| Name: string | **data-a...ry.html (line 14)** |

Figure 2-6: Finding the type of the results using the jQuery data( ) method with data attributes

Data Attributes in the Wild

Data attributes are so useful that some companies already take extensive advantage of them. Twitter was quick to adopt them, allowing them to be used as an option for adding a Tweet button to web pages. Certain parameters about the content are stored in a set of predefined attributes:

```
<a href="https://twitter.com/share" class="twitter-share-button"
data-url="http://broken-links.com" data-via="stopsatgreen">Tweet</a>
```

By including a call to Twitter's JavaScript elsewhere on the page, this element is replaced by a Tweet button using the supplied data. Many other social services, such as Facebook, Google+, and LinkedIn, use data attributes in the same way.

Web Components: The Future of Markup?

An exciting new approach to extending HTML is in the proposal for what's currently known as *Web Components*. This is a collective title for a group of technologies that aim to make it easy to create rich interfaces for web applications, using CSS and markup.

As I write this, the specification is at draft stage and very much subject to change, so instead of talking about it here, I'll cover Web Components in more detail in Chapter 11.

Summary

In this chapter, I've covered a core function of a good website or application: the underlying structure. Using markup in a correct and meaningful way lays the foundations for everything else I'm going to cover in this book and will be extremely important to making sure your own sites are maintainable and scalable.

I've been a little mean to HTML5 structural elements, but whether you use them or not, you should definitely consider using WAI-ARIA in your project, regardless of the context. Content accessibility is the bedrock of the Web, and even if you use roles and nothing else, you and your users win.

You also got a look at adding context to your sites through semantic and structured data, and you learned the importance of aboutness. The approach you take will, of course, depend on the context you're making it for. Building a large database-led website with lots of consumer-focused content probably means you want to add lots of semantic richness in order to get the most from search engines and crawlers. In this case, you'll want to consider RDFa, microformats, and/or microdata. Building a hybrid app for mobile devices, however, will make that much less of a consideration.

Further Reading

HTML5 Doctor is the best source information for most HTML5 topics, including the clearest definition of the new outline algorithm I've read so far, in this article by Mike Robinson: *http://html5doctor.com/outlines/*. You can download the element flowchart shown in Figure 2-1 from *http:// html5doctor.com/resources/#flowchart/*. See also Derek Johnson's article in *Smashing Magazine*: *http://coding.smashingmagazine.com/2011/08/16/ html5-and-the-document-outlining-algorithm/*.

For much more detail on the HTML5 structural elements problem, I strongly suggest you read Luke Stevens's book *The Truth About HTML5*; find it at *http://www.truthabouthtml5.com/*. If you want to read the full HTML5 specification and make up your own mind, I advise going for the developer's version at *http://developers.whatwg.org/sections.html*.

Read the full WAI-ARIA specification at *http://www.w3.org/TR/wai-aria/*. The *Paciello Group Blog* is worth reading for information about accessibility in HTML5, and this post on landmark roles is directly relevant: *http://www .paciellogroup.com/blog/2010/10/using-wai-aria-landmark-roles/*.

Divya Manian's article on semantics was published by *Smashing Magazine* at *http://coding.smashingmagazine.com/2011/11/11/our-pointless-pursuit-of-seman tic-value/*. For more on aboutness and the importance of semantics, I highly recommend the book *Ambient Findability: What We Find Changes Who We Become* by Peter Morville (O'Reilly, 2005). The website *http://webdatacommons.org/* provides information and statistics about sites that use structured data.

Read all about microformats at *http://microformats.org/*. A revision of the syntax, microformats 2.0, was started in 2010 and is still underway; learn more about that at *http://microformats.org/wiki/microformats-2*.

If you want to learn more about the RDFa format, the W3C published an excellent primer: *http://www.w3.org/TR/xhtml-rdfa-primer/*.

The best resource for learning about microdata comes from the HTML5 Doctor again: *http://html5doctor.com/microdata/*. If you're feeling masochistic and prefer to read the spec in detail, you'll find it at *http://www.w3.org/TR/ microdata/*.

You can get more information on Schema.org at—wait for it!—*http:// schema.org/*, and Google's documentation of rich snippets is at *http://support .google.com/webmasters/bin/answer.py?hl=en&answer=99170*. You'll find the testing tool at *http://www.google.com/webmasters/tools/richsnippets/*.

John Resig wrote a concise introduction to data attributes on his blog, *http://ejohn.org/blog/html-5-data-attributes/*, and the data() method is fully documented on the jQuery website at *http://api.jquery.com/data/*.

3

DEVICE-RESPONSIVE CSS

With a solid structure in place, the next step is to plan how you're going to display your content. You have many different approaches and methodologies to choose from. Among the development community's chattering classes, two of the most popular methods of building websites today are *adaptive* or *responsive*, both of which I explain later in this chapter. For now you just need to know that, at their core, they're similar, with only one mechanism separating the two.

This chapter will be more about learning the fundamental techniques that allow you to make great websites regardless of your approach, and the most important technique is something that both adaptive and responsive methods have in common, something that is absolutely essential to the new world of multi-device development: media queries.

Media Queries

In my opinion, media queries are the biggest agent of change in website design for many years—probably since CSS itself became mainstream. The widespread adoption of CSS allowed you to leave behind the rigid limitations of table-based websites, and media queries take that a step further, letting you style pages in a way that's sympathetic to the specifications of each device your sites are displayed on.

A *media query* is a logical statement: If the logic is true, the style rules within the statement are applied; if the logic is false, the rules are skipped. The parameters of the statements are known as *media features*, and the most commonly used today concern the dimensions of the device or the viewport. But before discussing media features in detail, let's see how they're used.

Media queries extend the media types syntax used in CSS 2.1 and HTML 4.01—remember, that's the syntax that lets you call media-dependent styles, such as when linking to an external stylesheet:

```
<link rel="stylesheet" href="foo.css" media="screen">
```

This code calls the external stylesheet *foo.css* only when the viewing device is a screen—in other words, not a different media type such as print. You extend this syntax by simply adding the word *and* and including the query itself in parentheses:

```
<link rel="stylesheet" href="foo.css" media="screen and (query)">
```

This modified code has two conditions: The media type should be a screen, and the logic of the media query should be true. If both of these conditions are met, *foo.css* is applied.

You can also use media queries to include external stylesheets from within other stylesheets, using the @import at-rule. The following code has the same logic as the previous code block, but it can be used within style tags or an external stylesheet:

```
@import url('foo.css') screen and (query);
```

WARNING   *Performance issues can occur when using @import in this way, so proceed with caution. For more details, see Steve Souders's blog post, "Don't Use @import" (*http://www.stevesouders.com/blog/2009/04/09/dont-use-import/*).*

Finally, you can use media queries inline, which is handy when you want to apply blocks of rules for specific cases rather than calling external stylesheets:

```
@media screen and (query) { ... }
```

So now that you know how media queries work and how to include them in your pages, let's move on to explore the media features themselves—starting with the most common, those that use the dimensions of your device or browser viewport.

Media Features Based on Dimensions

Media queries are most commonly used today for detecting the dimensions of the agent being used to view your content and then serving up the appropriate rules for display on that agent: large text and images for big monitors, small text and a single-column layout for smartphones, that kind of thing. Of course, there's more to media queries than those simple contexts, but you get the general idea.

You need to consider two sets of dimensions: first, those of the device itself, and second, those of the agent's viewport (for most people that is a web browser, but the viewport could also be an app window) on that device. A person may visit your site using an enormous wide-screen television, but that's of little concern to you if the app the person is using to view your site only occupies a quarter of the screen. On certain devices, the two sets of dimensions are the same—on most smartphones and tablets, for example, the browser's width is the same as the device's width.

NOTE *The viewport itself is subject to change on some devices; see "Device Adaptation" on page 48 for more details.*

The viewport's dimensions are probably the most important and the ones that you'll use the most, and the media features that are relevant to these are height and width. The viewport dimension features take as an argument a single length value that the logic is tested against; if the dimension in question is equal to the supplied length value, the logic is true and the rules are applied. In the following query, the rule inside the curly brackets is applied to the body element of the viewport when it is exactly 480px wide:

```
@media screen and (width: 480px) {
  body { background-color: #00f; }
}
```

NOTE *Working with width is much more common so I'm using width in the examples in this section, but the same techniques apply to height also.*

I've used a px value in this example, but any length unit is permitted. Regardless of which unit you use, an exact value is likely too specific for most purposes. A pair of extensions to the feature makes it more flexible, however.

Many media features, including `width`, allow the prefixes `max-` and `min-` before the feature name. These stand for maximum and minimum respectively, which you probably don't need me to explain, and in practice mean "no more than" and "no less than." For example, using `max-width` you can apply style rules to any browser that is no more than 480px wide, and using `min-width`, to any that is no less than 480px wide:

```
@media screen and (max-width: 480px) { ... }
@media screen and (min-width: 480px) { ... }
```

In the example file *mq-width.html*, you can see a simple demonstration of these prefixes in use. The page has three `iframe` elements with widths of 190px, 200px, and 210px respectively, and with a unique `id` value for your reference:

```
<iframe src="mq-hello.html" width="190" id="a"></iframe>
<iframe src="mq-hello.html" width="200" id="b"></iframe>
<iframe src="mq-hello.html" width="210" id="c"></iframe>
```

Because an iframe creates a new viewport, you can use the `width` media feature to apply rules to each differently sized viewport. The page that the iframes refer to, *mq-hello.html*, contains an inline style block in the header that applies different border-style properties to the elements, depending on the media features that are matched. This task is performed with the following three media queries:

❶ ```
@media screen and (width: 200px) {
  h1 { border-style: solid; }
}
```
❷ ```
@media screen and (min-width: 205px) {
  h1 { border-style: dotted; }
}
```
❸ ```
@media screen and (max-width: 195px) {
  h1 { border-style: dashed; }
}
```

The rules are applied like this: ❶ applies to iframe #*b*, which has a width of 200px; ❷ to iframe #*c*, as it's at least 205px wide; and ❸ to iframe #*a*, as it's no wider than 195px. You can see the result in Figure 3-1.

*Figure 3-1: Applying different rules to viewports of different widths using media queries*
```

Now, I'm sure it doesn't take much imagination on your part to see how the width feature could be useful: You could use smaller text on smaller screens and larger text on larger screens, for example:

```
@media screen and (max-width: 480px) {
  h1 { font-size: 2em; }
}
@media screen and (min-width: 481px) {
  h1 { font-size: 3.6em; }
}
```

NOTE *The queries I've used here are just for illustration. You can approach this in a better way, which I cover in "Mobile First and Content Breakpoints" on page 57.*

If you're sure you want to work with the dimensions of the device, not those of the viewport, you can use the device-width and device-height features—although, as before, I think width is a more commonly used dimension than height, so I'll concentrate on the former. The way you use the device-width feature is, for all practical purposes, the same as for the width feature—only the metric it responds to is different. As with width, device-width can be extended with max- and min- prefixes:

```
@media screen and (max-device-width: 799px) { ... }
@media screen and (device-width: 800px) { ... }
@media screen and (min-device-width: 801px) { ... }
```

Another way to serve rules depends on the device's or viewport's aspect ratio. The *aspect ratio* is the ratio of width to height (or device-width to device-height); a 1024×768 monitor, for example, has an aspect ratio of 4/3—that is, four horizontal pixels to every three vertical pixels—which is common for older screens. Newer widescreen devices (such as the iPhone 5) tend to use a 16/9 ratio.

NOTE *I discuss pixels further in "A Quick Digression: All About Pixels" on page 45.*

To target a screen with a 4/3 aspect ratio, you'd use the device-aspect-ratio feature:

```
@media screen and (device-aspect-ratio: 4/3) { ... }
```

The max- and min- prefixes apply to these features as well, so to create a query where you wanted to target only viewports—not devices—which are currently in at least an 8/5 ratio, you'd use the min-aspect-ratio feature:

```
@media screen and (min-aspect-ratio: 8/5) { ... }
```

A quick way to work out which aspect ratios are greater than others is to divide the first figure by the second; a 4/3 ratio works out to 1.333, whereas 8/5 works out to 1.6. The larger the result, the wider the ratio. The example shown here applies only to screens for which that number is 1.6 or more.

Probably more useful than the very precise figure of an aspect ratio is the orientation of the viewport—whether it's in *portrait mode* (height is greater than width) or *landscape mode* (width is greater than height). You query this with the orientation feature. This feature is especially useful for handheld devices like phones and tablets that can change orientation often:

```
@media screen and (orientation: portrait) { ... }
```

The max- and min- prefixes don't apply to this feature for (hopefully) obvious reasons.

Combining and Negating Media Queries

You can add a series of logical statements by repeated use of the and keyword with extra media queries. When and is used, the rules are applied only if *all* of the media query logic is true; for example, to test if a viewport is both in landscape mode and at least 800em wide, you could use this code:

```
@media all and (orientation: landscape) and (min-width: 800em) { ... }
```

You can actually simplify this more; the all media type is the default state, so you can leave it out of queries, also making the first instance of and unnecessary:

```
@media (orientation: landscape) and (min-width: 800em) { ... }
```

You can create a series of media queries and apply the rules if any *one* of them is true, using the comma separator to act like an or operator. In this example, the rules are applied if either the device is in landscape mode or the width of the viewport is at least 800em:

```
@media (orientation: landscape), (min-width: 800em) {}
```

Finally, you can reverse the logic of a media query by using the not operator; added to the start of the query, this operator means the rules are applied if the logic of the query is false. In this code the rules are applied to any device that has an aspect ratio other than 8/5:

```
@media not all and (device-aspect-ratio: 8/5) {}
```

Finding the right balance of media queries for your site can be a quite complex act involving many different variables, but the end result can be extremely satisfying. I highly recommend spending time really coming to grips with how they work. Zoe Mickley Gillenwater wrote an excellent post on the topic, *Essential Considerations for Crafting Quality Media Queries*, in which she says:

> Designing web layouts with media queries is a *process*. You need to keep them in mind from the very beginning and make decisions at several points about how to integrate them in ways that will make the most sense for your site. There are very few always-right or always-wrong answers.

This post is a great piece of work that deserves to be read and digested fully.

A Quick Digression: All About Pixels

As we've moved into the multi-device era, a point to consider beyond the dimensions of the screen is its resolution. Many new devices, especially smartphones, now ship with high-resolution screens, so if you want to provide an optimal experience for everyone, you need to consider how images and other objects will display on those screens. Before I get into that, however, I need to talk briefly about pixels.

To talk about resolution-dependent media queries, first I need to define some terms, starting with those related to pixels (I presume that readers know what a pixel is). The *physical pixel count* of a screen is the number of pixels contained in the width of the screen. For example, a 1280×800 screen has a physical pixel count of 1280 along its broad edge. The iPhone 3GS, in its default (portrait) position, has a physical pixel count of 320, whereas the iPhone 4 and above, using the "retina" display, has a count of 640.

The *pixel density* of a screen is traditionally measured in *pixels per inch (PPI)*—actually if you prefer the metric system, you can use *pixels per centimeter (PPC)* instead, but I'll stick to imperial measure for this description. Imperial measure is sometimes known as *dots per inch (DPI)*, even by popular desktop image-editing software, and the two terms—PPI and DPI—can be considered interchangeable. Regardless, pixel density is a measure of the number of pixels that can be placed in a line that spans one inch of the device's screen.

For the vast majority of screens in use until recently, the PPI is 96. With the rise of smartphones, however, the PPI count has been steadily increasing; the original iPhone (and all versions up to the 3GS) has a 163 ppi resolution, whereas the iPhone 4 and above has double that, an incredible 326 ppi (despite the screen staying the same size—you'll see why in a second).

So far, so straightforward—but that's not the whole story. The majority of high-density screens now have an extra, virtual pixel unit: the *density-independent pixel (DIP)*, sometimes referred to as a *CSS pixel*. This is a relative unit; one physical pixel is equal to any number of DIPs. This allows you to scale websites up (and down), generally to provide better usability on smaller screens.

The ratio of virtual pixels to physical pixels is known as the *device pixel ratio*. I'll use the abbreviation *DPR* for this, although it is also known as *DPPX (dots per pixel)*. Devices that don't have DIPs have a DPR of 1—that is, one virtual pixel to one physical pixel. The most common high-resolution devices as I write this (such as the Samsung Galaxy S III or the iPhone 5) have a DPR of 2—two virtual pixels to one physical.

Figure 3-2 illustrates this. On the left is a 2×2 block of physical pixels; in the center, a screen with a DPR of 1.5 fits 9 DIPs into the same space; and on the right, a screen with a DPR of 2 fits 16 DIPs into the space.

Figure 3-2: Comparing different DPR values: 1 (left), 1.5 (center), and 2 (right)

You can find out the DPR of any device by using JavaScript, as most browsers now support a DOM property called `devicePixelRatio` on the `window` object. To find out the DPR of the device you're using, just type this into your browser's developer console:

```
window.devicePixelRatio;
```

If your browser doesn't have a developer console, I've written a script in the example file *mq-dpr.html* that you can use instead.

This discussion has all been quite technical, and to be honest I've barely scratched the surface, but hopefully you understand enough about resolution and pixels to be able to get the most out of the rest of this chapter.

Screen Resolution Media Queries

As you've just seen, many devices now ship with very high-resolution screens. Although certainly a positive thing, these screens do have one or two drawbacks, mainly around the display of graphics. As you're probably aware, two types of graphic exist: *vector*, such as SVG, is a series of coordinates used to display shapes on screen regardless of resolution (I discuss SVG in more detail in Chapter 7); and *bitmap* or *raster*, such as JPG and PNG, is a series of different colored dots that are more explicitly tied to pixels.

The practical difference between the two types is that bitmaps are saved with a PPI setting, and a bitmap graphic that looks fine on a screen with a low DPR will look pretty poor on a device with a high one. That means you will most likely want to use higher PPI bitmaps for higher-resolution screens, which is why media features exist to do just that.

In fact, two media features are available. The first, and most widely used owing to WebKit's popularity on mobile devices, is a proprietary feature called -webkit-device-pixel-ratio. This feature—along with the related max- and min- prefixes—lets you target a device's DPR. For example, here's how to add a high-resolution image to devices with a DPR of at least 2:

```
E { background-image: url('foo.png'); }
@media screen and (-webkit-min-device-resolution: 2) {
  E { background-image: url('foo-hi-res.png'); }
}
```

WARNING *Remember that a high-resolution device doesn't automatically mean a good Internet connection. The user might not thank you for making him or her download a 600kB image over a low 3G connection.*

All pretty straightforward, right? Wrong. -webkit-device-pixel-ratio is, as mentioned, a WebKit-proprietary CSS extension and not part of the Media Queries specification. The spec actually contains a similar query, resolution. This query immediately improves upon -webkit-device-pixel-ratio by being more flexible in the values it accepts; you can, for example, use the dpi unit. Remember, a standard monitor resolution has a DPI (or PPI) of 96; that being the case, you can target those monitors with this code:

```
@media screen and (resolution: 96dpi) {
  E { background-image: url('foo.png'); }
}
```

But you can also target higher-resolution screens by multiplying the standard count, 96, by the DPR. For example, the following query applies to devices with a DPR of 2 or above, just like in the -webkit-device-pixel-ratio example a few paragraphs ago:

```
@media screen and (min-resolution: 192dpi) {
  E { background-image: url('foo-hires.png'); }
}
```

You can do this in an even better way, however, by using the dppx unit. This unit is equivalent to the DPR, so an updated version of the previous example employs this code:

```
@media screen and (min-resolution: 2dppx) {
  E { background-image: url('foo-hires.png'); }
}
```

-webkit-device-pixel-ratio has been around since the iPhone was launched in 2006, and an awful lot of legacy devices are out there, so this extension is not going anywhere in a hurry. That being the case, you're probably going to have to test for both by extending the media query with a little extra logic. As previously mentioned, using a comma-separated list of media queries means the rules are applied if any one of them is true:

```
@media screen and (min-resolution: 2dppx),
       screen and (-webkit-min-device-resolution: 2)  {
  E { background-image: url('foo-hires.png'); }
}
```

This logic tests that the device has a DPR of at least 2 but works in both legacy WebKit browsers and in ones that are compliant to the spec.

NOTE *To complicate matters further, some browsers—such as Opera Mobile—allow you to change the device pixel ratio.*

Device Adaptation

Mobile browsers are capable of scaling websites for better presentation on small screens but presume that most websites are aimed at desktop browsers. This presumption means that, by default, they show a site zoomed out/scaled down in order to accommodate the whole thing (or as much as possible) on screen. This is generally known as the *layout viewport*, and the drawback of the layout viewport is that the zoomed-out view can leave sites that are optimized for mobile looking very small indeed (you can see it in the "before" state in Figure 3-3).

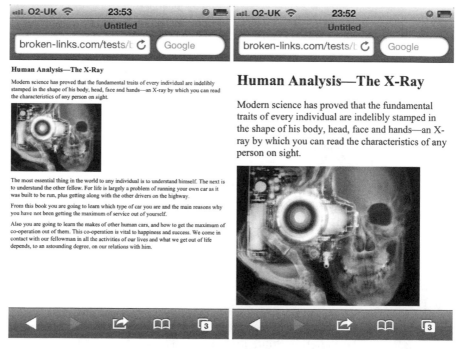

Figure 3-3: The same page displayed on an iPhone before (left) and after (right) the application of the viewport meta tag

The solution that Apple came up with when they created Safari for iPhone was to ask developers to add a special tag, known as the *viewport meta tag*, in the head of their documents. This tag is used to control the dimensions and scaling of the browser viewport. Here's an example:

```
<meta name="viewport" content="width=device-width">
```

You can use a number of different values in the content attribute, but the ones in this code mean: "Make the width of this document the same as the width of this device." The difference can be clearly seen in Figure 3-3, which shows the same document before and after this tag is applied. In the before shot, the browser has automatically adjusted the main body text to better fit the screen, but the heading and image are very small; in the after shot, the heading and image are more naturally sized for the screen.

A device's width will vary, but it is also affected by DPR. The iPhone 3GS screen is, as mentioned, 320px. But although the iPhone's "retina" screen has a physical pixel count of 640px, as it has a DPR of 2, it only counts 320px—the DIPs—when the viewport meta tag is used with the device-width value.

Other parameters used in this tag control the initial zoom level of the page and whether the user has control over zooming it. In this example, the initial zoom level is 1.5x, and the user will not be able to change that:

```
<meta name="viewport" content="initial-scale=1.5,user-scalable=no">
```

WARNING   *Taking the option to zoom out of users' hands can be extremely annoying; think carefully before applying this option.*

Although the viewport meta tag fulfills its main function well, it does have a drawback: Using a meta tag means you can define only one set of parameters per page. For example, rather than using the default device width, you could specify a fixed size instead:

```
<meta name="viewport" content="width=480">
```

The problem is that all devices that recognize the viewport tag will set their zoom level at 480px, which is fine for smaller handheld devices but less useful for large tablets.

The solution is to set the viewport parameters in CSS. You do this with the @viewport at-rule. Where the viewport meta tag uses different parameters in the content attribute, @viewport uses CSS syntax to perform the same functions with a subset of specialist properties. To illustrate, I've repeated the previous example:

```
@viewport { width: 480px; }
```

The reason this solution is more useful is that you can combine `@viewport` with media queries to have different viewport parameters, depending on the viewing device. Consider this example:

```
@media screen and (max-width: 480px) {
  @viewport {
    width: 480px;
  }
}
@media screen and (min-width: 481px) {
  @viewport {
    width: device-width;
  }
}
```

For screens with a 480px width or lower, the viewport will be displayed at 480px, and on larger screens, at their natural size.

This approach is known as *device adaptation* and has the advantage of making sitewide changes much easier by requiring the modification of only a single CSS rule, rather than an unknown number of individual pages.

Input Mechanism Media Features

Although I've talked a lot about the dimensions or resolution of screens, I have to cover other key factors as well; for instance, the ways in which a user interacts with the device is just as important. The mouse and keyboard pairing has been the dominant input mechanism for many years, but the new device landscape accommodates not only that but also touch, stylus, and voice—and who knows what else in the future.

In recognition of the variety of input mechanisms, two new media features were proposed in the Media Queries Level 4 specification. These allow you to provide style rules sympathetic to the way users interact with your pages.

The first of these is the `pointer` feature, which has three available parameters: Of today's most common input mechanisms, a device with keyboard or voice control has no pointer, so is classed as `none`; finger-based touch screens like a tablet or smartphone are most likely classed as `coarse`; and a mouse or stylus, which provides very close control, is classed as `fine`.

That being the case, here's an example query adding extra padding to link elements on sites viewed using touch-screen (or other less precise) devices:

```
@media screen and (pointer: coarse) {
  a { padding: 1em; }
}
```

One feature unique to devices with mouse input is the hover state, which detects when an on-screen pointer is positioned above an element. Obviously, this feature doesn't exist for touch or voice input. To address this, a hover feature is available for testing the existence of a hover state in the device. As the hover query is Boolean, no second value is required:

```
@media screen and (hover) {}
```

If you want to set rules on devices that don't have a hover state, you could use either the 0 value or the not operator, so these rules are analogous:

```
@media screen and (hover:0) {}
@media not screen and (hover) {}
```

 These are only proposals, and although they were already implemented in WebKit at the time of writing, they are subject to change.

Further Media Features

A handful of other media features are available, many of which deal with device capabilities that will be out of the scope of most developers. A few of those features are related to color; for example, if you're developing for ebook readers, some of which use grayscale "liquid paper," you might want to investigate using the monochrome query and its opposite, color:

```
@media screen and (color) {}
@media screen and (monochrome) {}
```

I have to point out that in my (limited) tests, browsers on grayscale devices don't always identify themselves as monochrome, even when these features are fully supported. As always, test on as many devices as possible.

For the remaining features in the Media Queries spec, I can do little more than repeat what's in the documentation, as they're largely aimed at specialist devices that I don't have access to. I urge you to take a look at the spec for yourself and see if those features are relevant to your project.

Proposed in the draft version of the Media Queries Level 4 spec is the useful script feature, which tests whether JavaScript (or, more correctly, ECMAScript) is both supported and enabled by the browser. script is Boolean, so it requires no extra value to detect if script support is present:

```
@media screen and (script) {}
```

At the time of writing this chapter, this feature is still only a proposal and not implemented by any browser and, as such, may be removed at any time, but I felt it was worthy of inclusion based on just how useful it could be.

Media Queries in JavaScript

The benefit of media queries in CSS is obvious, so you shouldn't be surprised that they have been adopted into JavaScript as well. This means you can run functions or load in more external scripts depending on device capabilities, leading to sympathetic and improved behavior as well as presentation.

The `matchMedia()` method is used to run the queries, which are provided in a string as an argument. Try running this in your developer console:

```
window.matchMedia('screen and (min-width: 800px)');
```

The result of this code is a `MediaQueryList` object, and how it appears in your console depends on the browser and tools you use; Figure 3-4 shows the result when I enter this query into Firebug.

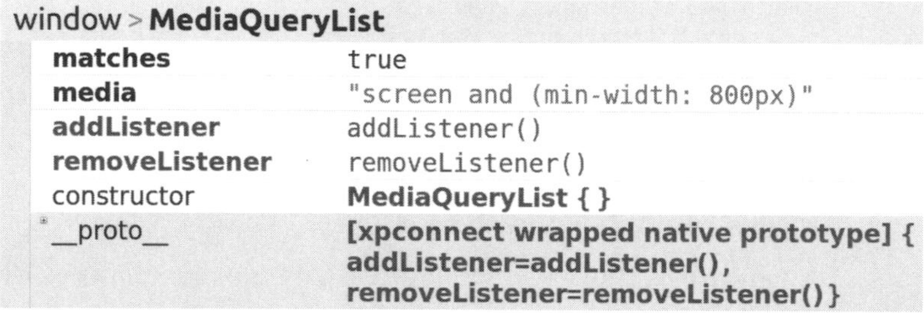

window > **MediaQueryList**	
matches	true
media	"screen and (min-width: 800px)"
addListener	addListener()
removeListener	removeListener()
constructor	**MediaQueryList { }**
__proto__	**[xpconnect wrapped native prototype] { addListener=addListener(), removeListener=removeListener() }**

Figure 3-4: The result of running a `matchMedia()` query in the console of Firebug

What I want from this object is the value of the `matches` property, which will return `true` or `false` depending on the query logic. Using this value, you can easily build an `if` statement to perform actions depending on the result; in this example, if the viewport is at least 800px wide, the function `foo()` runs:

```
var mq = window.matchMedia('screen and (min-width: 800px)');
if (mq.matches) { foo(); }
else { // do something else }
```

In the file *mq-matches.html*, you can see a short script I've written based on this logic, which simply shows an alert that tells you whether your browser window is at least 800px wide; try resizing your browser window and refreshing the page to see different results.

Taking advantage of JavaScript's dynamic nature, you can extend this with a listener that fires if the device's state changes, for example, if the user resizes his or her browser window or changes the orientation of his or her device. I can extend my previous code snippet by adding a new function, `widthWatch()`, containing the original `if-else` logic, which is called whenever the viewport changes and fires the listener:

```
function widthWatch(mq) {
  if (mq.matches) { foo(); }
  else { // do something else }
}
var mq = window.matchMedia('screen and (min-width: 800px)');
mq.addListener(widthWatch);
widthWatch(mq);
```

In the example file *mq-widthwatch.html*, you can see the results of a script based on this; it returns the same results as in the previous example, but you won't need to refresh the page to get a different result; just resize the window.

Adaptive vs. Responsive Web Design

As mentioned at the start of this chapter, two main methodologies, known as adaptive and responsive, are used for modern website development. Both share the concept of using *breakpoints*, which are the limits created by using media queries, at which point a change to the site layout is imposed.

The difference between adaptive and responsive methodologies comes down to how the site changes between breakpoints; *adaptive* is essentially a series of fixed-width layouts, whereas *responsive* uses flexible dimensions so even between breakpoints sites have fluidity.

My opinion is that, given the enormous variability in device screen sizes, making a series of fixed-width pages to accommodate even the most common configurations is probably a fool's errand. The better approach, and the key to building responsively, is to use what's known as *fluid design*, which involves using percentages for length values to make the dimensions of the elements on the page relative to the size of the viewport.

Making a page that's a fixed 960px wide was acceptable when you knew your users were mostly using desktops or laptops with monitors at least 1024px wide, but those days are over, and designing that way nowadays means users with mobile devices see a scaled-down screen that they have to zoom in and out of and scroll around to see. Not the end of the world, but also not ideal.

Using percentages instead of fixed values means your page elements scale up or down along with the size of the viewport, making the content flow inside the boundaries of the screen—hence the name, fluid. Combine this with media queries for content or devices, and you have the very core of responsive design and a tailored, sympathetic experience for your user, regardless of his or her device.

Working with percentages is not without its problems, however, one of which is the difficulty of mixing length units. Consider, for example, a page with three columns: a central column that's 50 percent wide, and a column on either side that's 25 percent wide:

```
E, G { width: 25%; }
F { width: 50%; }
```

Now say you want to add 20px of padding to the left and right of the central column, to act as a gutter, but you don't want this width to be variable—it must always be exactly 20px:

```
F {
  padding: 0 20px;
  width: 50%;
}
```

Maybe you can already see the problem. As you know, the CSS box model makes padding, borders, and margins extra to the content's dimensions, so now these elements have a combined width of 100 percent, plus 40px, making them wider than their container.

A further problem when using percentage widths is that nesting elements leads to some pretty weird numbers. For example, imagine you have an element that you want to be 85 percent of the viewport, and inside that there's a child element you want to be 55 percent of the viewport. Unfortunately, as percentages are relative, you can't just set the width to be 55 percent; you have to calculate 55 percent of 85 percent, which gives you this:

```
E { width: 85%; }
F { width: 64.70588%; }
```

Note that I stopped after the fifth decimal place. So working in this way can involve a lot of calculations, and what's even worse is the various browsers round these numbers up or down in different ways, so pixel perfection can't be guaranteed.

This drawback might be enough to put you off of working responsively, but a few features in CSS3 should help eliminate these problems.

The box-sizing Property

You can, to some degree, work around the unit mixing problem that I just mentioned by using the CSS box-sizing property. To explain, let me recap the current code example: I have three columns with a 20px gap between them, meaning the total width is greater than that of their parent, causing them to overflow:

```
E, G { width: 25%; }
F {
    padding: 0 20px;
    width: 50%;
}
```

With box-sizing, you can change the boundary from where the width is measured—so the stated width includes the border and the padding. In this example, I can change element F so its width includes the padding, using the border-box value for box-sizing:

```
F {
    box-sizing: border-box;
    padding: 0 20px;
    width: 50%;
}
```

Now the entire element F, including the padding, is 50 percent wide, so the combined width of the elements is 100 percent again, making them fit neatly inside their container.

Some people find box-sizing so handy that they advocate applying it to every element, using the universal selector:

```
* { box-sizing: border-box; }
```

I think this is overkill and could cause unwanted difficulties, so my preferred approach is to apply it only where it's actually required:

```
div, .etc { box-sizing: border-box; }
```

Using box-sizing does have its limitations, however; for one, it doesn't affect margins at all. To accommodate that, having some way to perform dynamic calculations on length values instead would be better.

Dynamic Calculations on Length Values

When mixing units, a new value function eliminates all of the problems mentioned in the previous section. This function is called calc(), and with it, you can perform simple calculations using any numbered length units. At its very simplest, the argument supplied to the function would be two figures and a mathematical operator:

```
E { height: calc(10px + 10px); }
```

For a more practical illustration of what it can do, let's return once again to the simple three-column example. Say you now want to have a 4px border on the left and right sides of the central column as well as the 10px padding and 20px margin. You could use box-sizing to cover the border and padding, as before, but this time also use the calc() function to subtract the left and right margins from the width:

```
F {
  border: 4px solid black;
  border-width: 0 4px;
  box-sizing: border-box;
  margin: 0 20px;
  padding: 0 10px;
  width: calc(50% - 40px);
}
```

You could, instead of box-sizing, use further calc() values to set the width and even mix up the values a little more by using different length units. In the following example, I use em units for the margin and then an extra calc() function to calculate the combined border, padding, and margin values, before subtracting them all from the total:

```
F {
  border: 4px solid black;
  border-width: 0 4px;
```

```
    margin: 0 20px;
    padding: 0 1em;
    width: calc(50% - calc(48px + 2em));
}
```

You're not limited to using `calc()` only for `width` or `height` properties, however; you can use it on any property or function where length values are permitted.

Viewport-Relative Length Units

As mentioned previously, one problem with using percentages for widths is the fact that they're relative to their parent elements; that may not seem like a problem at first, but it can soon become quite complex. A better approach is to use a unit that's relative to a fixed value, rather than a value inherited from a parent; this is what the `vh` and `vw` units are for.

The `v` stands for viewport, and you may then be able to extrapolate that `h` is for height and `w` for width. In other words, this unit is relative to the dimensions of the viewport. Each number you use with this value is equal to 1 percent of the respective length of the viewport. So to make an element that's half the height of the viewport use this:

```
E { height: 50vh; }
```

And as they're always relative to the viewport rather than the parent, that means no more long strings of numbers after the decimal point. If you return to the earlier example of an element that's 85 percent the width of the viewport with a child element that's 55 percent of the viewport, the values are much more straightforward and easier to manage:

```
E { width: 85vw; }
F { width: 55vw; }
```

Two companion units, `vmax` and `vmin`, are also available; the first means use the greater length of the viewport, whether height or width, and the second means use the lesser value. So given a viewport with a resolution of 800×600, `vmax` would be equivalent to `vw`, and `vmin` equivalent to `vh`.

Root-Relative Units

Units that are relative to the dimensions are helpful, but if you want to use a unit over which you have a little more control, you can use one that's relative to a value that you set. The *root em* (`rem`) is a typographical unit, which like `em` is based on the width of a capital *M* character; the definition is not really important though, all you really need to know is that you can use `rem` for relative sizing.

Where rem differs from em is that the latter is inherited, whereas the former is fixed. For example, say you set a font size of 10px on the root of a document:

```
html { font-size: 10px; }
```

If you want to make a p element that's 12px in size, you could use either one of them in this way:

```
p { font-size: 1.2em; }
p { font-size: 1.2rem; }
```

So far, so identical. But now presume that you have a b element inside that p, like this:

```
<p>This is <b>bold</b>.</p>
```

And you want the b to be 13px in size. Because em is inherited, you would have to divide the larger figure by the smaller to get the new font size:

```
p b { font-size: 1.08333em; }
```

Using em has the same two drawbacks you saw earlier in the chapter: long, unwieldy numbers that become harder and harder to work with and differences in rounding values between browsers. But the rem value, which is always relative to the root, doesn't have these problems, making it much easier to work with:

```
p b { font-size: 1.3rem; }
```

Of course, although it's a typographic unit, you can still use rem for length values in the same way that many people use em.

NOTE *I'm using 10px as the root font size only for the sake of illustration, but you shouldn't do that in real life as it ignores the user's custom font settings. Better to use 62.5 percent, which equates to 10px for most users (16px is the default font size, 62.5 percent of which is 10px) but still makes allowances for users with vision impairment.*

Mobile First and Content Breakpoints

Two systems that I find really useful when building responsive websites are *mobile first* and *breakpoints*. These aren't hard and fast rules—you don't have to implement them if you think they're not appropriate for what you're making—but certainly for browser-based websites I can't imagine building without them.

The mobile first methodology targets the smaller (and most probably lower-powered) devices first and then adds layers of complexity to accommodate larger devices. What this means in essence is you start with a set of styles that's served to all devices—such as color, typography, iconography, and so on—as well as the minimal layout rules required for a small-screen device.

The next step is to add a media query that adds a new set of rules for larger devices/agents; this might be a tablet, for example. For anyone using an even larger device, add extra rules and so on, until you've catered to a core set of devices. If you imagine your core devices are mobile, tablet, and desktop, you'd end up with a set of style rules that looked something like this:

```
<link rel="stylesheet" href="base.css" media="screen">
<link rel="stylesheet" href="tablet.css" media="screen and (min-width: 481px)">
<link rel="stylesheet" href="desktop.css" media="screen and (min-width: 801px)">
```

The actual breakpoints you use are completely up to you; they depend on the devices you want to optimize for and should be based on analysis of existing visitors, if that information is relevant and available to you. The examples I've used here are simplistic and employed only to illustrate the method.

Luke Wroblewski is one of the leading proponents of this method. In the introduction to his book *Mobile First* (A Book Apart, 2011), he says:

> Designing for mobile first now can not only open up new opportunities for growth, it can lead to a better overall user experience for a website or application.

The other approach to consider is setting breakpoints for content rather than devices. With the huge range of web-enabled devices on the market now (and plenty more to come in the future), the boundaries between phone, tablet, laptop, and desktop are incredibly blurred. The phone I own has a 4.65" screen. Samsung's Galaxy Note has a 5.3" screen. Google's Nexus 7 has a 7" screen. At what point does the device stop being a phone and become a tablet?

In my opinion, labels like phone and tablet (and especially portmanteau terms like *phablet*) are fast becoming obsolete. As the functionality of all our Internet-enabled devices converges, we'll have to find a new vocabulary to describe these things (although I'm not going to presume to know what that new vocabulary will be).

My point in mentioning this is that the idea of building breakpoints based on device dimensions may well be a snipe hunt. Think about making breakpoints based on content instead; rather than thinking "how wide should my content be on a tablet," think "what's the maximum width this content can be before it becomes unreadable."

What this means in practice is using media queries to change content, not when an arbitrary device size has been reached, but when that content becomes awkward. To illustrate what I mean, imagine I have a stylesheet applied to wide viewports using a media query:

```
<link rel="stylesheet" href="foo.css" media="screen and (min-width: 1000px)">
```

And within that stylesheet I set the width of an article element to be some 60 percent of the viewport's width and a font to be 120 percent of the root:

```
article { width: 60vw; }
article p { font-size: 1.2rem; }
```

Many studies have shown that for optimal readability the maximum number of characters in a line of text is between 45 and 75, with 66 considered ideal, but if the user has a device with a very large viewport width, the width of 60vw may well lead to lines of text that could double that. Using the theory of content breakpoints, you may want to add an extra rule within the larger device stylesheet to make the text larger on much wider devices to restore some of the readability:

```
@media screen and (min-width: 1200px) {
  p { font-size: 1.4rem; }
}
```

Working in this way isn't going to be easy—quite the opposite, in fact. You will have to perform a lot of testing and analysis and make decisions based on best practice and instinct. Some people, such as Thierry Koblentz in his article "Device-Agnostic Approach to Responsive Web Design," have advocated using content breakpoints solely and not considering devices at all:

> If we consider that content is king, then it makes sense to look at it as the corner stone of the solution. In other words, we should set break-points according to *content* instead of devices.

My opinion is that a combination of the two serves you best. As always, experiment and find your own system.

Responsive Design and Replaced Objects

One sticking point I haven't yet addressed is when you have objects on a page—notably images, but also plug-ins like video and Flash. You can't do much with the latter (especially as Flash won't be supported on most of your users' mobile devices anyway), but images present a unique set of obstacles to building responsively, which I'll come to shortly.

Resizing most objects with percentages (or viewport-relative units if you go that way) is not a problem; you could quite simply set the max-width property to 100 percent to prevent the object ever being wider than its container:

```
img {
  height: auto;
  max-width: 100%;
}
```

Notice that I also set the auto value on the height property to maintain the object's original aspect ratio—having a fixed height and a dynamic width (or vice versa) could distort the object displayed. Sometimes preserving the aspect ratio is going to mean empty spaces on your page on either the horizontal or vertical axis, as the object is too small for its container (you can see an example of this in Figure 3-5). If that's the case, you can take advantage of the object-fit and object-position properties to better control how the object is displayed inside its parent.

The first of those properties, object-fit, controls how the object in question is resized within its container. If you use the contain keyword value, the object is resized so the whole of it shows inside the container, with its aspect ratio preserved and with empty space being added on the horizontal or vertical axis as necessary. Alternatively, using the cover keyword makes the shortest length of the object equal to the shortest length of the container, with the longest length overflowing the container. Using the fill keyword would resize the object to match the container's dimensions.

Figure 3-5: An image that's been resized to keep its aspect ratio, leaving empty space around it. (This image is "Evolution of Expression!" by kabils: http://www.fotopedia.com/ items/flickr-2680214376/. It is used under a Creative Commons license.)

In the example file *object-fit.html*, you can see these three keywords compared. This example has three div elements with an img inside, each of which has a unique id value. To this markup, I apply the following code:

```
img {
  height: 100%;
  width: 100%;
}
#obj-fill { object-fit: fill; }
#obj-contain { object-fit: contain; }
#obj-cover { object-fit: cover; }
```

The results, which you can see in Figure 3-6, are as follows: The first element, *#obj-fill*, has been resized to the same dimensions as its parent, causing it to be squashed horizontally and stretched vertically, and that distortion obviously doesn't look great; the element in the middle, *#obj-contain*, has kept its original aspect ratio but been resized so the entire img fits inside its parent, causing the "letterboxing" effect; finally, *#obj-cover* has also kept its aspect ratio but been resized so the whole of its parent is covered. To achieve this, the image has been scaled up and overflows the parent (I've hidden the overflow in this example).

Figure 3-6: Different values for the object-fit *property (left to right):* fill, contain, cover

By default, the object sits dead center of its parent when object-fit is applied, but you can change that with the object-position property. This property works like the background-position property in that you can use either two values to specify an offset from the top left of the container or extra positional keywords (top, right, bottom, left, center) to offset from another side. For example:

```
E { object-position: bottom 10px right 2em; }
```

The example file *object-position.html* shows three different values for the object-position property. The markup is essentially the same as in the previous example, but the relevant CSS for this has been updated:

```
img {
  height: 100%;
  width: 100%;
  object-fit: contain;
}
#obj-1 { object-position: center top; }
#obj-2 { object-position: center bottom; }
#obj-3 { object-position: right; }
```

The result is shown in Figure 3-7. All three img elements have the contain value applied to the object-fit property, but that's just for the sake of illustration and not required. The first image, *#obj-1*, is positioned in the horizontal center of its parent and the vertical top; the next, *#obj-2*, is still at the horizontal center, but now the vertical bottom; the last image, *#obj-3*, has been cropped to portrait dimensions to better show it positioned to the right of its parent.

Figure 3-7: Different values for the object-position property

The Image Problem

Although you've seen that resizing and positioning objects using responsive techniques is quite straightforward, images are still a source of major problems in responsive design for a number of reasons. Chief among them is the question of file size; although not always the case, the chances are good that someone using a mobile device will be using 3G or 4G and will have reduced bandwidth compared to a desktop user. That being the case, you don't want to have to serve them a large, heavy image that they have to download over their limited connection.

This is exacerbated by the increase in high-resolution screens. Standard-resolution (1DPR) bitmap images (like JPG and PNG) can look quite low quality on higher-resolution (2DPR) screens. HTML currently offers no way to provide higher-resolution images to devices, and even if it did, you still have the bandwidth problem. What's the solution?

The HTML5 Responsive Images Solution

Unfortunately there is, as I write this, no native solution. Although a number of proposals have been put forward, none has been officially blessed yet. The proposal that seems to be the most popular is to use a new picture element, like so:

```
❶ <picture alt="Description of image subject.">
❷   <source srcset="small.jpg 1x, small-highres.jpg 2x">
❸   <img src="small.jpg" alt="Description of image subject.">
  </picture>
```

Three key activities are at work here: ❶ is the new picture element with the alt attribute describing the image (other standard attributes could also be used here); ❷ is the source element, which lists different source alternatives using the srcset attribute—what you see here are two alternative image sources, one for standard screens and one for higher-resolution screens, using the number of the screens DPR, which you saw earlier in this chapter; finally, ❸ is the current img element, which you use as fallback for older browsers that haven't implemented picture yet.

Remember this suggestion is only the most prominent as I write this; it may not be the final syntax.

So this syntax allows for testing device resolution, but what about other media queries? You can add those with further source elements:

```
<picture alt="Description of image subject.">
  <source srcset="small.jpg 1x, small-hi-res.jpg 2x">
  <source media="(min-width: 481px)" srcset="med.jpg 1x, med-hi-res.jpg 2x">
  <img src="small.jpg" alt="Description of image subject.">
</picture>
```

In this example, you can see an extra source element using the media attribute to set up a media query and serving a different set of images if that query is true. I have to say that although this syntax works, I don't like it much; it's repetitious for a start and, if used on a page with multiple images, leads to maintainability issues. That said, no other simpler suggestion has been proposed.

The WHATWG's current proposal is to also use the srcset attribute, but only on the img element. This option allows images to be served dependent on screen resolution, but not with any other media query. I want to make this really clear: This is not "official," only a proposal.

Plenty of third-party solutions have been created, notable among them Matt Wilcox's Adaptive Images, which uses PHP and Apache to resize images on the server and serve them to users depending on their device's attributes. But while this option works well, it does depend on a specific server configuration that isn't available to everyone and also adds a reliance on JavaScript. This problem still waits to be solved natively.

Summary

I've covered a lot of ground in this chapter, discussing media queries, device resolution, the difference between physical and virtual pixels, responsive web design, and the problem with responsive images. If you're working cross-device, this information should be useful at least, critical at most.

What I haven't discussed in any great detail is how to actually create your page layout—the way to present content at its best. A lot of work has been done in this area in recent years, and in the next chapter, I talk about that.

Further Reading

First port of call for learning more about media queries should be Zoe Mickley Gillenwater's post "Essential Considerations for Crafting Quality Media Queries": *http://zomigi.com/blog/essential-considerations-for-crafting-qual ity-media-queries/.*

The authority on mobile devices is PPK, and if you want to find out more about physical and virtual pixels, I suggest you start with his article "A Pixel Is Not a Pixel Is Not a Pixel": *http://www.quirksmode.org/blog/archives/2010/04/a_pixel_is_not.html*. Wikipedia has a list of common device resolutions and pixel density: *http://en.wikipedia.org/wiki/List_of_displays_by_pixel_density*.

Patrick Lauke wrote an article about user-controlled DPR, "devicePixelRatio in Opera Mobile": *http://my.opera.com/ODIN/blog/2012/07/05/devicepixelratio-in-opera-mobile*. Matt Wilcox's article "The Responsive Design Process" has a good glossary of key terms as well as plenty of practical advice on the design side: *http://mattwilcox.net/archive/entry/id/1078/*.

Read more about the way that different browsers round decimal places in John Albin Wilkins's post "Responsive Design's Dirty Little Secret": *http://www.palantir.net/blog/responsive-design-s-dirty-little-secret/*.

Paul Irish's blog post "box-sizing: border-box FTW" sets out his reasons for applying this property globally: *http://paulirish.com/2012/box-sizing-border-box-ftw/*.

Luke Wroblewski's book *Mobile First* is published by A Book Apart: *http://www.abookapart.com/products/mobile-first/*.

To learn more about content breakpoints, read a pair of articles from Australian web design studio Jordesign (*http://www.jordesign.com/blog/responsive-breakpoints-from-the-content-out/*) and developer Thierry Koblentz (*http://coding.smashingmagazine.com/2012/03/22/device-agnostic-approach-to-responsive-web-design/*).

The history of the current favorite responsive images proposal, and latest news on the state of its adoption, can be found on the website of the Responsive Images Community Group: *http://www.w3.org/community/respimg/*.

Find Matt Wilcox's Adaptive Images tool at *http://adaptive-images.com/*.

4

NEW APPROACHES TO CSS LAYOUTS

Once your markup is in place and you've considered how to best optimize your website or application for the devices they'll be used on, you can actually start to create the layout of your website or application. Layouts have been quite limited and formulaic using the features available in CSS2.1. Even though clever designers and developers have pushed the use of floats and positioning to their maximum, most websites use a variant of the three-column grid, a pattern dictated largely by the limits of available technology rather than the demands of the content those sites contain.

For the first time, CSS3 has new properties dedicated to the creation of varied and flexible layouts, using much of the knowledge gained from centuries of written and printed material while staying sympathetic to the capabilities of electronic screens. With these new features, designers can display content to best advantage, and an application's user interface can better respond to the devices that it will be used on.

Although many of the new features in this chapter have already been implemented in browsers, they should be considered experimental and subject to change until the W3C has finished the standardization process. Detailed information on current browser support is in Appendix A and will be updated on http://modernwebbook.com/.

Multi-columns

With their roots in scientific document markup, websites have followed a pretty straightforward pattern when it comes to text: everything is based on a single, unbroken column, like a document in a word processor or text editor. This characteristic is largely because of the Web's dynamic nature, with variable font sizes and numbers of characters making it hard to control positioning precisely. Print, with its fixable letter sizes and known character count, allows for much greater flexibility in how text is laid out on the page.

Pick up just about any printed magazine or newspaper (younger readers: ask your parents what those are) and you're bound to find examples of text being flowed into multiple columns—often two, sometimes three or more. Columnar formats make it easy to fit more text on a page without sacrificing readability.

Until recently, replicating this columnar style on the Web hasn't been possible without JavaScript, but the Multi-column Layout Module addresses this shortcoming. To be honest, I think this feature is often more suited for print than for screen, where scrolling up and down to read columns of text can be a pain, but for some occasions, multiple columns is definitely the better pattern to use.

Multi-column properties make flowing inline content into columns straightforward. On the parent of the elements in question, you apply the `column-count` property, with an integer value for the number of columns. For example, this is the code you'd use to flow the content into three columns:

```
E { column-count: 3; }
```

The inline content is now in three columns, with a 1em gap between each. If you prefer to be more prescriptive about your columns, you could instead set their width using the `column-width` property with a length value:

```
E { column-width: 120px; }
```

This markup would make as many columns of 120px—plus the 1em gap between each column—as would fit into the width of the parent element. For example, given a parent width of 600px, four columns of 120px would be created, plus a total gap of 3em between them, leaving some space to spare. That spare space would then be equally distributed among each column, increasing the width until the full width of the parent is filled; that is, the `column-width` value is treated as a minimum rather than an absolute.

Figure 4-1 shows a comparison of the two approaches. The upper example uses `column-count` to create three equal columns that fill the parent's width; the lower example has a `column-width` value of 120px, but the actual width of the columns is slightly different as each has been resized to better fit the parent.

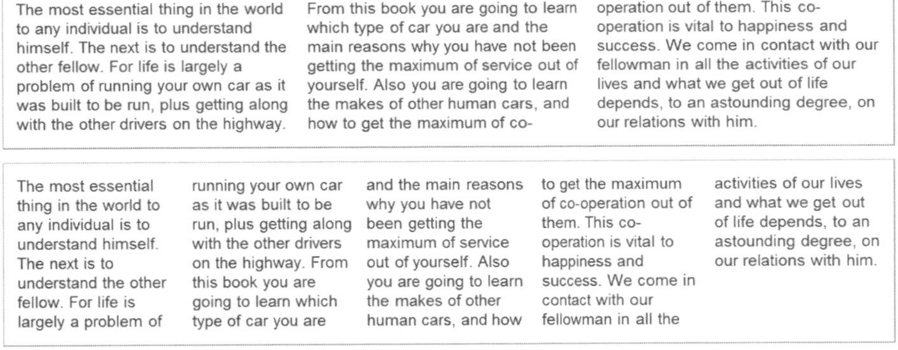

<table>
<tr><td>The most essential thing in the world to any individual is to understand himself. The next is to understand the other fellow. For life is largely a problem of running your own car as it was built to be run, plus getting along with the other drivers on the highway.</td><td>From this book you are going to learn which type of car you are and the main reasons why you have not been getting the maximum of service out of yourself. Also you are going to learn the makes of other human cars, and how to get the maximum of co-</td><td>operation out of them. This co-operation is vital to happiness and success. We come in contact with our fellowman in all the activities of our lives and what we get out of life depends, to an astounding degree, on our relations with him.</td></tr>
</table>

<table>
<tr><td>The most essential thing in the world to any individual is to understand himself. The next is to understand the other fellow. For life is largely a problem of</td><td>running your own car as it was built to be run, plus getting along with the other drivers on the highway. From this book you are going to learn which type of car you are</td><td>and the main reasons why you have not been getting the maximum of service out of yourself. Also you are going to learn the makes of other human cars, and how</td><td>to get the maximum of co-operation out of them. This co-operation is vital to happiness and success. We come in contact with our fellowman in all the</td><td>activities of our lives and what we get out of life depends, to an astounding degree, on our relations with him.</td></tr>
</table>

Figure 4-1: Comparing columns laid out using the column-count (top) and column-width properties (bottom)

You can also apply `column-width` and `column-count` to the same element. When you do, the `column-count` value becomes the maximum number of columns allowed. In this case, the logic is: "Make columns of 120px, up to a maximum of three columns; then resize them as necessary to fill the parent width." You could also use the `columns` shorthand for this, where the two values provided are `column-width` and `column-count`, respectively:

```
E { columns: 120px 3; }
```

When inline content is flowed into columns in a parent element with no fixed height, the browser evenly distributes (as much as possible) the number of lines in each column, possibly leaving some empty space at the bottom of the parent element. But if the element has a set height, you can choose how the text will flow, using the `column-fill` property.

The default value for `column-fill` is `balance`, which distributes the lines evenly. The alternative behavior is for the columns to be filled sequentially, to their maximum height, more than likely leaving a final column with many fewer lines and lots of unused space. If this is your preference, you can set it with the keyword value `auto`.

Gaps and Rules

As mentioned earlier, between each column is a default 1em gap. You can alter that gap with the `column-gap` property. This property accepts a single length value, and it increases the gap between each column to the specified length. Here's an example:

```
E { column-gap: 2em; }
```

You can also add lines between each column, known as *rules*, with the column-rule property. The effect is essentially the same as the border property from CSS2.1, and it requires the same three values—one for width, one for style, and one for color—but it applies only to a single vertical rule, not to all four sides. So to add a dotted, gray, 2px-wide rule between each column, you'd use this code:

```
E { column-rule: 2px dotted gray; }
```

When used with column-gap, the gap width is distributed equally on either side of the rule. Using this example, you would have a 2em gap: 1em gap on each side of the 2px rule, as shown in Figure 4-2.

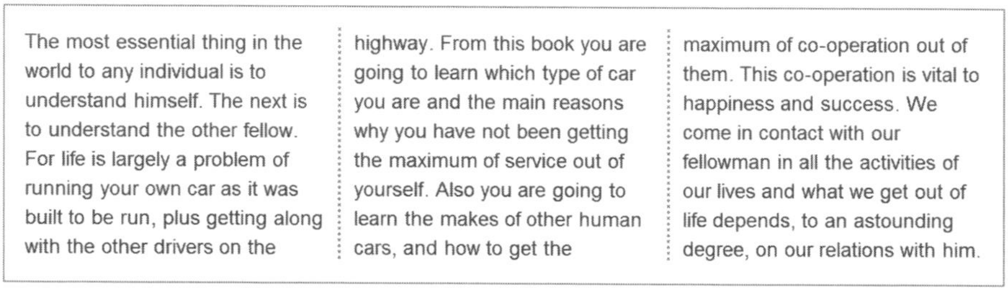

The most essential thing in the world to any individual is to understand himself. The next is to understand the other fellow. For life is largely a problem of running your own car as it was built to be run, plus getting along with the other drivers on the	highway. From this book you are going to learn which type of car you are and the main reasons why you have not been getting the maximum of service out of yourself. Also you are going to learn the makes of other human cars, and how to get the	maximum of co-operation out of them. This co-operation is vital to happiness and success. We come in contact with our fellowman in all the activities of our lives and what we get out of life depends, to an astounding degree, on our relations with him.

Figure 4-2: Controlling the gap and rule between columns

Spans and Breaks

Columns are fine when you're flowing text and other inline content into them, but at other times you will want to use objects or block elements that don't fit nicely into columns. A couple of related properties help in those circumstances.

The first is column-span, best for when you want to break the flow of the columns with a new element that spans all of them. This is a Boolean property—an element spans either all columns or none. As such, the permitted values are either all or none:

```
F { column-span: all; }
```

When the all value is used, the flow of the inline text stops before the element it's applied to and continues afterward, as shown in Figure 4-3.

When you have elements within a grid, you may encounter a situation where the end of a column causes a break in the middle of that element. This isn't ideal if you have, for example, a subheading that could be broken over two columns. To avoid this situation, a set of properties tries to control where the breaks occur. These properties—break-after, break-before, and break-inside—all work in more or less the same way.

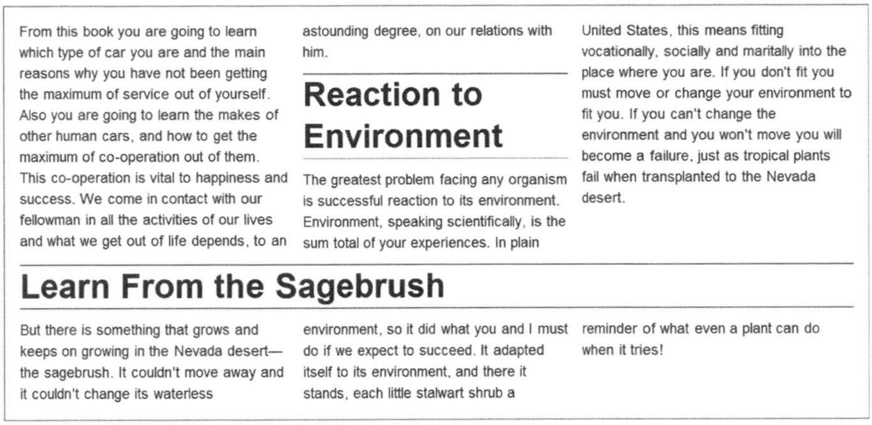

From this book you are going to learn which type of car you are and the main reasons why you have not been getting the maximum of service out of yourself. Also you are going to learn the makes of other human cars, and how to get the maximum of co-operation out of them. This co-operation is vital to happiness and success. We come in contact with our fellowman in all the activities of our lives and what we get out of life depends, to an astounding degree, on our relations with him.

Reaction to Environment

The greatest problem facing any organism is successful reaction to its environment. Environment, speaking scientifically, is the sum total of your experiences. In plain United States, this means fitting vocationally, socially and maritally into the place where you are. If you don't fit you must move or change your environment to fit you. If you can't change the environment and you won't move you will become a failure, just as tropical plants fail when transplanted to the Nevada desert.

Learn From the Sagebrush

But there is something that grows and keeps on growing in the Nevada desert—the sagebrush. It couldn't move away and it couldn't change its waterless environment, so it did what you and I must do if we expect to succeed. It adapted itself to its environment, and there it stands, each little stalwart shrub a reminder of what even a plant can do when it tries!

Figure 4-3: The second subheading spans all the columns, interrupting the content's flow.

I'll use break-before as an illustration. The values you can apply to this property (and its siblings) set whether a column break occurs before an element. A value of column forces a break before the element (where relevant, of course). A value of avoid-column (or just plain avoid—a marker that this property is also available to other CSS features) forbids the browser to break before the element unless absolutely necessary for page flow. The default value auto lets the browser decide the best way to lay out the columns.

If this still sounds a little opaque, the example file *column-breaks.html* shows the column value at work. Here is the code in this example:

```
h2 { break-before: column; }
```

The results are shown in Figure 4-4. In the upper example, the default value auto means the subheadings are inline, in the middle of the columns. But using the column value means that in the second example, the column breaks always occur before the h2s, or subheadings.

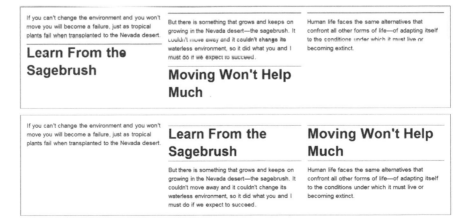

Figure 4-4: The effects of the column value on the break-before property are clearly shown in the lower example.

The break-after and break-inside properties work the same way, except for the location where the break occurs. (Do you need me to tell you where that is, or would you like to guess?)

Flexbox

If you're building more of an app than a content-rich website, especially if you're building an app with lots of buttons and options in the UI, or with lots of form elements or interactive regions, you'll find the Flexible Box (*Flexbox*) module extremely useful.

The roots of Flexbox are in XUL, the language used to create the Firefox browser's layout, which should tell you that it's aimed at user interfaces. Flexbox makes elements resize flexibly to better fit their available space and reorders them or changes their orientation quickly.

The Flexbox syntax has undergone an awful lot of changes in the past few years, but it's finally quite stable and well implemented, so we can discuss it without worry!

Declaring the Flexbox Model

The first step to using Flexbox is to create the *flex container*. The flex container is the parent element that will hold all the *flex items* (I'll get to those soon). To declare a flex container, simply use a new value for the display property:

```
E { display: flex; }
```

Now you have your flex container, but what is it good for? That becomes apparent when you add child items to the container. Example file *flexbox.html* has two child items inside the container, using the following markup:

```
<div id="container">
  <div id="a">...</div>
  <div id="b">...</div>
</div>
```

In Figure 4-5, notice that the two elements are positioned horizontally inside the container at equal widths, even though I haven't used any floats or positioning properties. This behavior is the default for flex items (children of a flex container): They are laid out in a row inside the container. Or, rather, they are laid out in the direction of the language of the document—in left-to-right languages, such as English, the direction in a row is from left to right.

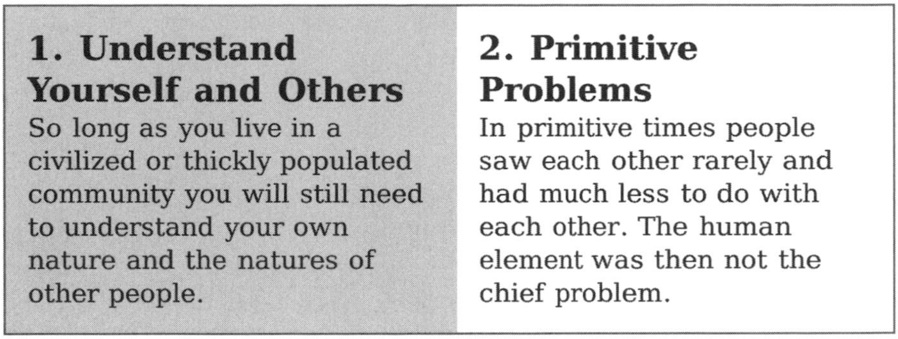

1. Understand Yourself and Others	**2. Primitive Problems**
So long as you live in a civilized or thickly populated community you will still need to understand your own nature and the natures of other people.	In primitive times people saw each other rarely and had much less to do with each other. The human element was then not the chief problem.

Figure 4-5: Child items of a flex container are automatically laid out horizontally.

You can alter this direction by using the flex-direction property on the container. Its default value is row, which gives the behavior just discussed, whereas a value of column lays the items perpendicular to the direction of text—in this case, into a column. (A few other permitted values are available, which I'll cover shortly.):

```
E {
  display: flex;
  flex-direction: column;
}
```

This syntax makes your flex items look like the page layout default behavior, where one item follows the next in vertical sequence.

Changing the Content Order

One of Flexbox's other great capabilities is that you can quickly change the order that items are displayed in, regardless of their order in the DOM. For example, in the previous section, I had two items laid out in a row, but what if I wanted to change them around so that *#b* came before *#a*?

You can do this quickly with the flex-direction property that I just discussed, using the new value row-reverse. This property reverses the order in which the flex items are displayed, as you can see in Figure 4-6.

```
E { flex-direction: row-reverse; }
```

The column-reverse value does the same thing to flex items displayed in columns: They are laid out in reverse order, vertically. Play around with the values of flex-direction in the example file to see their different effects.

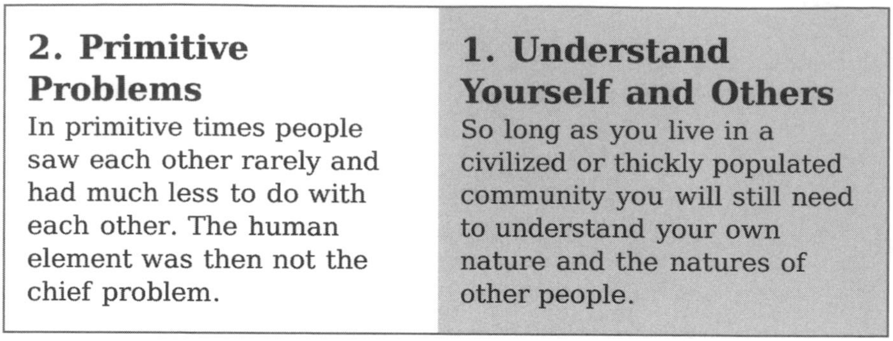

2. Primitive Problems

In primitive times people saw each other rarely and had much less to do with each other. The human element was then not the chief problem.

1. Understand Yourself and Others

So long as you live in a civilized or thickly populated community you will still need to understand your own nature and the natures of other people.

Figure 4-6: The row-reverse value quickly reverses the order of flex children.

By using the flex-order property, you can go beyond this reverse ordering to make completely bespoke ordering patterns. This property is applied to the flex items, not the container, and the value is a number that creates an *ordinal group*, so items with the same value are grouped together. The items are ordered by their ordinal group: All items in the lowest numbered group come first, followed by all items in the second-lowest numbered group, and so on. Any items without a declared value are shown first because they have the default value of 0.

Items with the same ordinal group number will subsequently be shown in the order in which they appear in the DOM. This ordinal group ordering may sound confusing at first, so I'll illustrate using four flex items, marked up like so:

```
<div id="container">
  <div id="a">...</div>
  <div id="b">...</div>
  <div id="c">...</div>
  <div id="d">...</div>
</div>
```

Without any explicit values being set, the children are displayed in the order they appear in the DOM: #*a*, #*b*, #*c*, #*d*. But let's reorder them by using different values on the flex-order property:

```
#a { flex-order: 2; }
#b, #d { flex-order: 3; }
#c { flex-order: 1; }
```

With these rules applied, the items are laid out in this order: #*c*, #*a*, #*b*, #*d*. Item #*c* comes first because it has the lowest ordinal group number, followed by #*a* with the next highest, and then #*b* and #*d*—both are in ordinal group 3, and #*d* comes last because it's also later in the DOM order.

Alignment Inside the Container

Flex items with explicit dimensions might be smaller than their container, but one of the other benefits of Flexbox is tight control over alignment and placing.

Before getting into this fully, I'll quickly explain the two different axes used for alignment. The *main axis* goes in the direction that the items are placed: By default, when the value of flex-direction is row, the main axis is horizontal; when the value is column, the main axis is vertical. The *cross axis* is the perpendicular: vertical when the flex-direction is row, horizontal when it's column. Figure 4-7 shows the difference.

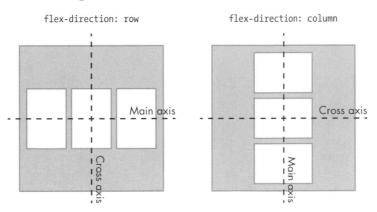

Figure 4-7: The main and cross axes depend on whether the flex children are in rows or columns.

Now on with the alignment properties. Imagine you have a flex container that is 600px wide, with three flex items that are each 150px wide. By default, the three items display in a row, aligned to the left, with 150px of unused space after them (as shown in the first row of Figure 4-8).

You can redistribute this unused space with the justify-content property. This property accepts a series of keyword values that apply differently depending on the direction of the flex parent (row, column, reversed row, and so on). For the purpose of demonstration, let's presume the standard English left to right row. The default value is flex-start, which aligns all flex items to the left of the parent with the unused space occupying the remaining horizontal width to the right, as I mentioned in the previous paragraph.

The alternative values are: flex-end, which aligns the items to the right of the container with the unused space to the left; center, which distributes the unused space to either side of all items, centering the items in the container; space-between, which adds an equal amount of space between each item but none before the first or after the last item; and space-around, which puts an equal amount of space on both sides of each item.

Have a look at *flexbox-alignment.html* and try changing the value of justify-content to see its effect. Figure 4-8 shows a few different values for comparison.

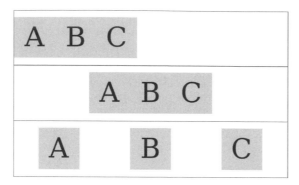

Figure 4-8: Different values for the justify-content property: flex-start (top), center (middle), and space-around (bottom)

But what about alignment on the cross axis? After all, at times the height of your flex items is less than the height of the flex container. (To avoid repetition, I'll continue to assume we're dealing with items in a row.)

The property that applies is align-items, and the values are a little different. The default is stretch, which makes the item the same height as its parent. This value works only when no height has been specified on the items, however; if a height has been specified, the default becomes flex-start, which aligns the items to the top of the container. Of the other values, flex-end aligns items to the bottom of the container; center to the vertical center of the container, with equal unused space above and below; and baseline aligns the items according to the baseline of the first line of their content.

Have a look at *flexbox-alignment.html* and update the value yourself to see the different effects in action. Figure 4-9 shows some different values at work.

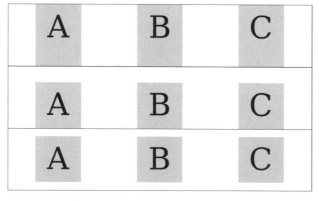

Figure 4-9: Alignment on the cross axis is controlled with different values for align-items: stretch (top), flex-end (middle), and center (bottom).

To control the alignment of individual items, use the `align-self` property. This property applies to the item, not the container, but the values are the same as `align-items`, and they have the same effects (although on the selected item only—sibling items remain unaffected).

Adding Some Flexibility

You've seen how items can be aligned and ordered, but so far a better name for the module might be Versatile Box. What about the titular flexibility? This comes in the shape of dynamic growing or shrinking of items to better fit the container and is provided by a new property called `flex`. This property is applied to items, rather than the container, and takes three values:

```
E { flex: 1 2 150px; }
```

The `flex` property is actually a shorthand, and each of the values are for a further property; in order, they are `flex-grow`, `flex-shrink`, and `flex-basis`. If I wrote the same rule out again using all three properties, it would be:

```
E {
  flex-grow: 1;
  flex-shrink: 2;
  flex-basis: 150px;
}
```

But what do these properties actually do? I'll start by explaining `flex-basis`, which essentially acts like (and takes precedence over) the value of the `width` property. The `flex-basis` property is like a "preferred width" property, meaning these boxes will be flexible, but their flexibility will be based on this number.

In the example code I've used so far in this section, I've included three flex items, each with a `flex-basis` of 150px, in a flex container that is 600px wide, leaving 150px of unused width. This is where the other properties come in.

The `flex-grow` and `flex-shrink` property values are basically a ratio. Ignore `flex-shrink` for a moment, and note that each item has a `flex-grow` value of 1. This value means the 150px of unused width is divided up using the ratio 1:1:1—that is, equally. Fifty pixels are added to each element so they each become 200px wide, filling the container. But what if I changed the `flex-grow` value for one of the children?

```
#a, #b { flex: 1 2 150px; }
#c { flex: 3 2 150px; }
```

Now the ratio has changed to 1:3:1, meaning the 150px will be distributed between the items in that ratio; for every 1px that's distributed to items #*a* and #*b*, 3px is distributed to item #*c*. Therefore #*c* becomes 240px wide, and items #*a* and #*b* are 180px wide. Changing the `flex-grow` value alters that ratio and the flexibility of your items.

For example, Figure 4-10 shows the effect of a change to flex-grow; in the upper example, all items have an equal value of 1; in the lower example, item *B* has a value of 3, meaning it grows proportionally larger.

Figure 4-10: A greater flex-grow value means item B in the lower example becomes proportionally larger than its siblings.

The flex-shrink property works in reverse. If you keep the same items as in the examples but reduce the width of the container to 300px, the combined width (or flex-basis) of the items creates a 50px-surplus width, which is removed from each of the items in the ratio given by flex-shrink: 2:2:2. Notice this is an equal ratio, so it's actually the same as 1:1:1 or 5:5:5. The result is the same: each item is reduced in width by 50px to fit the container.

Now what if you change the flex-shrink value of one of the items?

```
#a, #b { flex: 1 2 150px; }
#c { flex: 3 3 150px; }
```

Now item *#c* is reduced by 3px for every 2px from items *#a* and *#b*; it flexes to 86px in width, compared to its siblings' 107px.

This flexibility is really useful when you have a series of elements that must fit into variable spaces, such as a user interface on an app that has to work across multiple devices. Flexbox is also good for those times when you don't know how many interface elements you'll have, but you know they should all be proportional regardless.

Wrap and Flow

Even with the extra flexibility provided by Flexbox, at times you will have too many items to fit comfortably into one row (or column) of a container. Should this occur, you can break items onto multiple lines using the flex-wrap property. Its default value is nowrap, which preserves all the items on the same line, but a value of wrap makes the items break onto extra lines if required:

```
E { flex-wrap: wrap; }
```

The wrap value makes new lines below the first (or to the right in column view), but an alternative value of wrap-reverse changes the direction of the cross axis so new lines appear above (or to the left) instead. Figure 4-11 compares the two different values.

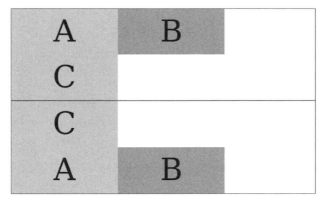

Figure 4-11: Comparing values for the flex-wrap property. The upper example has a value of wrap, so element C appears in a new line below; whereas in the lower example, the value is wrap-reverse, so element C is on a new line above.

You can combine flex-wrap with flex-direction in the shorthand flex-flow property. To set a column with multiple lines and a reversed cross axis, use this:

```
E { flex-flow: column wrap-reverse; }
```

When items wrap over multiple lines, you can control their alignment with the align-content property. This property works like the justify-content property but on the cross axis. It has the same possible values plus one extra, stretch, which resizes the items to fill all unused space. Figure 4-12 compares two different values.

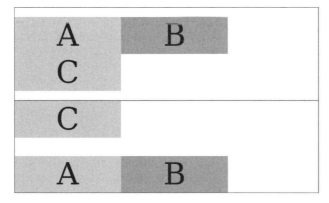

Figure 4-12: Alignment on the cross axis when flex items are wrapped is controlled with align-content: center (top) and space-between (bottom).

Although you can create entire page layouts with Flexbox, that's not really what it's intended for, and you would probably be hacking it around to get the exact layout you want. A better option is to use a dedicated set of page layout properties, and that's where the Grid Layout module comes in.

Grid Layout

Grids are a fundamental design element. Simple grids have been used by calligraphers since medieval times and the modern typographic grid since the second half of the 20th century. For a few years now, efforts have been made to bring grid-based design to the Web, with a number of frameworks being created that use floats, padding, and margins to emulate the possibilities of print.

Recently browsers have begun to implement a native CSS Grid Layout system, which provides a series of properties designed specifically to create grids on screen, meaning the developer no longer has to hack them together from existing properties and behaviors. But before I introduce the new grid syntax, I'll explain some of the terminology used in the Grid Layout module. Even if you're a designer familiar with using grids, you should take time to understand these terms, as the terminology used in CSS grids is distinct from that used by designers.

Here I've defined the key terms used in the module:

Grid element   The container element that acts as the boundary and sets the dimensions of the grid.

Grid items   Each child element that is placed onto the grid is known as an *item*.

Grid lines   The dividing lines between rows and columns; these lines are notional, not actual.

Grid tracks   The shorthand name for both rows and columns. Each column or row created in the grid is referred to as a *track*. Tracks are the spaces between lines.

Grid areas   Each intersection of a column and a row creates an *area*. Think of these like cells in a table.

A grid is created by first setting a number of lines on the grid element to create a series of tracks. Grid items are then positioned in the grid using the tracks as coordinates and either fit into an area or span a series of areas, as shown in Figure 4-13.

If you've used spreadsheet software such as Excel, a grid should be easy to visualize. The grid lines—the lines between cells—define a series of rows and columns that are numbered for coordinate placement. (If you haven't used spreadsheet software or you don't know about typographical grids and are confused about what all this means, don't worry—I explain it in stages.)

NOTE   *The syntax I'm using in this section is what shipped with Internet Explorer 10; however, the specification has undergone changes since then. The new syntax will be listed later in "The September 2012 Grid Layout Syntax" on page 84.*

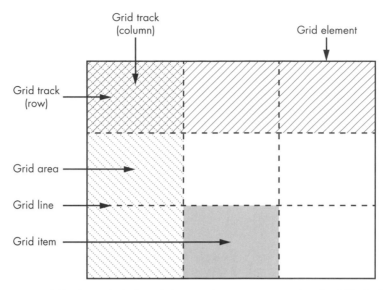

Figure 4-13: A simple 3×3 grid showing the core terms used in the CSS Grid Layout syntax

Declaring and Defining the Grid

The first step in creating a grid is to declare the grid element. As explained in the introduction to this section, this is the container element that is used as the grid's foundation: Its dimensions will be the limits of the grid, and all the grid properties will be applied to it. The grid element is declared with the existing display property, using the new value grid:

```
E { display: grid; }
```

Next, you define the grid tracks with the grid-columns and grid-rows properties. The value for each of these properties is a length unit, which sets the width of the column or height of the row. As a simple first example, here's how to create two columns, one that is 75 percent of the width of the grid element and one that is 25 percent:

```
E { grid-columns: 75% 25%; }
```

You're not confined to percentages here; any length units are permitted, and a new length unit, fraction (*fr*), has been created especially for defining grids. One fr means one equal share of the remaining space. In the previous example, you could use the fr unit instead of percentages to achieve the same result:

```
E { grid-columns: 3fr 1fr; }
```

But fractions really come into their own when mixed with other units. For example, say you want to have one fixed-width column and two equal and dynamic columns as part of a responsive layout. Using fr is perfect for this. In the following code, three columns are created: one at 15em wide and the remaining two at half of the remaining width each:

```
E { grid-columns: 15em 1fr 1fr; }
```

Adding rows is done in the same way, using all of the same possible units. Say, for example, I want to create three rows: The first is 100px high; the second has a value of auto, so it is as high as the content contained within it; and the third is 15em high. Here's the code to create these rows:

```
E { grid-rows: 100px auto 15em; }
```

Putting all these properties together lets you fully define your grid. As a simple example, let's create a basic grid of three columns and three rows, for a total of nine cells. Here's the code for that:

```
E {
  display: grid;
  grid-columns: 1fr 4fr 1fr;
  grid-rows: 100px auto 15em;
}
```

The columns of this grid are distributed in the ratio 1:4:1, and the rows are 100px at the top, 15em at the bottom, with a central row of automatic height to accommodate all the content within it. The grid will look something like Figure 4-14.

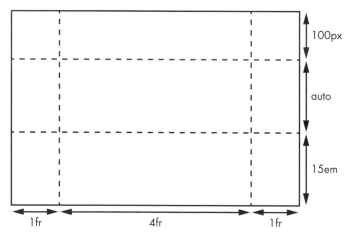

Figure 4-14: A simple 3×3 grid

Repeating Grid Lines

The simple grids defined in this chapter so far are good for learning and for some real-world situations, but you'll often want to use quite complex grids for finer control over content. A 12- or 16-column grid is fairly commonplace, and each of those columns usually has a *gutter* (empty space) between itself and its neighbor. But using the Grid Layout syntax, even a 6-column grid with gutters can be quite repetitive:

```
E { grid-columns: 1fr 10px 1fr 10px 1fr 10px 1fr 10px 1fr 10px 1fr; }
```

Now imagine how repetitive that would be with 16 columns! To get around this problem, you can use the repeat() function to manage repetition. This function takes two values: an integer that sets the number of repetitions and then the grid line values to be repeated:

```
E { grid-columns: 1fr repeat(5, 10px 1fr); }
```

This defines one track, one fraction wide, and then repeats a pattern alternating 10px and 1fr, five times, matching the code in the previous example.

Internet Explorer 10 uses syntax from an older version of the spec, where the number of repetitions is placed after the parentheses in square brackets. If you're building apps for the Windows 8 UI, use this syntax:

```
E { -ms-grid-columns: 1fr repeat(10px 1fr)[5]; }
```

Placing Items on the Grid

To place an item on the grid, you assign it a cell reference using the grid-column and grid-row properties. Each property takes a single whole number as a value, which refers to a track (either a column or a row). For example, to place an item in the cell positioned in the second column, second row, you would use this code (the result is shown in Figure 4-15):

```
F {
  grid-column: 2;
  grid-row: 2;
}
```

The default value of both grid-column and grid-row is 1, so omitting either would place the item in the first row or column. Given the following code, the item would be placed in the cell in the second column of the first row, as you can see in Figure 4-16.

```
F { grid-column: 2; }
```

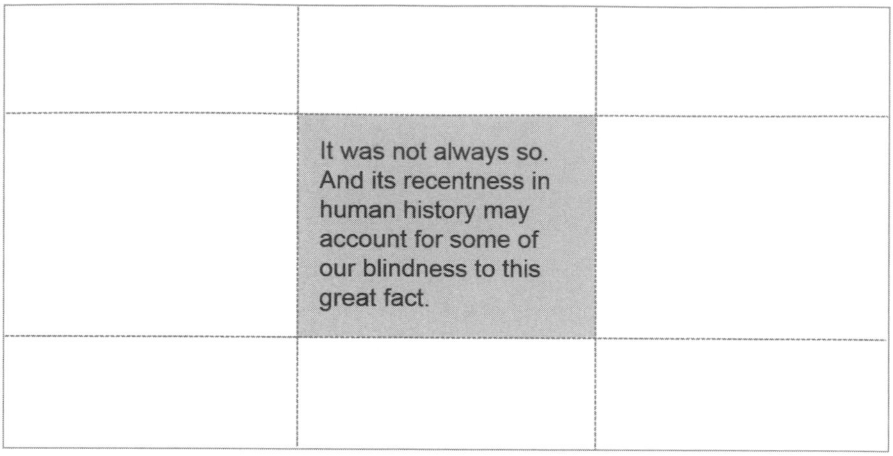

It was not always so.
And its recentness in
human history may
account for some of
our blindness to this
great fact.

Figure 4-15: An item placed on the grid in the second column, second row (grid lines added for clarity)

It was not always so.
And its recentness in
human history may
account for some of

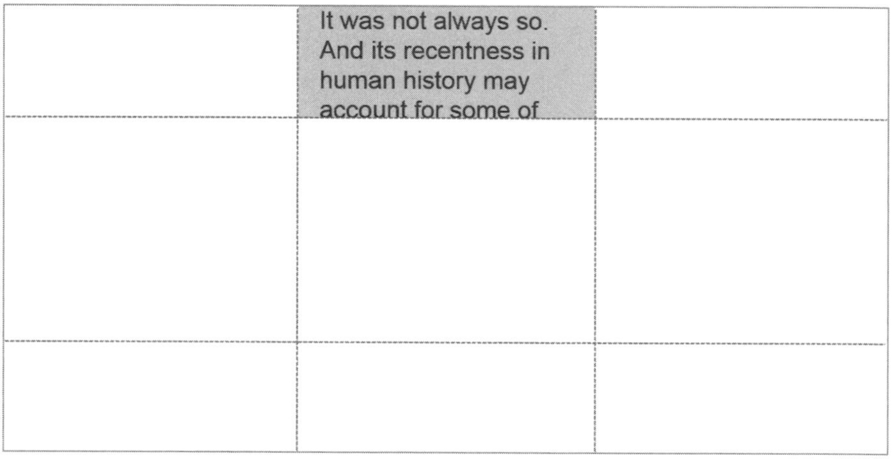

Figure 4-16: An item placed on the grid in the second column, first row (grid lines added for clarity)

By default, the item is sized into the nominated cell, but you can expand the item's size by making it span multiple cells in rows or columns. You do this with the `grid-column-span` and `grid-row-span` properties, each of which, again, takes a single whole number value that determines how many tracks the item should span. For example, here's an item that spans the first three rows of the first column:

```
F { grid-row-span: 3; }
```

Remember, you don't need to define `grid-column` and `grid-row` in this instance, as they both default to 1. The item is placed in the first column of the first row—right where you want it—and it spans all three rows, as shown in Figure 4-17.

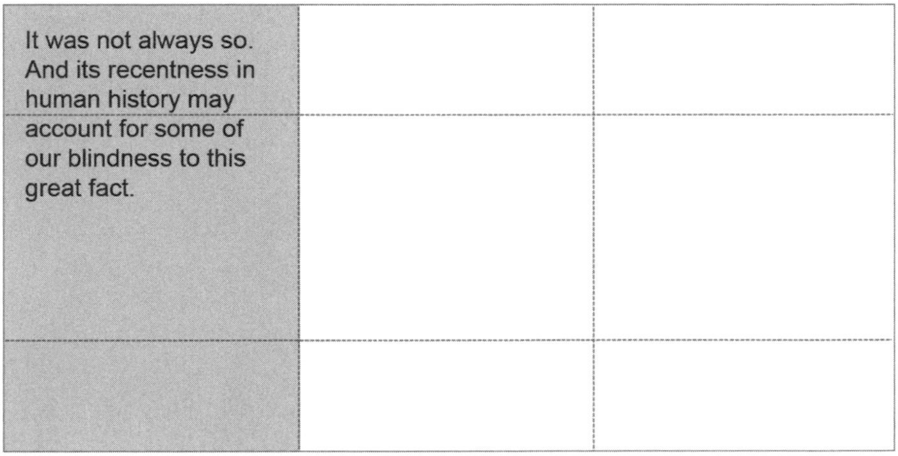

Figure 4-17: An item on the grid spanning three rows of the first column (grid lines added for clarity)

Alignment and Stacking

By default, the items you place on the grid are positioned so their top-left corner is at the top-left corner of the designated cell, but you can change this default positioning with the `grid-column-align` and `grid-row-align` properties. These properties each take a series of keyword values (center, end, start, and stretch). These values set the alignment of the item within its cell.

The center value obviously aligns the item to the horizontal or vertical center of the cell, whereas start and end depend on the direction of writing in your document. For those of us using English and other left-to-right languages, start aligns the item to the left or top of the cell, and end to the right or bottom. The stretch value makes the item expand to fill the whole width or height of the cell.

To show how these values work, take a look at the example file *grid-align .html*. You'll find a grid of three equal cells with an identical item in each. I've positioned each differently, using the following code:

```
#a { grid-row-align: end; }
#b { grid-row-align: stretch; }
#c { grid-row-align: center; }
```

As you can see, each item is aligned differently within the row: *#a* is aligned to the end (bottom), *#b* stretches to fill the whole cell, and *#c* is vertically centered. You can compare the results in Figure 4-18.

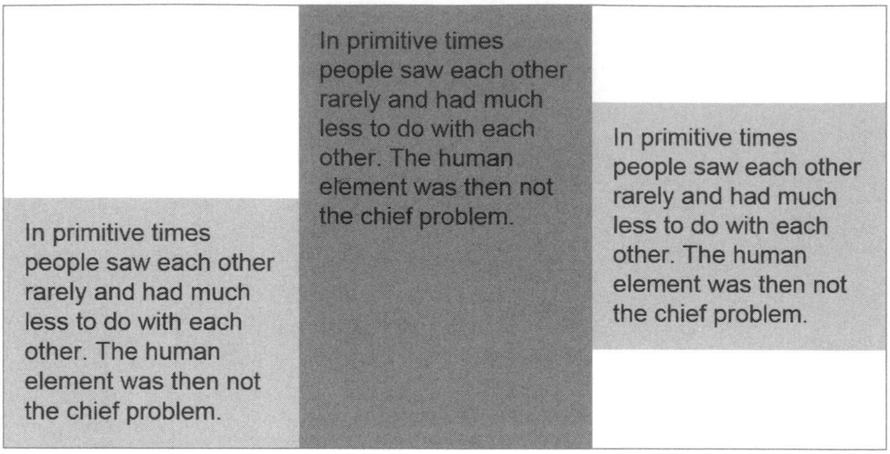

Figure 4-18: Each item is aligned differently within its cell with the `grid-row-align` *property.*

As you're placing items into the grid, you may find that items overlap in the same cell. By default, items are stacked in DOM order, with items that appear later in the DOM stacked on top of items that appear earlier, as in the following markup, for example.

```
<div id="a">...</div>
<div id="b">...</div>
```

If the div items #*a* and #*b* were placed into the same cell, the latter would show above the former because it's later in the DOM order. You can change this order by using the z-index property (from absolute positioning in CSS2.1). For example, to have item #*a* appear above #*b*, you do this:

```
#a { z-index: 10; }
```

(I'll discuss another approach to dealing with stacking conflicts later in "Exclusions and Grids" on page 208.)

The September 2012 Grid Layout Syntax

As I mentioned previously, the syntax of the Grid Layout module was updated after Internet Explorer 10 had implemented its version. The updated specification still has draft status and is a long way from being approved, and as I write this, the new syntax has yet to be implemented in any browser.

The good news is that the core concepts remain the same, and the main changes come in the form of new and updated property names. For example, when defining a grid, the grid-columns and grid-rows properties are now known as grid-definition-columns and grid-definition-rows, respectively. That was easy, but pay attention to the next part.

The roles played by the grid-column and grid-row properties are now filled by grid-column-position and grid-row-position, although the former properties still exist as shorthands: grid-column is shorthand for grid-column-position and grid-column-span, and grid-row is shorthand for grid-row-position and grid-row-span. That makes more sense than it might seem to at first.

Other shorthands include the following: grid-position is shorthand for grid-column-position and grid-row-position; grid-span for grid-column-span and grid-row-span; and grid-area for (deep breath) grid-column-position, grid-row-position, grid-column-span, and grid-row-span (or grid-position and grid-span, if you prefer shorthands of shorthands).

WARNING *Remember that because the spec is still draft, this syntax is not necessarily final. Updates will be posted on this book's companion website,* http://modernwebbook.com/.

On the Grid Layout Terminology

The terminology used in the Grid Layout module is really quite distinct from that of the typographic grids used by designers, a fact that has caused some designers to be quite vocal about their displeasure. Mark Boulton, one of the chief instigators in explaining the importance of grid systems on web pages, wrote an open letter to the W3C about the terminology used in the Grid Layout module:

> I'm confused as to the need to invent new terminology with regards to grids that have existed for centuries. I'm also a little concerned that the mental model this terminology builds is one more similar to tables and spreadsheets (where these terms could be interchangeable) than to grids and layout.

Tab Atkins, of Google and the CSS Working Group, was forthright about why CSS grids seem to have more in common with tables than typographic grids:

> Because Grid Layout is basically just the good parts of table layouts, without the shitty parts, so we reused the same terminology.

Grid Template

The Grid Layout module offers another way to define grids. Though as of this writing no browsers have implemented grid templates or indicated that they will, I think it deserves a brief explanation because it's such a clever and different approach.

The grid-template property allows you to define grid areas by using a series of unique identifiers in strings of text. Each identifier represents an area, and each string represents a row. For example, to make a grid of one row with three columns, you would use this:

```
E {
  display: grid;
  grid-template: 'a b c';
}
```

New Approaches to CSS Layouts   **85**

To make multiple rows, add more strings, and make cells span rows and columns, add an extra instance of the letter in the direction you want to span. For example, in the following code, cell *a* will span two rows, and cell *b* will span two columns. I've formatted the strings to make it easier for you to visualize how these will appear:

```
E {
  display: grid;
  grid-template:
    'a b b'
    'a c d';
}
```

To place an item in a grid declared with a template, just use the letter of the cell as a value for the grid-area property. For example, to place an item in cell *b*, use this code:

```
F { grid-area: 'b'; }
```

As mentioned, I have no idea whether grid templates will ever see the light of day in a browser, but they offer an interesting way to approach the creation of simple grids.

The Further Future

The three key layout modules I've covered in this chapter already provide a seismic shift in the way we'll lay out web pages in the near future, but looking still further ahead, there are even more incredible modules being proposed. As these are in varying states of proposal and stability, I've chosen not to cover them in this chapter, but I include them in "Even Further Future Layouts" on page 209. If rich, dynamic web layouts excite you (and why wouldn't they?), I think you'll be quite satisfied with that section.

Summary

This chapter has covered the many new approaches now available to you as a developer when you decide how to best lay out your pages. From the easy creation of grids to DOM-independent UI layouts via unique and dynamic text reflowing, the new methods should make the old three-column layout a thing of the past. Combining each of the new methods with the power of the media queries introduced in Chapter 3 means you can now make flexible, dynamic layouts and interfaces that are custom-tailored for every device.

And the future of CSS layouts looks even more exciting. Although as I write this many of the proposals and specifications are still in a state of high flux, the new possibilities mean that in five years we'll have whole new sets of tools at our fingertips that will change the paradigms of website and application development.

Further Reading

The ever-dependable MozDev has a really clear introduction to multiple columns, "Using CSS multi-column layouts," at *https://developer.mozilla.org/en-US/docs/CSS/Using_CSS_multi-column_layouts/*.

The Flexbox syntax has changed so often that almost every current online resource is out-of-date! That said, I recommend Stephen Hay's article "Learn You a Flexbox for Great Good!" at *http://www.the-haystack.com/2012/01/04/learn-you-a-flexbox/*, even though it refers to an outdated syntax, as Stephen's knowledge of CSS layouts is second to none.

The best explanation of the Grid Layout module, at least in regard to the IE10 implementation, is contained in the "Internet Explorer 10 Guide for Developers": *http://msdn.microsoft.com/en-us/library/ie/hh673533%28v=vs.85%29.aspx/*.

Read Mark Boulton's open letter on the subject of grid terminology at *http://www.markboulton.co.uk/journal/comments/open-letter-to-w3c-css-working-group-re-css-grids*.

5

MODERN JAVASCRIPT

The third column of front-end web development, along with markup and style, is behavior, which on the Web is performed by JavaScript. The activity around HTML5 and its related APIs has also brought many new features and (dare I say it?) improvements to this scripting language, making JavaScript both easier to use casually for front-end developers and more powerful for those who really like to get into the hard-core mechanics. In the first section of this chapter, I look at some of those features.

But probably the biggest change in the world of JavaScript has been not in the language itself but in the number of libraries and frameworks that use it. There's been a Cambrian explosion of libraries, and in the second section of this chapter, I present my Burgess Shale—a small but illuminating snapshot of what's available.

New in JavaScript

From many new ways of DOM traversal to a whole new range of events, JavaScript has changed plenty in the past three or four years. If you don't actively follow or keep up with the JavaScript community, you can easily miss it.

In this section, I run through some of the new features of JavaScript, chosen on the massively unscientific basis of how useful *I* think they are. This section includes by no means everything that's new in the language— just a handful of methods, attributes, and events you might use often in your day-to-day web builds.

The async and defer Attributes

A browser's default behavior is to load all page elements in order and execute JavaScript files as soon as they're encountered, which blocks HTML parsing. Sites on slow connections, or those that include a lot of script to execute, can lag considerably. This is generally why best practice is to link to script files toward the end of your document, after the rest of the page has loaded.

A solution that prevents this blocking has been developed, however. The `defer` attribute, when added to the `script` element for external files (that is, when the `src` attribute is present), downloads scripts without pausing the parser but delays executing them until the HTML has finished loading. As `defer` is a Boolean attribute, no value is required:

```
<script src="foo.js" defer></script>
```

HTML5 has another new option, which is to execute the scripts asynchronously. As with deferred loading, external scripts are downloaded without pausing the parser; the difference is that the parser then executes those scripts as soon as possible. This approach is a kind of "best of both worlds" approach: not pausing the parser while downloading but not waiting until the end before executing. This option requires the `async` attribute, which is also Boolean:

```
<script src="foo.js" async></script>
```

One drawback is that your scripts may very well be executed in a different order from the way you call them in the document, so you can't rely on dependencies between script files. But if order is not an issue and the script is self-contained, this option may be best.

You can see the difference in the way the three approaches work in Figure 5-1. The first row shows default behavior, where HTML parsing is paused while the scripts are loaded and executed. The second row shows deferred execution, where the scripts are loaded without pausing the parser and then executed when the DOM is ready. In the final row, the parser still isn't paused while the script is loading, but it is paused as it then executes.

HTML parsing
Script loading
Script executing

Figure 5-1: The effects of deferred and asynchronous loading of JavaScript files

The addEventListener Method

The standard way to add event handlers to elements used to be with the series of event properties, such as `element.onclick` or `element.onmouseout`, which were fine as things went but had the drawback of allowing only a single handler of that type on each element. The W3C created a more flexible approach in the form of the `addEventListener()` method.

Honestly, this method isn't all that new, but only fairly recently, after being implemented in IE9 in 2011, has `addEventListener()` had a good level of support across browsers. A generic method, `addEventListener()` takes two mandatory and one (semi-)optional parameter:

```
el.addEventListener(type,listener,useCapture);
```

The *type* parameter is the type of event to listen for; the *listener* is the object that gets notified when the event occurs and is most commonly a function; and *useCapture* is a Boolean to indicate event bubbling. I won't go into detail on the latter parameter, as describing event bubbling is beyond the scope of this book, but although the parameter is supposedly optional, you have to include it, as certain older browsers will throw an error if it's not present. If you don't need it or know what it is, set *useCapture* to *false* and don't worry about it.

Here's a quick example of a simple use of `addEventListener()`; this code listens for a click event and runs an anonymous function to log a message into the console when that even occurs:

```
el.addEventListener('click', function () {
  console.log('Click!');
},false);
```

Even at this basic level, addEventListener() is useful enough, but it's even more valuable than it might seem, as you can use it to add multiple events of the same type to an element. This means you can use scripts from different sources without worrying about accidentally overwriting an event listener. The next example shows two named functions applied to the same element; each could be in a completely different script file yet still be executed when the element is clicked:

```
el.addEventListener('click', foo, false);
el.addEventListener('click', bar, false);
```

Using named functions (as I've done in this example) rather than anonymous functions is a good idea. Named functions are simply easier to refer to elsewhere in your scripts, which is essential when you want to remove event handlers as discussed in "Removing Event Listeners" on page 93.

The event Object

The addEventListener() method returns an object with details of the event after it's been fired. You can access this object using an anonymous function with a unique identifier as an argument. This identifier will be the name of the object. In this example, I call it *ev* and log it to the console so you can see the result:

```
el.addEventListener('click', function (ev) {
  console.log(ev);
},false);
```

Figure 5-2 shows the event object output in Firebug. You can see a number of different property-value pairs, giving quite substantial information about the event as it happened (there's more information off-screen too).

This method also works with named functions; you just have to supply the unique id value as an argument when defining the function:

```
var foo = function (ev) {
  console.log(ev);
};
el.addEventListener('click', foo, false);
```

Among the event object's more useful properties is currentTarget, which holds information about the element that the event occurred on; you can then apply behavior to that element easily, as in this code where the element that is clicked has its color set to *#F00*:

```
el.addEventListener('click', function (ev) {
  ev.currentTarget.style.color = '#F00';
},false);
```

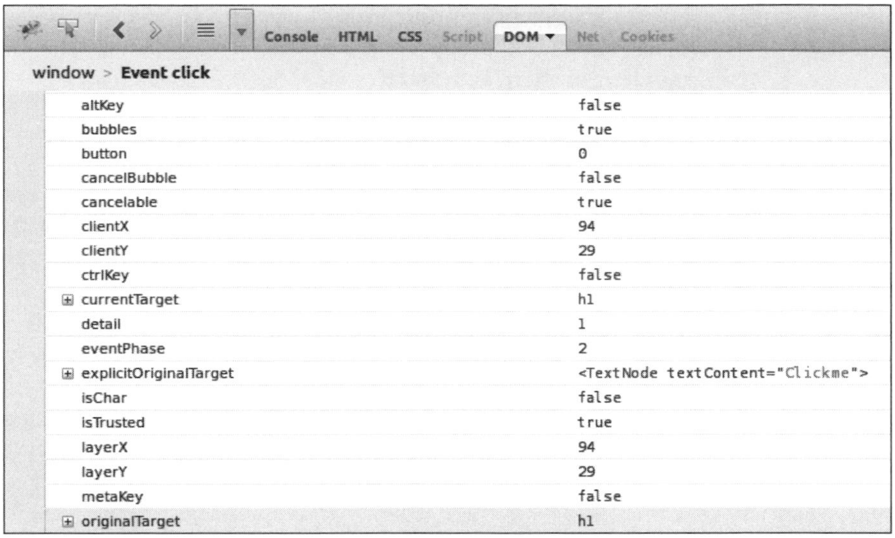

Figure 5-2: Some of the information contained in the object created by a click event

The event object is also useful when you want to stop a default action from occurring on an element. For example, you may attach an event to an a element that contains a link, but you don't want the browser to follow the link before the function attached to the event has run. Use the preventDefault() method for this:

```
el.addEventListener('click', function (ev) {
  ev.preventDefault();
  ...
},false);
```

Removing Event Listeners

Sometimes you want to remove a handler from an element to prevent it from firing again. You remove handlers with the removeEventListener() method, which has the same three parameters as addEventListener():

```
el.removeEventListener(type,listener,useCapture);
```

To remove an event, you have to provide removeEventListener() with the exact parameters used by the addEventListener() method, which is why I mentioned previously the importance of using named rather than anonymous functions. The following code illustrates what I mean; first an event listener is added to run the function *foo*, and then the listener is removed by using exactly the same parameters:

```
el.addEventListener('click',foo,false);
el.removeEventListener('click',foo,false);
```

You can remove anonymous functions from event handlers, but these methods are being deprecated in the latest revisions of JavaScript, so steering clear of them is best.

The DOMContentLoaded Event

The old way to initiate scripts when a page had finished loading was to use the load event, but this method had the drawback of only firing after every resource—images, stylesheets, and so on—had fully loaded, which could sometimes lead to quite a delay. Developers then created a custom event, domready, which fires when the DOM has loaded but before the resources.

The domready event was quickly adopted by many JavaScript libraries; it began to be adopted natively in browsers as DOMContentLoaded; and it is now standardized in HTML5. DOMContentLoaded is fired on the document object like so:

```
document.addEventListener('DOMContentLoaded', function () {...}, false);
```

Notably, the behavior layer of the site can be initiated much sooner, meaning the user can start exploring your site more quickly—especially useful over slow connections or for image-heavy pages that could take some time to load. If you have scripts that you want to run only when every resource has finished loading, you can continue to use load.

Input Events

The massive rise in the number of devices with touch-enabled (whether finger, stylus, or sausage) input has meant the creation of a new series of events to cater to them. Although click events are still fired by touch input, simply relying on them is not sufficient, as there are major differences in the ways that mouse- and touch-enabled devices operate. For example, when a user clicks his or her mouse button, a slight pause occurs as the browser waits to see if the action is a single or double click. This delay is small but noticeable on touch screens and makes them appear to be unresponsive.

The W3C is currently considering two different input event models: *Touch Events* is aimed squarely at touch input, has been under active development for some time, and is already implemented in some browsers, but this model has been criticized in some quarters and may also fall foul of some existing patents; *Pointer Events* is a new proposal for a unified input model that has been accepted for consideration by the W3C but not yet formally approved or implemented.

Which—if either—model eventually becomes the standard remains to be seen, although indications are that Pointer Events is preferred. Given the uncertainty, I'll just briefly explain how each works.

Touch Events

The Touch Events Level 1 specification has four events:

- touchstart fires when a finger (the word I'll use from now on to avoid repeating the word "sausage") touches the screen.
- touchend fires when the finger is removed from the screen.
- touchmove fires when a finger moves between two points on the screen.
- touchcancel fires when the user agent interrupts a touch or when the finger leaves the active area.

Touch Events Level 2, still in development as I write this, introduces two additional events:

- touchenter fires when a finger already on the screen moves over the target element.
- touchleave fires when the finger moves out of the target area without leaving the screen.

To closely parallel a mouse click, you probably want to use the touchend event, which fires when the finger is lifted from the screen, denoting that the user has completed his or her action:

```
el.addEventListener('touchend', function () {...}, false);
```

Every time a touch event fires, it creates a TouchEvent object, which contains more information about the event. This information includes TouchList, an object containing the touches child object, which holds information about how many fingers are touching the screen, obviously useful for multitouch events. Bear in mind that each touch creates a touch event, and when using multitouch, each touch event includes all the preceding touches. So the TouchList object created when the first finger touches the screen holds information about touch 0; the TouchList created by the second finger holds information about touches 0 and 1; the TouchList of the third finger about touches 0, 1, and 2, and so on.

Pointer Events

As I mentioned, Pointer Events presents a unified approach to creating events regardless of the actual input mechanism—whether finger, mouse, stylus, or other. This approach is similar to DOM Mouse Events in the way that it records an action's stages but uses the agnostic pointer* events: pointerdown, pointerup, pointercancel, pointermove, pointerover, and pointerout. For example, to fire an event when the pointer is released, use pointerup:

```
el.addEventListener('pointerup', function () {...}, false);
```

When fired, each event creates a `pointerEvent` interface that combines properties from the `MouseEvent` interface—`currentTarget`, coordinates where the event occurred, and so on—with a series of new properties, including the type of pointer used (`pointerType`), the amount of pressure applied, and the pointer's tilt (where relevant).

Without an implementation, I can't give any examples of these events in use, but certainly the spec makes sense and seems to logically extend existing events and be more general—and, therefore, more useful—than dedicated Touch Events. Although not confirmed as I write this, Pointer Events seems to be the specification that the W3C will develop. In the meantime, a number of community-built libraries exist to fill the functionality gap: among the multitude, the PointerEvents polyfill is the one to consider.

CSS Selectors in JavaScript

Selecting elements from the DOM used to be a little problematic. You had `getElementById()` and `getElementsByTagName()`, but too often getting the exact elements you wanted involved a lot of DOM traversal or filtering. Libraries like jQuery (I get to this in "Pointer Events" on page 95) solved this problem with methods that allow CSS selectors as arguments:

```
var foo = $('p.foo');
```

The obvious benefit this brings soon fed back into JavaScript through two new native methods: `querySelector()` and `querySelectorAll()`. Both work in a similar way, taking CSS selectors as arguments; the difference is that `querySelector()` selects only the first matched element, so its result is a single node, whereas `querySelectorAll()` matches all instances of the element, so its result is returned as a `NodeList`:

```
var foo = document.querySelector('p.foo');
var foo = document.querySelectorAll('p.foo');
```

In Figure 5-3 you can see the results of the different selectors logged in to the console; `querySelector()` is the first result, `querySelectorAll()` the second.

You can use any complex selector or series of selectors with these two methods; the only proviso is that they can't be relative selectors—that is, they can't begin with a combinator like > or +. This argument is, therefore, invalid:

Figure 5-3: Comparing the results of querySelector() and querySelectorAll()

```
var el = document.querySelectorAll('+ h2');
```

A proposal to resolve this problem is a pair of similar methods called find() and findAll(), which would work in basically the same way but allow selectors relative to the target. To create a valid version of the previous code, use this:

```
var foo = el.findAll('+ h2');
```

Although these aren't really vital methods, they make DOM traversal a little easier, so I hope to see them broadly adopted soon.

The getElementsByClassName() Method

One fairly big (and surprising) gap in using JavaScript to access the DOM was a method for selecting elements by their class name. As with DOMContentReady, this absence led developers to write their own custom scripts to carry out that task, many of which consolidated around the name getElementsByClassName(). This solution was also standardized in HTML5, and the method is now present natively in modern browsers. getElementsByClassName() takes a single string value and returns a NodeList of all elements that have a class name matching the string:

```
var el - document.getFlementsByClassName('foo');
```

You can also match multiple class names by separating them with spaces in the string; the following code selects all elements that have a class name of both *foo* and *bar*:

```
var el = document.getElementsByClassName('foo bar');
```

Interacting with Classes

With the introduction of the classList object, JavaScript has also made interacting with the class names of elements easier. Every element in the DOM has an associated classList, which is just what it sounds like: a list of all the classes applied to that element. To get the classList of an element and log it to the console, do this:

```
var el = document.querySelector('.foo');
console.log(el.classList);
```

The classList object contains a series of properties and methods for manipulating the classes. You can query for the existence of a class with the contains() method, which returns true if the provided class is present and false otherwise. You add a class with the add() method and remove one with remove(). The following code tests for the class name *foo*, adds it if it isn't present, and removes it if it is:

```
if (el.classList.contains('foo') {
  el.classList.remove('foo');
```

```
} else {
  el.classList.add('foo');
}
```

A quicker way to do this is with the `toggle()` method; `toggle()` simply removes a class if it's present or adds it if it's not:

```
el.classList.toggle('foo');
```

JavaScript Libraries

JavaScript libraries are collections of prewritten scripts that aim to reduce the cost of developing applications, and in the past few years, their number has exploded—to the point where you will rarely work on a large project where no libraries are used. From light single-purpose libraries to extensive frameworks, the range is truly wondrous. Whatever you want to do with JavaScript, the odds are good that someone has already written a library for it.

At times writing your own scripts from scratch is the best approach, especially if you don't want the overhead of some libraries' large file size. But when working on large teams—when having everyone work to the same standard is advantageous—or when you need to get something into production quickly or for many other reasons, a library is the way to go.

Here I briefly introduce four JavaScript libraries that are useful for front-end developers. Bear in mind that I am barely scraping the surface of what's available, and just about every developer you talk to will have his or her own favorite (and probably won't be shy about telling you why it's superior).

To use each library, in most cases you only have to download or link to a copy of the library and place any code that relies on the library in subsequent files. Remember the warning about using the `async` attribute in this case. Where installation is more complicated, each library's documentation will have full instructions.

WARNING *Using JavaScript libraries can add significant weight to your page and adversely affect loading times. Think carefully before you use them, especially if you're building sites that may be accessed by visitors on mobile devices, where performance can be a major issue.*

jQuery

I would say almost certainly you have heard of jQuery, as it has quickly become a de facto standard for working on the Web. In August 2012, it was estimated that it's used on some 50 percent of the top 1 million websites. If you're comfortable with jQuery and happy that you know all about what it does, you can skip this section. For everybody else, I provide a short overview.

jQuery is a JavaScript framework that simplifies the way you write scripts, abstracting common functions and providing a unified experience across all browsers. It works by creating a set of methods that require simple arguments from the author but perform some quite complex tasks. Here's a simple example, which I'll talk through in a second:

```
$(document).ready(function () {
  $('h1').addClass('foo');
});
```

The first line is required to use jQuery; it acts basically like the `DOMContentLoaded` event, running the anonymous function when the DOM is ready. The second line contains a simple jQuery statement: The first part is a CSS selector that selects a node or group of nodes for the action to be applied to, and the second part is a method that states the action to be applied. In this case, a class of *foo* will be added to all h1 elements.

Using the selector at the beginning of the statement can sometimes confuse people, as we construct sentences in English in the opposite way; it's like saying "apple I will eat." If it makes it easier for you to remember, imagine this is how Yoda would say it.

Using jQuery doesn't limit you to DOM traversal or manipulation; it does plenty more as well. For example, you can use the on() method to attach events to elements—on() is like addEventListener with a few extra advantages, one of which is you can specify multiple event listeners to be added to a single element. In this example, an anonymous function runs whenever any h1 element is clicked or touched:

```
$('h1').on('click touch',function () { ... });
```

Another fantastic feature of jQuery is its ability to chain methods in sequence, mixing selectors and actions to create long statements. The following code is a little more complex than I've used so far, so see if you can work out what it does before I explain it:

```
$('.foo').on('click', function (ev) {
  $(ev.currentTarget).find('.bar').css('background-color','#f00');
});
```

Here's the sequence: first, add a click event listener to all elements with the class of *foo*; next, run an anonymous function when that event is fired, and assign the event object to the variable named *ev*; in that function, find all elements with a class of *bar* that are children of the element that the event was fired on and change their background color to *#f00*.

The range of different methods that jQuery gives you access to is far greater than I could possibly list here, so I suggest you take a look at the documentation, which is absolutely exemplary—especially for an open source project.

jQuery has a companion called *jQuery Mobile*, which might at first sound like a mobile-optimized version of the library, but it's not that simple; jQuery Mobile is actually an extension to jQuery that provides cross-platform widgets and styles, as well as new events and methods that take advantage of the new capabilities provided by mobile devices. It requires the jQuery library to run, meaning extra weight is added to your pages.

If you need a lightweight mobile-optimized library, you may want to consider an alternative such as Zepto.js, which features a jQuery-compatible API but is only 25 percent of its size. jQTouch is a library that provides many of the same features as jQuery Mobile but weighs in much lighter and is compatible with both jQuery and Zepto, although its browser support may not be as broad as that of jQuery Mobile. I advise you to evaluate each fully to find which one is best suited to your purposes.

YepNope

I've already covered (back in Chapter 3) using media queries in CSS and JavaScript for loading resources depending on device dimensions, but what about all the other variable capabilities and functionality you could be testing against? Maybe you want to load resources depending on whether a browser has support for the console or a certain API (you'll read more about those in Chapter 6). You could write custom functions that test for each critical dependency in turn, but using a conditional loader like YepNope.js might be a better option.

The idea of YepNope is incredibly simple: You give it a condition to test and then specify a resource to be loaded depending on the result. As a simple example, let's test to see whether the browser has a console and load a virtual one if it doesn't:

```
yepnope({
  test: window.console,
  nope: 'foo.js'
});
```

You can see what's going on here pretty easily. The yepnope function is called. It has two properties: test, which is the condition to return either true or false; and nope, which is a resource to load if the value of test is false. So if window.console is supported, do nothing; if not, load *foo.js*.

A few further properties are available, such as yep, which specifies a resource to run if the value of test is true; both, which loads a resource regardless of the value of test; and callback, which runs a function when the test is complete. Let's make the previous code example a bit more complex by adding a few of those in:

```
yepnope({
  test: window.console,
  yep: 'bar.js',
  nope: 'foo.js',
```

```
  both: 'foobar.css',
  callback: function () { ... }
});
```

Here I'm running the same test as before but now loading *bar.js* if test is true, *foo.js* if it's false, and *foobar.css* regardless of the result. When the test has finished, the anonymous function runs.

Any test that returns a result of `true` or `false` can be run in test, but where YepNope.js really comes into its own is when it's combined with Modernizr—the next library I discuss.

Modernizr

Browser support for experimental features, whether HTML, CSS, or JavaScript, can be quite variable, and providing safe fallbacks if a feature isn't present in a user's browser is not always easy. Modernizr, which runs a series of tests for features you define and then returns a result of `true` or `false`, addresses this problem.

Modernizr can be used in two principal ways: the first is through CSS. Say, for example, you want to check whether Flexbox properties are available in the user's browser. First, you build a custom version of Modernizr with the build tool, being sure to click the `flexbox` option and include a link to the generated file in the head of your document. When the document has finished loading, a class of either *flexbox* or *no-flexbox* (depending on whether it's available) is added to the `html` element.

That class could then be used to style the page depending on the level of Flexbox support; for example, you might have something like this, which makes an element display as a block by default but as a flex container for supporting browsers:

```
.foo { display: block; }
.flexbox .foo { display: flex; }
```

The second use of Modernizr is for conditional JavaScript. Each test you run creates a property for the `Modernizr` object, which has a true or false value for use with conditional functions; in this example, the code inside the curly brackets executes if Flexbox is supported:

```
if(Modernizr.flexbox) { ... }
```

If you want to extend it to load external resources, you can use the `Modernizr.load()` method, which may look somewhat familiar if you've been paying attention so far:

```
Modernizr.load({
  test: Modernizr.flexbox,
  nope: 'foo.js'
});
```

Yes, it uses YepNope.js as a basis. All the properties of YepNope can be used in Modernizr. You can use `Modernizr.load()` alone, or, if you're using YepNope already, use the `Modernizr` object as the test:

```
yepnope({
  test: Modernizr.flexbox,
  nope: 'foo.js'
});
```

Both work the same way. Your preference depends on your configuration, but whichever you opt for, the flexibility that Modernizr gives you is incredibly useful for building enhanced applications with graceful fallback.

The Modernizr concept of conditional style rules is so useful that it's been adopted into CSS itself, using the `@supports` at-rule. `@supports` works similarly to media queries, but rather than testing for media features, it tests for CSS property-value pairs. For example, to test whether Flexbox is supported in a browser, use this rule:

```
@supports (display: flex) { ... }
```

The declarations inside the curly brackets are applied to any browser that supports the `flex` value for the `display` property. You can read more about `@supports` and its associated API in "Feature Queries" on page 210.

Mustache

If you're building without a server backend or just want to get some static templates built quickly, you may want to consider a client-side template system. Preeminent among these is *Mustache*, a logic-less syntax that has proved its popularity by being ported to just about every major web programming language including, most appropriately for our purposes, JavaScript.

A logic-less syntax is one that doesn't use any logical statements—no `if`, `else`, or `or`—instead using a system of tags that can be replaced by values. Here's a basic example, substituting a single tag for a value:

```
var view = {
  name: 'Bonobo'
}
var output = Mustache.render('The {{name}} is funny.', view);
```

You can see that I've created an object called *view*, with a single property *name*, which has the value *'Bonobo'*. In the *output* variable, I use the `Mustache.render()` method to create the tag replacement. This method has two arguments. In this example, the first is a string of text that contains the *name* property in double curly brackets (or "mustaches")—this is the syntax for a tag. The variable inside it, known as the *key*, will be replaced by the property value with the same name from the object that is the second argument of the method—in this case, view. The final output will be the text 'The Bonobo is funny.', which you can see in Example 1 in the file *mustache.html*.

Using Mustache you can easily create sections of content that repeat—known, cleverly, as *sections*. Sections are useful for, for example, cutting the repetition needed for creating lists or tables. The first step is to set up the property-value pairs in the *view* object:

```
var view = {
  'apes' : [
    {'name':'Bonobo'},
    {'name':'Chimpanzee'},
    {'name':'Gorilla'},
    {'name':'Orangutan'}
  ]
}
```

The syntax of a section is like a tag, but it has an opening and closing tag marked with # and /, respectively. In the following code, I output the section called *apes* with the text or HTML to be repeated:

```
var templApe = '{{#apes}}The {{name}} is funny.{{/apes}}';
```

Here I've created a new variable called *templApe*, which contains the repeating section. I could have added this directly inside Mustache.render(), but keeping my template rules separate in this way is more manageable. Anyway, I have my content and my template, so now I render it, outputting a list of four statements saying that each of the great apes is funny:

```
var output = Mustache.render(templApe,view);
```

You can see the result of this in Example 2 of *mustache.html*.

Sharing resources between pages makes templates more useful. The best way to share resources is to call an external file. Doing this is quite simple in Mustache; you just load the results of a JSON file into the *view* variable:

```
  var request = new XMLHttpRequest();
  request.open('GET', 'apes.json', true);
  request.onreadystatechange = function () {
    if (request.readyState != 4)  { return; }
    var view = JSON.parse(request.responseText);
❶ var templApe = '{{#apes}}The {{name}} is funny.{{/apes}}';
❷ var output = Mustache.render(templApe,view);
  };
  request.send();
```

❶ and ❷ are essentially the same as the previous example; the only difference is that the source of *view* is now data that has been parsed from the file *apes.json*, which contains the same information as the previous example but is held externally. You can see the output in Example 3 of *mustache.html*.

This example may look complicated because of the script required for getting the external data with an XMLHttpRequest; if you prefer to use jQuery, you could get the same result in fewer lines of code:

```
$.getJSON('json/apes.json', function (view) {
  var templApe = '{{#apes}}The {{name}} is funny.{{/apes}}';
  var output = Mustache.render(templApe,view);
});
```

This function is the same, but jQuery has abstracted away the XHR and JSON to make it all much simpler and to work cross-browser, which is what jQuery does best.

If you don't like the idea of keeping templates in script, separate from your main content, you can use templates in the markup instead. Use inline script tags, with a type of *text/template*, with the template markup inside. For example, you could do this:

```
<div id="ape_area">
  <script id="apeTpl" type="text/template">
  <ul id="apes">
{{#apes}}<li>The {{name}} is funny.</li>{{/apes}}
  </ul>
  </script>
</div>
```

The script is similar to the previous example, except now you use a reference to the ID of the script tag, *#apeTpl*, to declare the template and overwrite the inline script to remove it from the markup at the time of rendering:

```
$.getJSON('json/data.json', function (view) {
  var templApe = document.getElementById('apeTpl').innerHTML;
  var output = Mustache.render(templApe,view);
  document.getElementById('ape_area').innerHTML = output;
});
```

Example 4 of *mustache.html* shows this in action. Whether you use the inline templating system comes down to your personal preference, but Mustache offers the advantage of making these alternative approaches available.

Polyfills and Shims

A *shim* (sometimes called a *shiv*) is a piece of code that intercepts an API call and provides a layer of abstraction, and a *polyfill* is a specific type of shim that adds support for new or experimental features in browsers that don't support them natively. CSS multi-columns aren't supported in many older browsers, for example, so a multi-column polyfill would use JavaScript to replicate their functionality in those browsers.

The idea behind a polyfill is that it happens invisibly; other than including a link to the polyfill file, no (or very little) more should be required from the author. In the case of multi-columns, the CSS to create the columns should be all you need. Of course, multi-columns create a dependency on JavaScript so you have to consider an acceptable fallback state, but that should be part of your everyday workflow anyway.

Honestly, there are far too many polyfills covering far too many features for me to even think about providing a list here. The Modernizr wiki holds a regularly updated list that should be your first port of call; just think about the feature you want to consider a polyfill for, and it will most likely be on that page.

Modernizr and YepNope are actually perfect for providing polyfills only to browsers that need them, improving the performance for pages that don't. To return to the multi-column example once more, you might use this to load the polyfill only for browsers that don't support the feature:

```
Modernizr.load({
  test: Modernizr.csscolumns,
  nope: 'css3-multi-column.js'
});
```

Polyfills cause performance considerations, and they do create a dependency on JavaScript, so I suggest carefully considering the potential drawbacks before deciding to use them.

Testing and Debugging

If you want a safe environment in which to experiment and test your scripts, resources like JS Bin and JS Fiddle are ideal. Both work in basically the same way, but as I tend to use JS Bin, I'll cover it in this section.

JS Bin provides up to five columns for you to run your scripts in: The first three columns are for providing the HTML, CSS, and JavaScript that you'll use for your tests; a Console is available for logging results and information; and an Output panel shows the results of the tests.

A list of popular JavaScript libraries is available in a drop-down menu, and choosing any of them automatically adds them to the head of your example markup. You can also manually add any libraries that aren't in the list (such as YepNope).

The ability to version your tests, creating *snapshots* (known as milestones) of all the columns, makes it easy to branch your tests and try different approaches. Best of all, you can also share your tests with other users so they can add their own changes in a separate version, making collaboration really easy. You can make your tests public for showing off the results, and if you create an account, you can save your tests and revisit them in the future.

Summary

In this chapter, I've, by necessity, rushed through the basics of new JavaScript DOM and API features; there really are too many for me to cover, so I've chosen what I think are the most useful. I've focused on those that improve the loading of scripts, those that facilitate easier DOM traversal and manipulation, and those that make events work better, especially for touch-enabled devices.

I've also covered some popular and useful JavaScript libraries, from the power of the ubiquitous jQuery to the utility of YepNope, Modernizr, and Mustache. I strongly encourage you to find out more about the many different libraries that are available and find ones that suit you best.

Further Reading

The illustration in Figure 5-1 is adapted from Peter Beverloo's blog: *http://peter.sh/experiments/asynchronous-and-deferred-javascript-execution-explained/*.

Christian Heilmann wrote an in-depth introduction to JavaScript events for *Smashing Magazine*: *http://coding.smashingmagazine.com/2012/08/17/javascript-events-responding-user/*. The PointerEvents library is hosted on GitHub at *https://github.com/toolkitchen/PointerEvents/*.

The jQuery website, *http://jquery.com/*, has instructions for getting started, while the excellent documentation is at *http://docs.jquery.com/Main_Page*. Statistics about jQuery usage are from the blog post "jQuery Now Runs on Every Second Website" at *http://w3techs.com/blog/entry/jquery_now_runs_on_every_second_website/*.

All mobile libraries are fully documented: jQuery Mobile at *http://jquerymobile.com/*, Zepto.js at *http://zeptojs.com/*, and jQTouch at *http://jqtouch.com/*.

YepNope.js is available from *http://yepnopejs.com/*, and you'll find a good introductory tutorial at *http://net.tutsplus.com/tutorials/javascript-ajax/easy-script-loading-with-yepnope-js/*.

Modernizr's website, *http://modernizr.com/*, has full documentation plus a configurable build system and also plays host to "The All-In-One Entirely-Not-Alphabetical No-Bullshit Guide to HTML5 Fallbacks" (their title, not mine) at *https://github.com/Modernizr/Modernizr/wiki/HTML5-Cross-browser-Polyfills/*.

Christopher Coenraets wrote an excellent introductory tutorial to Mustache, although bear in mind that the syntax has changed a little: *http://coenraets.org/blog/2011/12/tutorial-html-templates-with-mustache-js/*. The full documentation of Mustache.js is at *https://github.com/janl/mustache.js/*.

Many different experimenting and debugging tools are available, and both *http://jsbin.com/* and *http://jsfiddle.net/* are excellent.

6

DEVICE APIS

In the previous chapters, I've discussed some of the many APIs that have been introduced as part of the HTML5 process, such as microdata and Touch Events. But there is a further range of APIs that, although not part of the spec, are certainly related; and these APIs offer something extremely attractive to developers in the multi-screen world: access to the device itself.

In this chapter, we take a look at some device APIs—from the new location and spatial features in portable devices to file and storage options across most modern browsers. Obviously not all APIs are going to be available on every device—knowing the position in three-dimensional (3-D) space of a television is of little practical use—but many APIs are useful across a broad range of user agents.

This is a curated list of those APIs I feel will be most practical, and the introductions to many are, for reasons of space, quite brief; often, the APIs will be much more extensive, and although I'll note where I think the scope is available for you to learn more, I urge you to discover for yourself the capabilities and possibilities of accessing the device through JavaScript.

NOTE: *The examples and demos in this chapter are interactive; I've included screenshots and illustrations in some cases, but if there's one chapter you really should download the example files for, it's this one.*

Geolocation

Location-based services are handy in all sorts of ways, from helping users with mobile devices find their way around to providing tailored information about the region they live in. The Geolocation API accesses a device's location services, which use GPS, wireless, or cell tower data to provide information about the device's location that will be used by your location-based apps.

Location data obviously involves privacy concerns, so in most (if not all) browsers, users must give explicit permission to access this data, usually in the form of an on-screen prompt that allows them to opt in or out of providing their location, as shown in Figure 6-1.

Figure 6-1: The Geolocation opt-in prompt in Chrome for Android

The data is held in the geolocation object, a child of `window.navigator`, which you can access using the `getCurrentPosition()` method:

```
navigator.geolocation.getCurrentPosition(function(where){
  // Do something
});
```

A successful callback returns an object (I've called it *where*) containing a coords child object. This child object has a series of properties pertaining to the user's position, such as his or her altitude and heading, but the ones I'm really interested in are `latitude` and `longitude`. In this code, I'm accessing these properties and displaying them in an alert:

```
navigator.geolocation.getCurrentPosition(function(where){
  alert(where.coords.latitude + ',' + where.coords.longitude);
});
```

You can try this for yourself in *position-current.html*; my results are shown in Figure 6-2.

The page at http://broken-links.
com says:

51.4707176,-0.0801178

OK

Figure 6-2: Coordinates obtained through the geolocation object, referencing the street I live on; please don't stalk me.

Occasionally an error is returned when looking for the position; an optional error callback can check for this. The following code creates two functions, one for successful location and one for an error:

```
var geo = navigator.geolocation,
    lcn_success = function(where) { ... },
    lcn_error = function() { ... };
geo.getCurrentPosition(lcn_success, lcn_error);
```

Sometimes a GPS device can take a little while to find the user's exact position, and, of course, the user may also be on the move, so instead of a one-off location, you can choose to watch the user's position, receiving updated results when location data changes. You do this with the watchPosition() method, also on the geolocation object, which works in the same way as getCurrentPosition():

```
navigator.geolocation.watchPosition(function(where){
  console.log(where.coords.latitude,where.coords.longitude);
});
```

To cancel watching a user's position, use the clearWatch() method with the unique ID created by the watchPosition() method; in this example, the process ends when the user clicks the *#stop* link:

```
var geo = navigator.geolocation,
    watchID = geo.watchPosition( ... ),
    endWatch = document.getElementById('stop');
endWatch.addEventListener('click', function () {
  geo.clearWatch(watchID);
}, false);
```

In *position-watch-clear.html*, you can see a demo of this in action. Open the page in a mobile device and move around, and you should see the location update as your device gets a better fix on your location.

Orientation

The Orientation API detects changes to the device's position in 3-D space—that is, movement up and down, left and right, and clockwise and counterclockwise. This movement is measured with an accelerometer, and the devices that are most likely to contain one are those that are most portable; mobile phones and tablets move frequently so are very likely to have one, laptops move to some degree so may contain one, and desktops and TVs move so infrequently that it's very unlikely they'll have an accelerometer or access to this API.

Using orientation events opens up new possibilities for interaction and navigation; some apps already provide an option to control page scrolling by tilting the device forward or backward, and navigation between tiles or pages by tilting to the left or right.

Before detailing the API, I should talk about three-dimensional axes (you can skip this paragraph if you know about them already). All movement in three dimensions has three directions, or *axes*, commonly referred to as *x*, *y*, and *z*. If you hold a device in front of you now (or imagine you are doing so), the *x*-axis runs from left to right, *y* from top to bottom, and *z* toward you and away from you, as shown in Figure 6-3. Movement is measured along these axes from the center of the device and is either positive or negative: Bringing the device closer to you moves it positively along the *z*-axis and away moves it negatively. Lowering the device toward your feet moves it negatively along the *y*-axis and moving it to your right moves it positively along the *x*-axis.

Figure 6-3: Movement along the three-dimensional axes (This image is taken from the Mozilla Developer Network [MDN] article, "Orientation and Motion Data Explained": http://developer.mozilla.org/en-US/docs/DOM/Orientation _and_motion_data_explained/. It is used under a Creative Commons license.)

To detect the movement along each axis, use the deviceorientation event on the window object. This event fires every time the device moves and returns an object with a series of useful orientation properties:

```
window.addEventListener('deviceorientation',function (orientData) {
    ...
}, false);
```

The three key properties that are germane to movement are alpha, beta, and gamma. Each is measured with a number representing degrees of rotation, although some are constrained within set limits.

- alpha measures rotation around, not movement along, the z-axis—that is, if the device were laid flat on a table, clockwise or counterclockwise movement. The value of alpha is a number from 0 to 360.

- beta is rotation around the x-axis, which you can picture as tipping the top edge of the device toward or away from you. beta has a value range of −180 (tip toward you) to 180 (tip away from you).

- gamma is rotation around the y-axis or tilting the device from side to side. The value of gamma ranges from −90 (tip left) to 90 (tip right).

As a very simple example, the code in the following script uses deviceorientation to detect changes to the orientation and then logs the three values to the console:

```
window.addEventListener('deviceorientation',function (orientData) {
  console.log(orientData.alpha,orientData.beta,orientData.gamma);
}, false);
```

In the example file *orientation.html*, you can see a slightly different version that updates the text on the page when orientation changes; open it on a mobile or tablet device and move the device around to see the page content update.

Fullscreen

We all know the Web is an immensely powerful distraction machine, so sometimes providing an option to focus only on the content at hand is useful. This functionality is provided by the Fullscreen API, which allows you to expand any element to fill the entire screen of the device, rather than just the browser viewport. This is especially handy for large-screen devices, for instance, when playing video to provide the "lean back" experience of television.

Before setting up this script, check whether the browser has a fullscreen mode. You can do this with the Boolean fullScreenEnabled attribute:

```
if (document.fullScreenEnabled) { ... }
```

Fullscreen mode is called with the requestFullScreen() method. As this introduces potential security risks (an often-quoted example is an attack website that fools you into thinking that you're seeing something else and copies your keystrokes), many devices provide an on-screen prompt to make sure you give permission to enter fullscreen mode. If you grant that permission, the element the method is called on scales up to 100 percent of the device screen's height and width.

In the next code snippet, a click event listener is applied to the element *#trigger*, which, when fired, will put *.target* into fullscreen mode, as long as permission is granted. You can see this for yourself in the file *fullscreen.html*, which is illustrated in Figure 6-4.

```
var el = document.querySelector('.target'),
    launch = document.getElementById('trigger');
launch.addEventListener('click', function () {
  el.requestFullScreen();
}, false);
```

Figure 6-4: An element launched into fullscreen mode with an on-screen alert in Firefox for Android

The browser should offer a means to exit fullscreen mode, but you can also provide your own with the exitFullScreen() method. The next code block shows a function that uses this method to leave fullscreen mode when the ENTER key is pressed. Note two further things in the code: First, it uses the fullscreenchange event, which is fired whenever an element enters or leaves fullscreen mode; and second, it relies on an if statement using the fullScreenElement attribute, which returns either information about the element that is in fullscreen mode or null if there is none.

```
document.addEventListener('fullscreenchange', function () {
  if (document.fullScreenElement !== null) {
    document.addEventListener('keydown', function (e) {
      if (e.keyCode === 13) {
        document.exitFullScreen();
      }
    }, false);
  }
}, false);
```

When an element has been put in fullscreen mode, you might want to style it (or its children) a little differently. It's proposed that you can do this with a new dedicated CSS pseudo-class, which will be called either :fullscreen or :full-screen:

```
.target:full-screen {}
```

Vibration

The Vibration API makes a device vibrate, providing some haptic feedback for your users. This API actually used to be called the Vibrator API, but I'm sure you don't need me to tell you why that name was changed very quickly. Obviously not all devices are capable of vibrating, especially larger ones, so this API is decidedly more useful in mobile devices.

The API is extremely simple, requiring only the vibrate() method on the navigator object. The value supplied to vibrate() is a figure representing the number of milliseconds for the device to vibrate; for example, to make the device vibrate for one-fifth of a second after the user has completed a touchend event, use this code:

```
document.addEventListener('touchend', function () {
  window.navigator.vibrate(200);
});
```

You can also use an array of values that alternate between vibrations and pauses; that is, the odd-numbered values are vibrations and the even values are pauses. In this example, the device vibrates for 200ms, pauses for 200ms, and then vibrates for 500ms:

```
document.addEventListener('touchend', function () {
  window.navigator.vibrate([200,200,500]);
});
```

Vibrating runs down the battery more quickly, so use this API with caution. You can manually stop a vibration by using a 0 or an empty array value. In this code, the device will begin to vibrate for 5 seconds when the touch event starts, and then stops when the event ends:

```
document.addEventListener('touchstart', function () {
  window.navigator.vibrate(5000);
});
document.addEventListener('touchend', function () {
  window.navigator.vibrate(0);
});
```

You can try the API for yourself in the example file *vibration.html*, even though obviously you'll need to open it on a mobile device with vibration capabilities if you want to actually feel the vibrations. If you don't have one on hand, Figure 6-5 shows a reconstruction of the experience.

Figure 6-5: The Vibration API in action (reconstruction)

Battery Status

One of the key concerns with portable devices is knowing their battery status. Mobile devices can get as little as seven or eight hours out of a full charge, whereas a laptop is lucky to get more than three or four hours. Knowing the status of the device's battery can be important before you begin power-hungry processes or commence to download large files.

You can get information about the battery with the Battery Status API, which brings a set of attributes on the navigator.battery object. For example, to find out if the battery is currently charging, you can use the charging attribute to get a true or false value:

```
var batteryStatus = navigator.battery.charging;
```

To find the current battery level, you can use the level attribute, which returns a value from 0 (empty) to 1 (fully charged). The following code is a simple demonstration of this in action: The battery level is obtained and its value used as the value of a meter element (which will be fully introduced in Chapter 8), and the current charging status ('*Charging*' or '*Discharging*') is appended below it. You can try it yourself in the example file *battery.html*. The result is shown in Figure 6-6.

Figure 6-6: A meter element showing the remaining battery level of my device, plus its charging status

```
var el = document.getElementById('status'),
    meter = document.querySelector('meter'),
    battery = navigator.battery,
    status = (battery.charging) ? 'Charging' : 'Discharging';
meter.value = battery.level;
meter.textContent = battery.level;
el.textContent = status;
```

The battery object has two further attributes: chargingTime and dischargingTime. Both of these return a value, in seconds, of the remaining time until the battery is fully charged or fully discharged, respectively.

The Battery Status API also has a series of events that fire when a change to any of the attributes is detected: chargingchange, chargingtimechange, dischargingtimechange, and levelchange. The following code uses chargingchange to detect a change to the device's charging status and fires an alert if the status has changed:

```
var status,
    battery = navigator.battery,
    chargeStatus = function () {
      (battery.charging) ? status = 'Charging' : status = 'Discharging';
      return status;
};
battery.addEventListener('chargingchange', function () {
  window.alert(chargeStatus());
}, false);
window.alert(chargeStatus());
```

You can try this one yourself using the example file *battery-event.html*—plug and unplug your phone from its charger to see the status update.

Network Information

Knowing the current strength of a device's Internet connection is extremely useful; you may want to serve lower-resolution images to devices with low bandwidth or stream different video qualities to users depending on their connection. Likewise, you may want to hold off on the background processes if the user has a limited or metered tariff.

The Network Information API is composed of two attributes on the connection object: bandwidth, which is a figure representing the *estimated* bandwidth in Megabytes (MBps) of the current connection (0 if the device is offline, infinity if the result is unknown); and metered, a Boolean that returns true if the connection is metered (such as on pay-as-you-go tariffs).

The following code shows a function that uses both attributes: bandwidth to return the current connection's bandwidth and metered to add an extra message to the status if the connection is limited.

```
var status,
    connection = navigator.connection,
    showStatus = function () {
      status = connection.bandwidth + ' MB/s';
      if (connection.metered) {
        status += ' (metered)';
      }
        alert(status);
    };
showStatus();
```

Network Information also has an event handler, change, on the connection object, which fires whenever the connection status changes; with this, you can easily add an extra call to the function when necessary:

```
connection.addEventListener('change', showStatus, false);
```

You can see both at work in the file *network.html*—try connecting or disconnecting your Wi-Fi service to see the change event fire.

Camera and Microphone

Cameras and microphones have been common on desktop and laptop computers for a long time, and with the rise of mobile devices they've become extremely prevalent—almost ubiquitous. But for years, we've had to rely on third-party plug-ins, such as Flash and Java, to get audio and video input on the Web, so a native input method is more than overdue.

This native input comes in the shape of the getUserMedia() method, part of the WebRTC project, which I'll discuss in more detail in Chapter 9. The getUserMedia() method is on the navigator object, and takes up to three arguments: The first is for options about the stream, such as whether to accept only audio, only video, or both; the second is a callback fired when a successful connection is made; and the third, which is optional, is a failure callback:

```
navigator.getUserMedia({options}, success, failure);
```

As with the Geolocation and Fullscreen APIs, accessing the user's camera or microphone has privacy implications, so many browsers provide an on-screen prompt asking for the user's permission to access the device. On devices with more than one camera, some user agents offer a native control to switch between them.

A media stream requires a special element in order to be displayed, either the new video or audio HTML5 element (depending on the stream content). I introduce these new elements fully in Chapter 9, but for the purposes of the following demonstration, using a video stream, you need the following markup somewhere on your page:

```
<video autoplay></video>
```

When the successful callback is fired from getUserMedia(), the media stream is returned with a unique ID (provided by you), which will be supplied to the video element. The following code shows a basic example, which I've annotated and will explain after:

```
❶ navigator.getUserMedia({video:true}, function (stream) {
❷   var video = document.querySelector('video');
❸   video.src = window.URL.createObjectURL(stream);
  });
```

In line ❶, I've supplied two arguments to the getUserMedia() method: The first is the stream options where I'm flagging that I want to get video, no audio; and the second is the callback function where I've given the result a unique ID of *stream*. In the next line ❷, I've used querySelector() to assign the video element to the *video* variable so that in line ❸, I can use the createObjectURL() method to convert *stream* into a URL and set it as the src attribute of the video element. No failure callback is supplied.

To try this for yourself, see the file *getusermedia.html*—you'll need to have a video on your device to see the file in action.

Web Storage

Recording information about previous activity is usually done with cookies, but one of their drawbacks is that you can store only small amounts of data. The Web Storage API was created to allow user agents to store more data on the user's device. This data can be stored only until the browser is closed, which is known as *session storage*, or kept until the user or another script actively flushes the data, which is called *local storage*. Both operate in essentially the same way, except for that one key difference—permanence.

To store data, you save it in key:value pairs, similar to how you store cookies now, except the quantity of data that can be saved is greater. The API has two key objects, which are straightforward and memorable: localStorage for local storage and sessionStorage for session storage.

NOTE: *In the examples in this section I use* sessionStorage, *but you can swap this for* localStorage *if you prefer more permanent storage; the syntax applies equally.*

The web storage syntax is pretty flexible, allowing three different ways to store an item: with the setItem() method, with square bracket notation, or with dot notation. As a simple example, the next code snippet shows how you might store this author's name; all three different ways of storing data are shown for comparison, and all are perfectly valid.

```
sessionStorage.setItem('author','Peter Gasston');
sessionStorage['author'] = 'Peter Gasston';
sessionStorage.author = 'Peter Gasston';
```

Some developer tools allow you to inspect the contents of storage, so Figure 6-7 shows the result of this code, regardless of which approach you use.

Retrieving items from storage is just as flexible a process; you can use the getItem() method, which accepts only the name of the relevant key as an argument, or the square bracket or dot notation method without any value. In the next code snippet, all three techniques are shown and are equivalent:

```
var author = sessionStorage.getItem('author');
var author = sessionStorage['author'];
var author = sessionStorage.author;
```

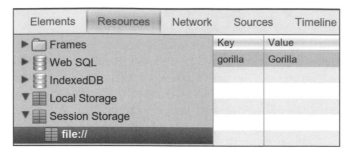

Figure 6-7: A key:value pair stored in the browser, shown in the WebKit Web Inspector

Although I'm storing only very simple values in these examples, in most browsers, you can store up to 5MB of data for each subdomain. This is the figure recommended in the specification, although it's not mandatory.

You can delete a single item from storage using the removeItem() method, which like getItem(), takes a single key name as an argument and deletes the stored item with the matching key:

```
sessionStorage.removeItem('author');
```

In the file *storage.html*, I've put together a simple demo that adds and removes items from the storage. To see the result, you need developer tools that show the contents of the storage, such as in the Resources tab of the WebKit Web Inspector. The contents don't update in real time, so you have to refresh to see changes.

The nuclear option to remove all items in storage (although only on the specific domain storing them, of course) is the clear() method:

```
sessionStorage.clear();
```

A storage event on localStorage is fired whenever storage is changed. This returns an object with some useful properties such as key, which gives the name of the key that has changed, and oldValue and newValue, which give the old and new values of the item that has changed. Note this event fires only on other open instances (tabs or windows) of the same domain, not the active one; its utility lies in monitoring changes if the user has multiple tabs open, for example.

The next code block runs a function that fires whenever storage is modified and logs an entry into the console. You can try it yourself in the file *storage-event.html*, but you'll need to open the file and developer console in two different tabs to see the changes occur—remember, changes to the value will show in the other window, not the one where the click occurs.

```
window.addEventListener('storage', function (e) {
  var msg = 'Key ' + e.key + ' changed from ' + e.oldValue + ' to ' + e.newValue;
  console.log(msg);
}, false);
```

Storage is being taken even further with the development of the Indexed Database (IndexedDB) API, which aims to create a full-fledged storage database in the browser that you access via JavaScript. Many browsers have already made an attempt at this, but the vendors couldn't decide on a common format. IndexedDB is an independently created standard aimed at keeping everyone happy. Its heavily technical nature takes it out of the scope of this book, but if you need advanced storage capabilities, keep it in mind.

Drag and Drop

Adding a "physical" aspect to your websites that allows users to move elements around the screen is a nice option. This "drag and drop" behavior is especially useful on devices with touch interfaces.

The Drag and Drop API is probably the oldest feature I cover in this book. It was first implemented in Internet Explorer 5 back in 1999 (that's about 150 Internet years ago) and has been adopted by other browsers for quite some time, although the effort to standardize it was only undertaken as part of the HTML5 movement. Unfortunately, Drag and Drop shows some signs of aging, being quite arcane and unintuitive at first.

By default the a and img elements can be dragged around the screen (I'll get to other elements momentarily), but you have to set up a *drop zone*, an area that the elements can be dragged into. A drop zone is created when you attach two events to an element: dragover and drop. All that's required of dragover is that you cancel its default behavior (for one of the arcane reasons I noted earlier, which you don't need to worry about). All the hard work happens with the drop event.

That may sound a little confusing, so this example shows a very simple setup: The *#target* element has the dragover and drop event listeners attached to it, the callback function of dragover prevents the default behavior with preventDefault(), and the main action happens inside the callback function of the drop event.

```
var target = document.getElementById('target');
target.addEventListener('dragover', function (e) {
  e.preventDefault();
}, false);
target.addEventListener('drop', function (e) {
  // Do something
}, false);
```

All of the events in the Drag and Drop API create an object called dataTransfer, which has a series of relevant properties and methods. You want to access these when the drop event is fired. For img elements, you want to get the URL of the item, so for this you use the getData() method with a value of *URL* and then do something with it; in this example, I'll create a new img element and pass the URL to the src attribute, making a copy of the existing one:

```
target.addEventListener('drop', function (e) {
  e.preventDefault();
  var newImg = document.createElement('img');
  newImg.setAttribute('src', e.dataTransfer.getData('URL'));
  e.currentTarget.appendChild(newImg);
}, false);
```

Note the use of preventDefault() again inside the function on the drop callback; using this is important, because in most (if not all) browsers the default behavior after dropping an item into a drop zone is to try to open its URL. This is part of Drag and Drop's arcane behavior. All you really need to know is to use preventDefault() to stop this from happening.

You can see a simple example based on the previous code in the file *drag-drop.html*—just drag the image from its starting position to inside the box.

I said previously that, by default, only a and img elements are draggable, but you can make that true of any element in two steps. First, apply the true value to the draggable attribute of the element in question:

```
<div draggable="true" id="text">Drag Me</div>
```

Second, specify a datatype for the element. You do this with the dragstart event, using the setData() method of dataTransfer to apply a MIME type (in this case, text/plain) and a value (in this case, the text content of the element):

```
var txt = document.getElementById('txt');
  txt.addEventListener('dragstart', function (e) {
  e.dataTransfer.setData('text/plain', e.currentTarget.textContent);
}, false);
```

You can detect the type of file being dropped by using the contains() method, which is a child of the types object, itself a child of the dataTransfer object created in the callback function of the drop event. The method returns true or false if the string supplied in the argument matches a value in types; for example, to find out if a dropped element contains a plain text type, you would use this:

```
var foo = e.dataTransfer.types.contains('text/plain');
```

Using the `contains()` method means you can perform different actions on different files.

The example file *drag-drop-2.html* shows two elements, an `img` and a `p`, which can be dragged into the marked drop zone, creating a copy of each, and the following code shows how this is done: The `contains()` method detects if the element being dragged contains a URL; if it does, it must be an `img`, so it creates a new `img` element with the URL of the dropped element in the `src` attribute; if it doesn't, it must be text, so it creates a new text node filled with the text of the dropped element.

```
target.addEventListener('drop', function (e) {
  var smth;
  e.preventDefault();
  if (e.dataTransfer.types.contains('text/uri-list')) {
    smth = document.createElement('img');
    smth.setAttribute('src', e.dataTransfer.getData('URL'));
  } else {
    smth = document.createTextNode(e.dataTransfer.getData('Text'));
  }
  e.currentTarget.appendChild(smth);
}, false);
```

Although what I've described in this section is more than sufficient for you to use the Drag and Drop API, the API contains plenty more that I haven't covered. If you're interested, a number of extra events are available: `dragenter` and `dragleave` are events for the drop zone, and `dragend` and `drag` are fired on the draggable item.

Interacting with Files

Working with different files is a common activity—although much more so on desktops or laptops than on mobile devices—so an API is available for doing this on the Web too. The File API is a fairly low-level API that allows you to get information about files and to access their contents, and there are a few higher-level APIs that I'll mention in due course.

To access files, you can either choose them using the `file` input element or drag them from a folder on your system (depending on the system you use) with the Drag and Drop API, which is the approach we'll look at here.

The `dataTransfer` object, which I just discussed in the previous section, contains a `files` child object that contains a list of all the files dropped into the drop zone. Each file has three properties—`name`, `size`, and `type`—and the meaning of these should be pretty obvious.

The following code example shows a function where files dropped into the drop zone will have their names listed. You do this with a `for` loop that runs through the `files` object and outputs the `name` property for each. Try it for yourself with the example file *files.html*.

```
target.addEventListener('drop', function (e) {
  var files = e.dataTransfer.files,
      fileNo = files.length;
  e.preventDefault();
  for (i = 0; i < fileNo; i++) {
    var el = document.createElement('li'),
        smth = document.createTextNode(files[i].name);
    el.appendChild(smth);
    e.currentTarget.appendChild(el);
  }
}, false);
```

If you need more than just information about the file, the FileReader interface allows you to get the content as a text file or data URL (where relevant). The following code snippet shows a simple example using an image file as the source; the syntax is a little complex, so I've annotated the code and will explain it next.

```
  target.addEventListener('drop', function (e) {
    e.preventDefault();
    var files = e.dataTransfer.files[0],
❶       reader = new FileReader();
❷ reader.addEventListener('load', function (evt) {
      var img = document.createElement('img');
❸   img.src = evt.target.result;
      target.appendChild(img);
    }, false);
❹ reader.readAsDataURL(files);
❺ reader.addEventListener('error', function (evt) {
      console.log(evt.target.error.code)
    }, false);
  }, false);
```

In ❶, a new FileReader object is created and assigned to the variable *reader*. To this object, a new event listener is added ❷, which will fire when the file has finished loading, running a function that will create a new img element using the content of the uploaded file. The src for the img element is obtained in ❸, using the result attribute of target, a child object of the event. The type of result is determined in ❹ using the readAsDataURL() method, which encodes the file content as a 64-bit data string. Finally, an error event listener is added to the object in ❺, which uses the code attribute of the error object of the target object of the event object (phew!) to log an error message.

Try this for yourself in *file-2.html*; drag an image from a folder on your system (if possible) to see it appear in the page. In addition to readAsDataURL(), a few other methods are available: readAsText() returns the content of the file as plain text, and readAsArrayBuffer() returns the content as a fixed-length data buffer (especially useful for images).

You can also use a number of APIs to go even further with files: The File Writer API allows you to modify the content of a file, and the File System API goes further still with the provision of a navigable filesystem on the user's device. These APIs are exciting but somewhat too technical for me to go into detail in this book.

Mozilla's Firefox OS and WebAPIs

A potentially quite interesting entry into the mobile OS market comes from Mozilla, makers of the Firefox browser. Mozilla is building a brand new OS from the ground up, all constructed with open web standards—HTML, CSS, JavaScript, and others. The OS has no middleware layer, as iOS or Android does, and the system APIs all use JavaScript to interact directly with the hardware. Building a new OS is a bold undertaking, and I look forward to seeing how it performs.

As part of that effort, Mozilla realized they needed to develop many of the existing device APIs and create many more. This project is called WebAPI, and although many of the included APIs have been covered already in this chapter, a few are unique to Firefox OS at the moment.

Here are some of the new APIs: WebTelephony, for sending and receiving calls; WebSMS, for sending, receiving, and managing text messages; Contacts, for accessing and managing the address book; and Device Storage, for accessing shared files or folders such as the picture gallery featured on many phones.

The fate of Firefox OS and broader implementation of these APIs remain to be seen, but I'm quite excited about a smartphone OS that is built using only open web technologies and the many possibilities that opens up for web developers with regard to device interactions.

PhoneGap and Native Wrappers

If you need deeper access to device APIs but still want to develop using web technologies, you might want to consider a native wrapper for your app. These wrappers act as a kind of layer between your web application and the device in question, providing hooks into the API but not using native code to display what's on the screen. Using a native wrapper around web technologies creates what's known as a *hybrid app*.

Which wrapper you use depends largely on your targets (I'll discuss this in more detail in Chapter 10), but as an example of what they can do, PhoneGap is perfect. It's a wrapper for mobile apps, providing a common API for developers to build hybrid apps that work across iOS, Android, Windows Phone, Blackberry, and more.

Summary

By necessity, I could detail only a few of the many APIs that make up the web platform, including those for location and spatial movement, status of the battery and Internet connection, access to the camera and microphone, local storage capabilities, interaction with files and elements in a tactile way, and access to information about the content of files. I hope that with this overview and the example files I've been able at least to hint at the creative possibilities that open up when you access a device through JavaScript.

Further Reading

Dive Into HTML5 has an in-depth explanation of the Geolocation API at *http://diveintohtml5.info/geolocation.html*, whereas the MozDev article "Orientation and Motion Data Explained" gives a good overview of three-dimensional orientation and movement: *https://developer.mozilla.org/en-US/docs/DOM/ Orientation_and_motion_data_explained/*.

The Fullscreen API is explained in the Sitepoint article "How to Use the HTML5 Full-Screen API" by Craig Buckler, although the API changed slightly as I was writing this, so some object names or properties may have been updated. You can find the article at *http://www.sitepoint.com/ html5-full-screen-api/*.

The Battery Status API is well explained by David Walsh at *http:// davidwalsh.name/battery-api/*, and a discussion of the previous and newly updated Network Information API is at *http://nostrongbeliefs.com/ a-quick-look-network-information-api/*.

HTML5 Rocks gives the best explanation of getUserMedia() in their article "Capturing Audio & Video in HTML5": *http://www.html5rocks.com/ en/tutorials/getusermedia/intro/*. The full aims of the WebRTC project are listed at *http://www.webrtc.org/*.

MozDev (again) gives a concise introduction to the Web Storage API: *https://developer.mozilla.org/en-US/docs/DOM/Storage/*.

The most accessible guide to the Drag and Drop API that I found was written by the HTML5 Doctors at *http://html5doctor.com/native-drag-and-drop/*, while the five-part "Working with Files in JavaScript" by Nicholas Zakas is an excellent resource for the File API: *http://www.nczonline.net/blog/2012/05/ 08/working-with-files-in-javascript-part-1/*.

The APIs that form the Firefox OS project are listed at *https://wiki .mozilla.org/WebAPI/*, and the slides from the presentation "WebAPIs and Apps" by Robert Nyman provide a great overview of the APIs: *http:// www.slideshare.net/robnyman/web-apis-apps-mozilla-london/*. "Are We Mobile Yet?" gives an at-a-glance guide to levels of API implementation: *http:// arewemobileyet.com/*.

7

IMAGES AND GRAPHICS

For many years the only way to display images on the Web was to use JPGs and GIFs, with the former generally used for photographs and the latter for icons and graphics. These formats were later joined by the PNG format, which largely ousted the GIF (for icons at least, although not for animations of cats). But they are all inert image formats; other than simple animation frames, they aren't capable of handling dynamic or interactive images or graphics, which was generally done with third-party plug-ins such as Flash.

Modern browsers, however, have the luxury of two new graphical formats: Scalable Vector Graphics (SVG), a scalable format that can be included in the DOM and manipulated using CSS and JavaScript, and canvas, an HTML5 element that can be drawn on using an API. Between these two, a whole new range of graphical possibilities has opened up, from interactive charts to on-the-fly image manipulation.

In this chapter, I'll walk you through the basics of each format, showing some common examples and giving you enough information so you can choose when each format is appropriate. Before I start, however, I'll briefly explain some key terms and concepts.

Comparing Vectors and Bitmaps

Vector graphics are made of geometrical shapes formed with a coordinate system; a series of points is plotted on a grid and lines are drawn between them to form the shapes, making them inherently scalable. If I make my grid larger, the same shape is drawn from the same coordinates, but the coordinates are now farther apart so my shape is bigger.

Bitmap graphics are a series of colored pixels laid out in a grid to form an image; if you open an image in Photoshop (or similar) and zoom in, you can see this grid for yourself. All of the common web image formats (JPG, PNG, GIF) are bitmap formats. Resizing a pixel grid means the computer has to use a scaling algorithm to increase or decrease the sizes of the pixels to fit the new space, removing pixels or adding new ones where necessary. These algorithms generally work impressively but are usually better at removing pixels than adding them, which is why a scaled-down bitmap often looks much better than a scaled-up one.

In Figure 7-1, you can see a comparison of the two different graphical approaches as I zoom in on an image. The vector image is crisp and clear, but the bitmap looks fuzzy, as the scaling algorithm had to make some estimates around adding new pixels to accommodate the larger scale.

Figure 7-1: Detail from a scaled-up image in SVG (left) and PNG (right); the SVG is noticeably sharper and clearer.

Vector graphics aren't suitable for photographic or photo-realistic images, but are great for illustrations such as logos, icons, and charts. Conversely, bitmap graphics are less useful in environments where scaling is common (such as mobile devices) but are much better for photographic images.

Scalable Vector Graphics

Vector graphics on the Web are created using the *Scalable Vector Graphics (SVG)* markup language. This language has been around for a long time without too much success, but two factors gave it a new lease on life: implementation in IE9 and the rise of the mobile and multi-device Web. All the major browsers have now implemented it.

The main reason SVG is so useful is its scalability, which I discussed in the previous section. Scalability is a real boon for responsive web design. You can reuse the same image across every platform, avoiding the problems with adaptive images, which I discussed in Chapter 3. In addition, the way that SVGs are made and embedded in a page can enhance accessibility and searchability, as you'll see in the following sections.

Of course, SVG doesn't work for everything—photographs, as mentioned, are still better off as bitmaps—but it is a really useful format for multi-screen design.

Anatomy of an SVG Image

Before I explain how you can use SVG in your pages, I want to run briefly through the code behind it. You see, SVG is actually an XML file that marks up the image that it creates; this means you can view it in a text editor and change it manually—something that is basically impossible with bitmap files.

Open an SVG file in your preferred editor, or view the source in a browser window, and inspect the contents. Although the actual markup varies wildly from file to file, you will at least be able to see the many common elements. To begin, all SVG files start with the XML declaration, which holds the version number of XML you're using, the text encoding method, and the standalone attribute that sets whether the file makes reference to other external files or stands alone (in most cases, just leave this as *no*):

```
<?xml version="1.0" encoding="UTF-8" standalone="no"?>
```

Next, you see the svg element—which is the root—and a series of namespaces with information about the syntax used. The following example is taken from an SVG file I opened at random. It tells me that the file uses Dublin Core metadata terms (see "RDFa" on page 30 for more on this), is licensed under Creative Commons, and uses RDF, SVG, and XLink schema to describe its contents:

```
<svg xmlns:dc="http://purl.org/dc/elements/1.1/" xmlns:cc="http://web.resource
.org/cc/" xmlns:rdf="http://www.w3.org/1999/02/22-rdf-syntax-ns#" xmlns:svg=
"http://www.w3.org/2000/svg" xmlns="http://www.w3.org/2000/svg" xmlns:xlink=
"http://www.w3.org/1999/xlink">
```

The simplest form of the svg element requires only the attributes for a link to the SVG namespace and the version of SVG that you're using:

```
<svg xmlns="http://www.w3.org/2000/svg" version="1.1">
```

All of the children of the svg element contain the information used to create the image itself. The bulk of this information is contained in a series of elements based on basic mathematical shapes used to make the drawing: circle, rect, ellipse, polygon, and line. Each of these shape elements also has a series of attributes to describe the shape's position, size, and color information. For example, here's how to draw a circle whose center is 50px from the left of the grid (cx) and 75px from the top (cy), has a radius of 25px (r), a black border (stroke) 2px wide (stroke-width), and a background color of silver (fill):

```
<circle cx="50" cy="50" r="25" stroke="black" stroke-width="2" fill="silver"/>
```

The element is closed with a trailing slash; SVG is strict XML and all empty elements must be closed.

In comparison to the previous code, here's a rectangle that is 100px wide (width) and 50px tall (height), is offset 25px from the left (x) and 50px from the top (y) of the grid, and has a blue background (fill):

```
<rect width="100" height="50" x="25" y="50" fill="blue"/>
```

I don't intend to go too much deeper into how an SVG file is made—for two reasons: First, the subject is too complex for a single chapter of a book to hope to cover; and second, I don't think you'll use it that often. You are more likely to use a graphical editor (such as Adobe Illustrator or the open source Inkscape) to edit SVG files, perhaps making only small adjustments to the code by hand.

Linked SVG Files

You'll use SVG on your sites in two main ways. One is to embed the code into the markup itself, which I cover in the next section. The second and easier way is to link to a premade SVG file as an image, in the same way you would a JPG or PNG. This method is great if you want a scalable, decorative image, although you don't get to access the SVG as part of the DOM.

To use a linked SVG, you must have an image saved with the file extension *.svg* (or *.svgz* for a compressed file); then just supply the path to the image at the relevant point in your code. You can use it in the markup with an img element:

```
<img src="/path/to/foo.svg">
```

Or you can call it in CSS anywhere that accepts a url() function as an argument, such as background-image:

```
.foo { background-image: url('path/to/foo.svg'); }
```

The drawback to using SVG in the img element or CSS is that you lose certain advanced SVG behaviors, such as scripting and animations. If having these is important to you, use an embedding technique (which I cover next) instead.

SVG Sprites

SVG's scaling capabilities are an especially good fit for using sprites for icons—that is, showing only a selected portion of a single large image to cut down on the number of file downloads and to speed up page load—although a little setup work is required. The way it works is that all of the desired icons are stacked one above the other in a single SVG image and then all except one are hidden using CSS (as illustrated in Figure 7-2).

Figure 7-2: In the SVG file, each of the icons is stacked one above the other (left) and hidden with CSS, except for one icon which is shown (right).

The code required to do this looks roughly like the following (and because there's a lot to explain, I've annotated it):

```
❶  <svg ...>
     <defs>
❷      <style><![CDATA[
         .icon { display: none; }
❸        .icon:target { display: inline; }
       ]]></style>
     </defs>
❹    <svg viewBox="0 0 30 30">
❺      <g class="icon" id="icon1">...</g>
     </svg>
     <svg viewBox="0 0 30 30">
       <g class="icon" id="icon2">...</g>
     </svg>
   </svg>
```

The root element ❶ requires no extra namespaces, so it can be the same as in previous examples. CSS can be put inline to the file itself ❷, which is handy for this technique as you can reuse the image on multiple pages; note that you must use a CDATA section to let the browser know that this is text, not XML to be parsed. In the style rules, you set all of the *.icon* elements to not display, except for the one the `:target` pseudo-class ❸ applies to, which is shown (I'll explain why shortly). Each sprite layer in the stack has a `viewBox` attribute ❹ with four coordinates inside; this attribute sets the limit of the box that will be displayed, using the first two numbers for the *x*- and *y*-coordinates of the top left of the box and the second two numbers as the width and height of the area to be displayed. Finally, the g element (used for grouping shapes) for each sprite ❺ has the same class name as the others but a unique id.

With this setup completed, you can link directly to the icon you want, using its id value in the URL, as shown here:

```
.bar { background-image: url('foo.svg#icon1'); }
```

The :target pseudo-class is applied when the hash of a URL matches the id of an element; in this case the URL hash is *#icon1*, so the :target selector applies to the svg element *#icon1*. As all other svg elements are set to not be displayed, *#icon1* is shown regardless of its order in the stock. You can see an example of this in *svg-icon.html* and illustrated in Figure 7-3.

Figure 7-3: The same source image is used for both buttons, but each has a unique icon because of the stacking technique.

WARNING   *Changes to the way browsers render SVG may possibly cause the stacking technique to break in the future. See the link in "Further Reading" on page 139 for more detail on this.*

SVG Sprites with Fragments

An alternative spriting technique uses Fragment Identifiers. This method doesn't require the icons to be stacked; the SVG sprite sheet can have all of the icons laid out distinctly, with their positions called using the four coordinates of viewBox as part of the URL in the svgView function. Here's an example:

```
.bar { background-image: url('foo.svg#svgView(viewBox(0 0 30 30))'); }
```

The advantage of this approach is that the SVG file isn't required to have a unique id for each sprite, and you can show multiple sprites or pieces of a sprite, which is more complicated to achieve with the stacking method.

Embedded SVG

If you want to manipulate the SVG, you can embed it directly into a page's HTML. The SVG then becomes part of the DOM and is, therefore, accessible through JavaScript and potentially CSS.

You can do this in a number of ways, the first of which is to use the embed element. This element has been used across the Web for embedding Flash files, although it was never made standard until the advent of HTML5. You can add SVG to your page with embed by supplying a link to the source file in the src attribute:

```
<embed src="foo.svg"></embed>
```

Similarly, you can use the object element, with the path to the SVG file used as a value for the data attribute:

```
<object data="foo.svg"></object>
```

With either of these approaches to embedding SVG, you can access the markup through the DOM by using the getSVGDocument() method, which returns an object that you can traverse using standard DOM methods. The following code shows how to get the SVG object from an embed element and then log the number of child nodes it contains, using the activeElement attribute:

```
var svg = document.querySelector('embed').getSVGDocument();
console.log(svg.activeElement.childNodes.length);
```

A much simpler and more powerful method of embedding SVG, however, is to put the markup directly into the page—something that is possible in most modern browsers. You can see a simple example of this in *svg-embedded.html*. Take a look at the code in the file and at what is shown here, and then compare it to the result displayed in the browser (also illustrated in Figure 7-4).

```
<svg version="1.1" xmlns="http://www.w3.org/2000/svg">
  <rect width="100%" height="100%" fill="#000" />
  <circle cx="150" cy="100" r="80" fill="#FFF" />
  <text x="150" y="125" font-size="60" text-anchor="middle">SVG</text>
</svg>
```

Figure 7-4: The SVG attributes state that the rectangle should be black and the circle white (left), but the example shows the opposite (right).

You should notice that the circle, despite having its fill attribute set to white in the code, actually displays black. This happens because the inline SVG becomes part of the DOM and I'm styling it with CSS. In the style tags in the file header, you find these rules:

```
rect, text { fill: #FFF; }
circle { fill: #000; }
```

As the SVG forms part of the DOM, you can manipulate it exactly the same way as any other element. Some of the elements and attributes, such as the fill attributes in this example, are presentational and, therefore, affected by CSS. And as SVG is part of the DOM, no special methods are required to interact with the element through script, meaning you can use standard DOM scripting like this:

```
var svg = document.querySelector('svg');
console.log(svg.childNodes.length);
```

This easy access makes direct embedding into the markup an especially useful way to display interactive data that responds to user input—adding, removing, or altering elements as required.

SVG Filters

SVG provides a range of graphical filters that you can apply to elements, letting you adjust color values, add dynamic blurring, and so on. The structure of this is first to create a defs element (immediately after the root), which is a container used for reusable elements, followed by a filter element that is a container for all of the individual filter elements. This probably sounds a little more complicated than it actually is. You can see it's quite straightforward in the following code sample, which applies a Gaussian Blur effect using the feGaussianBlur element:

```
<svg version="1.1" xmlns="http://www.w3.org/2000/svg">
  <defs>
    <filter id="filter1">
      <feGaussianBlur stdDeviation="3" in="SourceGraphic"/>
    </filter>
  </defs>
</svg>
```

You need to pay attention to two things in this code: first, the id attribute on the filter element, which I use to refer to the filter effect later in the markup, and second, the two attributes on the feGaussianBlur element. The two attributes are stdDeviation, which is specific to this element and is a number used to specify the amount of blur, and in, which is common to all filter effects and describes the input for the filter. The SourceGraphic keyword value is the default, so you could actually leave it out in simple cases like this.

The filter has been defined at this point and can be called by referring to its unique id. In the following code, I apply this filter to a bitmap image that is called using an image element and the xlink:href attribute. This is a namespaced attribute, so I need to call that namespace on the root element. Finally, I apply the filter using the filter attribute with the unique id as the argument in the url() function value. You can see this in the file *svg-filters.html*, and the result is shown in Figure 7-5.

```
<svg version="1.1" xmlns="http://www.w3.org/2000/svg"  xmlns:xlink="http://
www.w3.org/1999/xlink">
  <defs>
    <filter id="filter1">
```

```
    <feGaussianBlur stdDeviation="3" in="SourceGraphic"/>
  </filter>
</defs>
<image xlink:href="foo.jpg" filter="url(#filter1)"/>
</svg>
```

Figure 7-5: A photograph before (left) and after (right) an SVG filter is applied

You can combine multiple filter effects into a single filter by stacking them as children of the `filter` element. In the next code snippet, I apply the Gaussian Blur as before, albeit with a slightly lowered `stdDeviation` value, but I also add a second filter, `feMorphology`. This filter is used to erode or dilate the input image, and in this case I want to erode it, so I use the `erode` value on the `operator` attribute, with a `radius` attribute value of 2.

The code for my completed two-stage filter, which you can see for yourself in *svg-filters.html* (the result is shown in Figure 7-6), looks like this:

```
<filter id="filter1">
  <feGaussianBlur stdDeviation="2"/>
  <feMorphology operator="erode" radius="2" />
</filter>
```

Figure 7-6: The original image file (left) and after a two-stage SVG filter is applied (right)

You can apply filters to entire blocks of HTML using SVG's `foreignObject` element, which acts as a container for snippets of markup as long as the markup is correctly formatted XHTML. The next example shows how this works. There are a few things to note: First, `foreignObject` has a `requiredFeatures` attribute that checks to see whether the browser supports the feature of the required object type, in this case, extensions to SVG1.1; second, the same filter is used as in the previous examples; and third, the markup inside the element has the XHTML namespace.

```
<foreignObject filter="url(#filter1)" requiredFeatures="http://www.w3.org/TR/
SVG11/feature#Extensibility">
  <h1 xmlns="http://www.w3.org/1999/xhtml">SVG</h1>
</foreignObject>
```

Try it for yourself in the file *svg-foreignobject.html*. You can see the result in Figure 7-7.

Figure 7-7: SVG filter applied to HTML markup using `foreignObject`

The Convergence of SVG and CSS

Work on version 2 of SVG—which goes by the rather clever name of SVG2—is underway at the moment, and one of its goals is better integration with CSS, as many of their features are shared. The new Transforms module, for example, integrates the extremely similar CSS Transforms and SVG Transforms modules. Other new shared features include advanced image techniques such as Masking and Clipping (showing or hiding parts of an SVG image) and Compositing and Blending (combining shapes and colors).

Probably the first to arrive, however, will be Filter Effects. These are already implemented piecemeal in some browsers as I write this and come in two main components. The first is to use defined filters on any element in the page, even outside of the SVG code block; for example, using the filter defined in the previous section natively in CSS would be as easy as this:

```
.foo { filter: url(#filter1); }
```

The second component is to use function keywords—essentially, shortcuts to predefined SVG filters. For example, to add Gaussian blur to an element, you could use the `blur()` function and, for saturation, the `saturate()` function:

```
.foo { filter: blur(3) saturate(0.1); }
```

Like CSS3, SVG2 will be modular, allowing for staggered development and implementation, meaning you could start seeing elements of it sooner rather than later.

A Drawback of SVG

For all the advantages of including SVG in your documents, one of its key strengths—accessibility via the DOM—is also its key weakness: Being part of the page means slower loading times as the more complex page is rendered and more memory consumption as more objects are held in temporary storage.

You should consider this when deciding whether to include complex SVG objects in your page, especially as it might affect people who visit your site using a lower-powered mobile or portable device.

The canvas Element

The canvas element is so named because, like a blank canvas, it's there to be drawn on. The drawing is done with JavaScript using a dedicated API, creating a tailor-made bitmap graphic. And it really is like a painter's canvas in that once you've drawn on it, you can't then manipulate the things you've drawn. They are not objects like SVG elements, just pixels on the screen; you can only draw over them.

The basic setup is incredibly simple: Add a canvas element to your markup—perhaps with a unique id that will make it a little easier to reference—with size attributes and fallback content for browsers that don't support canvas (or JavaScript):

```
<canvas id="canvas" height="400" width="800">
  <p>Sorry, your browser doesn't support canvas (or JavaScript)</p>
</canvas>
```

NOTE *A quick note of disambiguation: When referring specifically to the element I'll use canvas; any other use of "canvas" throughout this book is a shorthand used to refer to the technique of drawing to a canvas element using the API.*

All subsequent actions are performed with JavaScript. The first step is to select the canvas and create a *context*, which is a fancy way of saying that you're going to draw on it. You do this using the getContext() method with a context as an argument, which for simple two-dimensional shapes is 2d. I'll also add some feature testing to make sure the browser supports the canvas API. My code ends up looking something like this:

```
var el = document.getElementById('canvas');
if (el && el.getContext) {
  var context = el.getContext('2d');
  if (context) { ... }
}
```

Then you begin drawing. As with SVG, drawings are carried out with a series of shapes and lines, using a coordinate system. For example, to draw a rectangle filled with a solid color you use the fillRect() method, which accepts four number arguments: The first two are *x*- and *y*-coordinates of the top-left corner; the next two are the width and height. The following code draws a 120×120 square, filled with a solid color, 20px from the top-left corner of the canvas element:

```
context.fillRect(20,20,120,120);
```

You can also change the appearance values of the objects you draw, using a series of properties in the API. These are applied the next time a method that draws to canvas is run. In the following code, I change the color of the fill and then set up a series of drop shadow properties that are rendered on the next rectangle drawn with fillRect() and all subsequent drawings until I change the properties again:

```
context.fillStyle = '#ff0000';
context.shadowOffsetX = 3;
context.shadowOffsetY = 3;
context.shadowBlur = 3;
context.shadowColor = 'rgba(0,0,0,0.5)';
context.fillRect(200,80,160,160);
```

Drawing circles is a little more complex, requiring the arc() method, which takes six arguments: the first two are the *x*- and *y*-coordinates of the center of the circle, the third is the radius, the fourth is the starting angle of the arc, the fifth is the finishing angle—I'm using π multiplied by 2 to draw a full circle—and the sixth and last argument is a Boolean to state whether the arc is drawn counterclockwise. When I've done all that, I use the stroke() method to draw the outline of my circle:

```
context.arc(360,240,160,0,Math.PI*2,false);
context.stroke();
```

You can see a few different shapes that I've drawn in the file *canvas.html* (and in Figure 7-8), but as with SVG, the canvas API includes so much that I can't possibly hope to cover it in a single chapter of this book, so if you're interested in learning more, I recommend taking a look at some of the great free resources available online, a few of which I list in "Further Reading" on page 139.

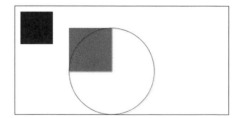

Figure 7-8: Simple shapes drawn on the canvas element

Image Manipulation

Canvas becomes extremely useful when manipulating images. You can load an image into a canvas and, once there, draw and manipulate it as you wish. Get the image data with the getImageData() method, which uses four arguments—the now familiar *x*, *y*, width, and height—to select the portion of the canvas you want to manipulate. Using this method inside a load event is a good idea; it ensures the script doesn't run before the image you're getting data from has finished loading.

In the next code snippet, I use querySelector() to find an image in the page and, when it has loaded, first draw it onto the canvas with drawImage() and then use getImageData() to select the whole canvas and assign it to the variable *newImg*:

```
var img = document.querySelector('img');
img.addEventListener('load', function () {
  context.drawImage(img,0,0);
  var newImg = context.getImageData(150,0,150,225);
}, false);
```

Once you have the image, you can begin to manipulate it using the data property. This is a huge array that contains information about every pixel in the image portion, where each item is a number from 0 to 255 representing the RGBA color model: The first item is the red value of the pixel, the second is the green, the third blue, and the fourth alpha. A fully opaque red pixel would be represented by the four array items [255,0,0,255]. These four values are repeated for every pixel in the image.

That means you can manipulate the color value of every single pixel, which is a pretty powerful ability to have. In the following code, I use a for loop to go through all the pixels and invert their values by subtracting their current value from 255. Once I've done this, putImageData() returns the modified image to the canvas at the same coordinates. You can see the result in Figure 7-9, and you can see for yourself how this looks in the file *canvas-image.html*.

```
var img = document.querySelector('img');
img.addEventListener('load', function () {
  context.drawImage(img,0,0);
  var i,
      newImg = context.getImageData(00,0,500,500),
      newLen = newImg.data.length;
  for (i=0;i<newLen;i+=4) {
    newImg.data[i] = 255 - newImg.data[i];
    newImg.data[i+1] = 255 - newImg.data[i+1];
    newImg.data[i+2] = 255 - newImg.data[i+2];
  }
  context.putImageData(newImg,0,0);
}, false);
```

Figure 7-9: The image on the right has been manipulated using canvas to invert the colors.

Rather excitingly, you can combine the canvas element with the live video stream obtained from the getUserMedia() method I described in Chapter 6, providing image manipulation on the fly. Although I don't have the space to go into that in any detail, I encourage you to look online for some great demos, such as Tim Taubert's "Building a Live Green Screen with getUserMedia() and MediaStreams." See "Further Reading" on page 139.

WebGL

You may have noticed that when I created the canvas context, I specified it was to be 2-D, which implies there is also a 3-D context—and there is, using a technology called WebGL to gain access to the device's graphics card and create hardware-accelerated 3-D objects in the browser. The actual context name is webgl. Test for support using something like this:

```
var el = document.getElementById('canvas');
if (el && el.getContext) {
  var context = el.getContext('webgl');
  if (context) { ... }
}
```

WebGL is not fully supported across every browser and may never be, and it uses a language that is extremely complicated for your average developer (me included), so obviously WebGL is far beyond the scope of this book. As before, if you're interested in learning more, I advise you to take a look at some of the fantastic free online resources that exist.

When to Choose SVG or Canvas

The two image methods in this chapter should really be viewed as complementary rather than competing, as they each fill a different role in web graphics. You could likely end up using both in your websites instead of being forced to make a choice between them.

Where SVG excels is in its scalability, which makes it suitable for any screen regardless of size or resolution. As it creates new elements in the DOM, SVG is very useful for interacting with and being manipulated by JavaScript. And it's also much easier to make accessible by adding alternative and fallback text to the created items. SVG is a good choice for logos, icons, and interactive charts and graphics.

Canvas is bitmap-based so is less suitable for scaling. It allows no external manipulation by JavaScript beyond its own API and has few to no accessibility features as it currently stands (although work is underway to improve that). Canvas is best suited for image manipulation, and as it doesn't access the DOM (which can slow a page considerably), it can be good for moving multiple items around the screen quite quickly, making it handy for gaming.

Both formats have their pros and cons, and for many purposes either would be suitable, so the best advice I can give you is that you should carefully consider the problem you want to solve and test each solution to see which is the more relevant one.

Summary

In this chapter, I covered the two different approaches to digital graphics—vectors and bitmaps—and the way they are implemented on the Web using SVG and canvas. I discussed the basic syntax of each and looked at the situations they are best suited for. You can explore much more about each different graphic format, but for reasons of space I've, by necessity, only touched briefly on each—hopefully, however, enough to make you want to find out more.

Further Reading

You can find a great introduction to SVG at the SVG Basics website: *http://www.svgbasics.com/*, and the W3C's own SVG Primer is a useful way to dig deeper: *http://www.w3.org/Graphics/SVG/IG/resources/svgprimer.html*. MDN has a quite complete list of elements and attributes: *https://developer.mozilla.org/en-US/docs/SVG/*.

The technique for stacking SVG icons was developed by Erik Dahlström and is described on the blog of Simurai: *http://simurai.com/post/20251013889/svg-stacks/*. Mozilla's Robert O'Callahan warns of the possible changes to the stacking technique: *http://robert.ocallahan.org/2012/10/impending-doom-for-svg-stacks-sort-of.html*. I detailed the svgView() method on my blog, *Broken Links*: *http://www.broken-links.com/2012/08/14/better-svg-sprites-with-fragment-identifiers/*.

The IE Testdrive site has a good hands-on tool for experimenting with SVG Filter Effects: *http://ie.microsoft.com/testdrive/graphics/hands-on-css3/hands-on_svg-filter-effects.htm*.

Dirk Schulze wrote a good, concise introduction to the features planned for SVG2: *http://dschulze.com/blog/articles/8/new-features-in-svg2/*.

You can find a good range of canvas tutorials, from beginner to expert level, at *http://www.html5canvastutorials.com/*, and an excellent cheat sheet with all of the core properties and methods on Jacob Seidelin's blog at *http://blog.nihilogic.dk/2009/02/html5-canvas-cheat-sheet.html* (last updated in 2009 but still relevant).

HTML5 Rocks has a tutorial on making more advanced image manipulation effects at *http://www.html5rocks.com/en/tutorials/canvas/imagefilters/*.

In his blog post "Building a Live Green Screen with getUserMedia() and MediaStreams," Tim Taubert explains the basics of live video image manipulalation: *http://timtaubert.de/blog/2012/10/building-a-live-green-screen-with-get usermedia-and-mediastreams/*.

The *Learning WebGL* blog has lessons for complete beginners on working in a three-dimensional context in canvas at *http://learningwebgl.com/lessons/*, and WebGL.com has frequent roundups of demos, tutorials, and developer meet-ups: *http://www.webgl.com/*.

8

NEW FORMS

The motivating factor behind the creation of Web Applications 1.0, the original proposal that evolved to become HTML5, was to extend the power of HTML forms to allow the creation of rich and flexible online applications. HTML5 doesn't disappoint, bringing a whole new range of elements, attributes, and controls to make forms richer, more interactive, and more informative in the modern web platform.

Many JavaScript frameworks, such as the popular jQuery UI, provide controls and widgets that extend the functionality of form elements; these range from simple enhancements such as automatically suggesting values as you type to more complex user interface elements such as those that allow you to pick a date. Given HTML5's stated aim of standardizing common design patterns, it comes as no surprise that these common form elements should become part of the specification.

Other than new widgets and form interactions, the most common use of JavaScript in forms is to check for errors while the user is filling out the form, and to ensure the data is correctly formatted and doesn't contain any nasty surprises before being sent to the server. HTML5 also provides a native implementation of this validation, with a series of new attributes and input types that require set patterns of data, including on-screen notes and alerts in many browsers, and an API that gives developers more flexibility when using script.

New Input Types

In HTML 4.01, a handful of form elements allowed user input, including textarea, checkbox, and radio, but the most common was without a doubt input, most often with a type attribute value of text. This hard-working field (from here on known as the *text input*) was used in every situation in which a specialized control was unavailable: as a search box, for telephone numbers and email addresses . . . you name it, the text input did it, with only some client- or server-side validation to give meaning to the different types of data being provided by the user.

When work on HTML5 was underway, with its stated emphasis on standardizing common patterns of existing usage, creating new input types to lift some of the burden from the encumbered text input was really a no-brainer. Now a handful of properties have the appearance of a text input but with different type values to give meaning to the data.

The first new value is search, which is (fairly obviously) used to mark up a search box. It looks like this:

```
<input type="search">
```

In some browsers, the appearance of the search box is differentiated from that of a regular text input, sometimes with rounded corners to match the OS it's running on or perhaps with a button to clear the contents of the field. A few different examples are shown in Figure 8-1. But although its appearance and behavior might differ from a text input, search has no limitation on the type of data that you can enter.

Figure 8-1: The search input rendered in different browsers: Chrome for Ubuntu (left) and Safari for iOS (right)

That's not the case with the next two values, email and url, which are provided for the user to enter—can you guess? that's right!—an email address and a URL. The fields look identical to a text input but have a key difference: They limit the data that users can enter into them. Here's how these values are used:

```
<input type="email">
<input type="url">
```

The email type accepts only a well-formatted email address—*peter@ broken-links.com*, for example—and the url type requires a correctly formatted URL, including the protocol, such as *http://broken-links.com*. If the user enters a value that doesn't match the required pattern into either field, the field will be declared invalid. I'll return to this subject a little later, in "Client-side Form Validation" on page 154.

Another commonly requested piece of information is a telephone number. The new dedicated input for this has a type of tel:

```
<input type="tel">
```

The actual format of telephone numbers can vary wildly, including numbers, letters, and symbols, so this field doesn't have any restrictions as to which characters can be entered.

As many browsers display these new input types mostly identically, what exactly is the point of using them instead of text? Well, I've already mentioned that they provide some native validation, which I'll cover in "Client-side Form Validation" on page 154, but aside from that, they also offer another big advantage: On many devices with on-screen (or *soft*) keyboards, they provide the user with a sympathetic keyboard layout.

Apple popularized sympathetic soft keyboard layouts when it invented iOS (called iPhone OS back in those heady pre-iPad days), and their implementation is probably still the standard-bearer. If you open the example file *input-types.html* on an iOS device and put the focus into each input in turn, you'll see the on-screen keyboard update to display a different layout for each (shown in Figure 8-2 in case you don't have an iOS device handy): The text input shows a standard keyboard layout; the email input adds an @ and a period, commonly used in email addresses; the url input displays a period, slash, and top-level-domain chooser; and the tel input displays a telephone number pad. All of these inputs help users enter the correct data in a faster and more convenient way.

Figure 8-2: The sympathetic soft keyboard on iPhone, optimized for (from left to right) text, email, url, and tel input types

The value of sympathetic layouts becomes really obvious when you use an on-screen keyboard that doesn't support them; switching among different views for letters, cases, numbers, and symbols becomes a real chore. So help your users out by implementing these new types wherever and whenever you can.

New Attributes

Before moving on to discuss more input types, I want to make a brief digression to talk about some of the many new attributes. These attributes bring some useful and crucial new properties and behavior to HTML forms and, once again, are based on popular script libraries and workarounds created by developers and made official as part of HTML5.

autofocus

The autofocus attribute, which is common to all input types, simply sets the focus on the specified element when the page is loaded. In a text input field, for example, the cursor would already be placed and ready for the user's input. autofocus is a Boolean attribute, so the value to activate it can be either autofocus or just left out entirely, as shown here:

```
<input type="text" autofocus>
```

If multiple instances of autofocus are used on a page, the first (in DOM order) will be respected.

WARNING *Keep in mind that some users, especially those requiring assistive technology, may be confused by being automatically focused on a form when the page loads. Check out Bruce Lawson's article "The Accessibility of HTML5 Autofocus" for a discussion of best practice (see "Further Reading" on page 160).*

placeholder

The placeholder attribute, which you can use on any text-like input element (the ones I've already introduced in this chapter, for example), takes a string of characters as its value; this string will be displayed inside the input when no value is present. Use the string for instructions on the type of value required; for example, in an email input you might include something like this:

```
<input type="email" placeholder="e.g. foo@bar.com">
```

WARNING *The placeholder text should not describe the value of the input—for example, "Work email"—as that's the role of the label element. Remember the placeholder text disappears when users click in the box, so they may not remember what field they're filling out if the label isn't present.*

Most browsers style the placeholder text lighter than the default color to show that it's holding text rather than a value, but depending on your website's color scheme that may not be ideal. Unfortunately, no standardized selector is available to change placeholder text properties, although some browsers have implemented their own proprietary pseudo-class (or pseudo-element):

```
input:-moz-placeholder {}
input:-ms-input-placeholder {}
input::-webkit-input-placeholder {}
```

autocomplete

The autocomplete attribute sets whether the browser should remember previous values entered into a field and offer them back to you in the future. The values are on and off; the default is on, but if you're creating a site with confidential form information, you may want to set this to off to increase the user's security by not offering suggestions to someone who may subsequently use the same device:

```
<input type="email" autocomplete="off">
```

spellcheck

Many browsers now offer native spellchecking facilities. These are usually applied, by default, to textarea elements only, but you can apply the spellchecker—if present—to any field by using the spellcheck attribute. This is a slightly strange attribute, as it's Boolean but doesn't behave like the other attributes of that type; it requires a value of true or false to enable or disable spellchecking:

```
<input type="text" spellcheck="true">
```

By default, the dictionary used will be in the language of the user's browser, but you can change this with the lang attribute. If the user has the stated language dictionary installed (Spanish, in the following example), that dictionary will be used for spellchecking:

```
<input type="text" spellcheck lang="es">
```

multiple

The multiple attribute is for situations when the user can enter or submit more than one entry in a field. You can pair it with the file input to select multiple files from a user's device or with the email input to enter more than one email address in the field. The attribute is a true Boolean, so only the attribute name is required:

```
<input type="file" multiple>
```

form

One of the limitations of forms in HTML 4.01 was that all form elements, including the submit button, had to be contained within the `form` element itself, meaning that, unless JavaScript were used, all the elements had to follow each other subsequently in the markup, limiting the ways they could be laid out on the page.

HTML5 has addressed this with the `form` attribute, which takes as a value the `id` of a `form` element, creating an association between the field and the form regardless of their position in the markup. The value of the element is then submitted along with the form. In this example, the input *#bar* will be submitted along with the form *#foo*:

```
<form id="foo">...</form>
<input type="text" id="bar" form="foo">
```

Datalists

Where elements accept text input—such as `text`, `url`, or `search`—you can provide a list of helpful suggestions to the user. The browser can offer these based on the user's previous input (controlled by the previously mentioned `autocomplete` attribute), but at times you may want to suggest a range of predefined terms. Implement this latter option with the `datalist` element.

The `datalist` element contains a list of suggestions, each of which is contained in an `option` child element (which you should be familiar with from the `select` element in HTML 4.01). To illustrate what I mean, here's a short datalist with only a few options:

```
<datalist id="apes">
  <option>Chimpanzee</option>
  <option>Gorilla, Eastern</option>
  <option>Gorilla, Western</option>
  <option>Orangutan</option>
</datalist>
```

The `datalist` element isn't rendered on the page and doesn't have to be close to the input that refers to it; it can be placed anywhere in the markup.

To create an association between the input field into which the user will enter data and the `datalist` element that holds the suggestions, the former uses the `id` value of the latter as the value for its own `list` attribute:

```
<input type="text" list="apes">
```

Now when the user types a letter (or sequence of letters), any `option` element values within the `datalist` that match that sequence will be displayed in a list of suggestions below the input. From here, the user can choose a matching option. You can see this for yourself in *input-types-more.html*, as illustrated in Figure 8-3.

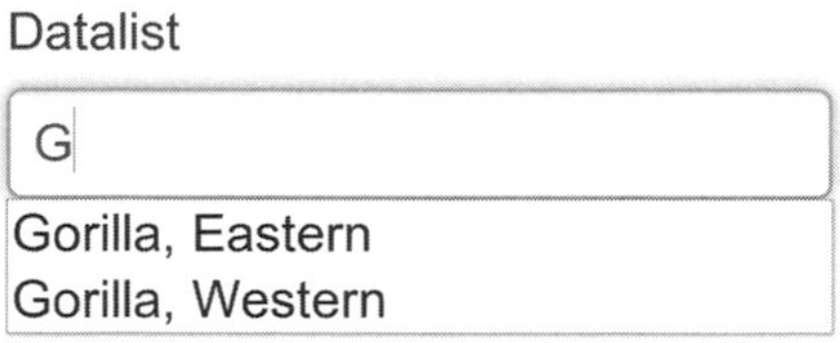

Datalist

Gorilla, Eastern
Gorilla, Western

Figure 8-3: Auto-suggested results from a
datalist element

This association between the id and list attributes means that multiple inputs can refer to the same datalist element, if required.

In browsers that don't support datalist, the input box falls back to a standard text input. Please keep this in mind if you require certain input values from the user, and ensure you have contingencies in JavaScript and on the server side.

On-Screen Controls and Widgets

The new elements you've seen so far are all based on a simple text box, but some form elements also provide richer on-screen controls; in HTML 4.01, for instance, think of select and checkbox. But as I mentioned in the introduction, many other widget types are commonly used by developers and designers—think of date pickers and number range sliders—so HTML5 has adopted and standardized these patterns.

How these controls and widgets appear depends on the browser and platform in which they've been implemented; the HTML5 specification notes only that these controls could be used and isn't prescriptive as to how they appear. If a browser doesn't support the controls natively, they should fall back to look like a standard text input.

Numbers

The new HTML5 input types discussed so far already cover various text formats. But, of course, many forms require that the user enter a number, for instance, credit card details, an area code, or a quantity.

The number input is the field for inputting numbers. It is often displayed as a text field, but some browsers also add controls—often a pair of arrows, one up, one down—for incrementing or decrementing the value.

Similar to number is the range input, which lets users enter a value without requiring them to be too precise about the exact figure; to allow this, many browsers style this element as a slider.

```
<input type="number">
<input type="range">
```

You can compare number and range as they're displayed in Chrome for Android in Figure 8-4.

Number   Range

Figure 8-4: The number and range types as displayed in Chrome for Android

Both of these types have some new attributes in common: `max` and `min` are number values that set the maximum and minimum (did you work that out for yourself?) permitted values, and `step` is the number by which the value is incremented or decremented. The following code shows how all three could work; the `number` input has an initial value of 50 and can be incremented or decremented by 10 at a time to reach a minimum of 10 or a maximum of 100:

```
<input type="number" max="100" min="10" step="10" value="50">
```

You can also manipulate these values with JavaScript using the `stepUp()` and `stepDown()` methods. Each takes a single integer value, which moves the value of the input by the specified number of steps; for example, this syntax reduces the range input value by 3 steps:

```
var foo = document.querySelector('input[type=range]');
foo.stepDown(3);
```

Each method returns an error if the specified number of steps causes the value to exceed the element's `max` or `min` values.

When working with numeric fields, you may want to take advantage of a new DOM property defined in HTML5, `valueAsNumber`. This property is similar to the existing `value` property but returns the value as a number rather than a string, meaning you don't need to convert between types using `parseInt()`. Using `valueAsNumber` is simplicity itself:

```
var foo = document.querySelector('input[type=number]');
bar = foo.valueAsNumber;
```

Dates

Another popular data pattern for forms is a date or time field, used in situations such as when asking the user to enter a date of birth or choose a delivery time and date. Often these are rendered using a JavaScript-created date picker, a common widget aimed at helping users choose a date from a range shown on screen so they don't have to worry about conforming to your chosen date pattern.

HTML5 has a range of new input types for date and form fields, and many browsers have added native date-picker widgets to enhance them. Probably the most commonly implemented is `date`, which lets the user select a single date from the widget:

```
<input type="date">
```

The implementation method varies across browsers, with mobile and tablet devices varying quite significantly from desktop and laptop browsers. You can see some examples of this variety in Figure 8-5.

Figure 8-5: The native date-picker widget on the Chrome for Android tablet (left), the iPhone (center), and the Chrome desktop (right)

HTML5 also has a series of other date and time inputs: If you need to be more general about dates, you can use month to select an entire month and week for an entire week; or if you require a time without any associated date, you can use time to choose hours and minutes. A couple examples of different time and date pickers are shown in Figure 8-6.

Figure 8-6: A time picker on Chrome for Android (left) and a month picker for iPhone (right)

If you require a date and a time, the datetime input requests both. This field requires a value in the format *YYYY-MM-DD*T*HH:MM*Z, where the Z is a shorthand code for the UTC time zone. For example, to submit a time of 2 PM on April 1st, 2014, you would use **2014-04-01T14:00Z**. If the time zone isn't required, you could use datetime-local. For both types, the picker widget would have fields for both date and time, as shown in Figure 8-7.

All the date-related input types are demoed in *input-types-dates.html*; open the page in different browsers and see how they're displayed.

As with the number input types, the max and min attributes are permitted, but they must use a valid date or time format; a full datetime would require *YYYY-MM-DD*T*HH:MM*Z, whereas the month would require only *YYYY-MM*. The step attribute is also allowed, but its time period depends on the element used: a day, a week, a month, or a time in seconds.

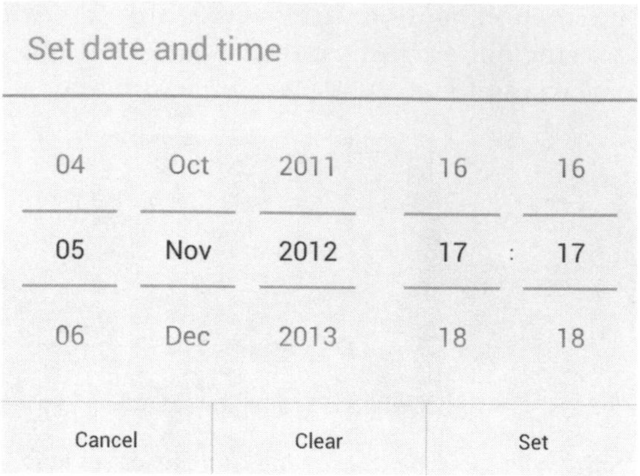

Figure 8-7: A datetime picker on Chrome for Android

So putting that all together, you could use attributes somewhat like the following, where the month input would allow the user to select only dates between January 2012 and June 2016; the step attribute would be in play only if the stepDown() and stepUp() methods were used:

```
<input type="month" max="2016-06" min="2012-01" step="3">
```

WARNING *If you have strict limits on required dates, don't rely on the max and min attributes, as they're not supported by some user agents; always use JavaScript and server-side validation to ensure dates are in range.*

As numbers have the valueAsNumber DOM property, so dates have valueAsDate. This property works in the same way, but returns a date-formatted value; for example, given the date *04/01/2014*, the value property would return *2014-04-01*, whereas the valueAsDate property would give *Tue Apr 01 2014 01:00:00 GMT+0100 (BST)* (in my time zone, at least).

```
var foo = document.querySelector('input[type=date]');
bar = foo.valueAsDate;
```

Color

If you're building an app that allows the user some level of customization, you may be interested to know that HTML5 has a color input, which will, if implemented, show either the system default color picker or a proprietary widget, depending on the browser:

```
<input type="color">
```

Try it for yourself in *input-types-more.html*. Figure 8-8 shows how Chrome implements it for Ubuntu.

Color

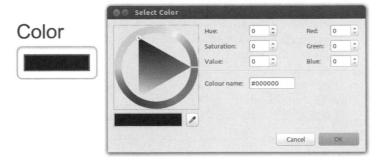

Figure 8-8: Chrome uses the native color picker of your OS for the color element; here's how it looks in Ubuntu.

Displaying Information to the User

As well as accepting input from users, sometimes displaying information back to users is helpful, perhaps to show their progress through filling out a long form or the results of a measurement. A new set of elements defined in HTML5 is aimed at exactly that purpose.

progress

Progress bars show movement toward a set goal and are commonly used in operating systems and on the Web, such as when loading data into a web application or installing software. The progress element gives you a standardized method for implementing progress bars in your own pages. In its simplest form, it shows progress between 0 and 1, using the value attribute to show the current position:

```
<progress value="0.5">0.5</progress>
```

Although this element is displayed as a bar in most browsers—as you can see in Figure 8-9—including the value inside the element is also good practice, as it serves as a fallback for browsers that don't have a graphical widget.

Progress   Progress

Figure 8-9: Different implementations of the progress element: Firefox for Android (left) and Opera for Ubuntu (right)

If the values you want to use can't be simply divided into a range of 0 to 1, you can set a different range with the max and min attributes:

```
<progress max="20" min="10" value="15">15</progress>
```

Updating the bar using script is easy, requiring only a change of the value attribute, perhaps in a function somewhat like this one, where any value supplied as an argument to the *updateProgress* function updates the progress bar accordingly:

```
var progressBar = document.querySelector('progress'),
    updateProgress = function (newValue) {
      progressBar.value = newValue;
};
```

You can get the current progress toward the target by using the position property, which returns the result of dividing the current value by that of the maximum value; in the case of the previous example, the max attribute is 20 and the value is 15, so the position is 0.75:

```
var currentProgress = progressBar.position;
```

meter

At first glance, the meter element seems superficially the same as progress, and indeed, some browsers style the two in the same way. They differ semantically, however; where progress shows movement toward a goal, meter shows a scalar measurement, such as a rating or a poll result. At its most simple, meter shows a value between 0 and 1.0, just like progress:

```
<meter value="0.5">0.5 of 1</meter>
```

The similarities to progress continue, as you should add a text child for browsers that don't represent this graphically, and max and min attributes are also available if you want to change the scale:

```
<meter max="20" min="10" value="15">15 of 20</meter>
```

Where meter differs significantly from progress is in displaying ranges of low, medium, and high values, using three new attributes: low sets the upper limit of the low range, high sets the lower limit of the high range, and optimum sets the ideal value. If these attributes are present, the meter's current value is either displayed as being within acceptable bounds or flagged as being outside them.

The following code example illustrates this. Here, any value less than or equal to 0.2 is considered low and will be displayed with a warning color (often yellow) in many browsers, whereas a value greater than or equal to 0.8 is considered high and will be likewise flagged (most commonly in red); any number between those two will be marked in the standard color (usually green) for the average range:

```
<meter low="0.2" high="0.8" value="0.65">0.65 of 1</meter>
```

Introducing the optimum attribute changes the behavior slightly, as it can introduce a third level of "acceptability" depending on where it's positioned. For example, given the meter element in the previous example, you could say there are three ranges: low for any value of 0.2 or less, high for any 0.8 or greater, and average for any greater than 0.2 but less than 0.8. If you were to set the optimum to be 0.9, any value in the high range would be optimal and colored green, any in the average range less optimal and colored yellow, and any in the low range less optimal still and colored red. Conversely, if the optimum value were 0.1, those ranges of optimality would be reversed.

If that all sounds a little complex, the following markup shows a few different examples, which you can see for yourself in the example file *input-types-meter.html* and illustrated in Figure 8-10; I advise you to view this example as it relies on color, which is hard to convey in a black-and-white book! I'll annotate this code and then explain it subsequently.

```
❶ <meter low="0.2" high="0.8" value="0.85">0.85 of 1</meter>
❷ <meter low="0.2" high="0.8" optimum="0.9" value="0.85">0.85 of 1</meter>
❸ <meter low="0.2" high="0.8" optimum="0.1" value="0.85">0.85 of 1</meter>
```

In all three examples, the low range is 0 to 0.2, the medium range is 0.21 to 0.79, the high range is 0.8 to 1, and the value of the meter is 0.85. The numerals correspond to the examples in Figure 8-10 in vertical order. In ❶ no optimum value is given, so the optimum range is medium (neither high nor low). The value of the meter is in the high range, one range away from optimum, so it's colored yellow. In ❷ the optimum value is 0.9, so the high range becomes optimum; as the value is 0.85, this value is within optimum range and colored green. In ❸ the optimum value is 0.1, so the low range becomes optimum; the value is 0.85, which is two ranges away from optimum, so colored red.

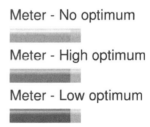

Figure 8-10: Different values for the meter element

As I said, this concept is a little hard to convey in black and white, so try the example for yourself. Once you see it, the concept is quite simple and easily grasped.

output

The output element displays the result of a calculation or user input and is especially handy for showing the result of interactions in other fields. A purely semantic element, output has no widget or on-screen presence if no value is supplied. At its most basic, it requires no attributes:

```
<output></output>
```

The output element becomes more useful when interacted with using JavaScript. Its key properties are value, which gets or sets the value, and defaultValue, which gets or sets a default value (if none is supplied). To show how this works, I've written a short script that updates the output element when a range input is changed. Here's the markup:

```
<label for="output">Output</label>
<input type="range" id="range">
<output id="output" for="range"></output>
```

The following script first selects the elements I'll interact with, sets a default value of 50 for the output element, and then adds an event listener to the range input, which fires whenever the value is changed. This listener runs an anonymous function to get the value of the input and set the value of the output. Here's the final script, which you can try for yourself in *input-types-output.html*:

```
var range = document.getElementById('range'),
    output = document.getElementById('output');
output.defaultValue = 50;
range.addEventListener('change', function (e) {
  var newValue = e.currentTarget.value;
  output.value = newValue;
}, false);
```

Client-side Form Validation

The new input types are really useful, but perhaps HTML5's greatest gift to developers is native client-side error checking. Checking the contents of a form before it's submitted is extremely important for security and usability, and until now, we haven't had a simple way to do so, although many hundreds of JavaScript libraries have been written to work around this.

Now, with native form validation, many browsers will automatically warn you that the value you've entered into a field doesn't match the input type. In Firefox, for example, if you type only numbers into an email input or omit the *http://* protocol from the start of a URL in a url input, a glowing red rule around the input field warns you that the values are incorrect, as you can see in Figure 8-11.

If you try to submit the form now, you'll receive an on-screen error message, such as the one in Figure 8-12—if, that is, your browser has implemented client-side validation. Each browser that has implemented it has its own style.

If you delete the content of the field and then click **Submit** again, no error is displayed. This field is optional by default, so not supplying a value is valid, but an incorrectly formatted value is invalid. To make the field not optional, you can add the Boolean required attribute:

```
<input type="email" required>
```

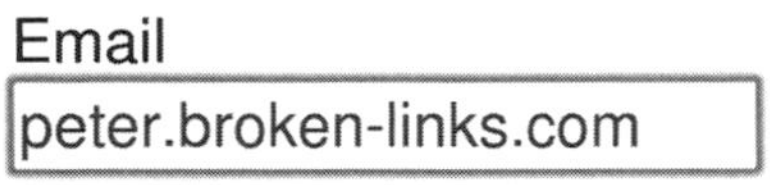

Email

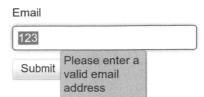

peter.broken-links.com

Figure 8-11: This email address isn't formatted correctly, so in Firefox the field is surrounded by a glowing red rule.

Figure 8-12: A warning message is displayed when the field doesn't validate, as shown here in Chrome.

This attribute forces the browser to check the value of the field; an empty or improperly formatted value is invalid and returns an error, and only a properly formatted value allows you to submit the form.

The field's type determines the pattern of the value format—email requires an email address, url requires a URL with protocol, date requires a year, month, and day, and so on—but you can override this requirement with the pattern attribute. The value for pattern is a *regular expression*, or *regex*, a standardized way of matching strings of data across many programming languages. As a simple example, you might want to allow only numbers in a tel input:

```
<input type="tel" pattern="\d*">
```

If you try to submit this input with letters or non-numeric characters, you'll receive a different error message, asking you to use the correct pattern. You can customize this error message in some browsers by adding extra text in the title attribute; in this example, the words "Numbers only" are added to the on-screen message, as you can see in Figure 8-13.

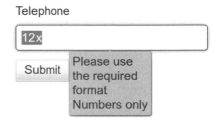

Figure 8-13: Extra information added to the warning using the title attribute

```
<input type="tel" pattern="\d*" title="Numbers only">
```

It's far, far beyond the scope of this book to explain regular expressions in any more detail (to be honest, I barely understand them myself). You can find some useful regex generators online that will help if you need it. (There's one listed in "Further Reading" on page 160.)

If you want to disable validation on an entire form, you can do so with the novalidate attribute. This attribute prevents any of the validation processes from running, regardless of the required state or pattern matching:

```
<form action="foo" novalidate>...</form>
```

And you can do this at a more local level with the `formnovalidate` attribute on an `input` or `button` element.

```
<button type="submit" formnovalidate>Go</button>
```

This option is useful when you want to have an option to submit without validation. For example, in a content management system, allowing the user to save a page for editing at a later date, without publishing it, is quite common; the data might be in an incomplete state and invalid, so running validation would only annoy the user.

The Constraint Validation API

Native form validation is great, but at times you may want to do more with it by perhaps adding some custom validation or creating your own error-reporting framework. The Constraint Validation API has a series of objects, properties, and methods aimed at giving you the flexibility to extend the browser's validation system or to roll your own.

The first property is `willValidate`, which returns `true` or `false` if the element it's called on will be validated—not if its value is valid, but if the validation process will be applied. You might find it more useful to think of the property as *willBeValidated*. By default, all form elements return `true`, unless they are explicitly set not to—for example, by using the `disabled` attribute.

You could use `willValidate` to run actions only on form elements that will be validated, as in this code:

```
var inputFields = document.querySelectorAll('input'),
    inputLen = inputFields.length,
    i;
for (i = 0; i < inputLen; i++) {
  if (inputFields[i].willValidate) {
    // Do something
  }
}
```

The simplest way to validate an element in a form is to use the `checkValidity()` method, which returns `true` or `false` depending on whether the element it's called on will validate with its current value. This method is at the core of the following script, in which the function *checkStatus* is used to run the `checkValidity()` method and update the contents of a sibling p element with a check or cross, depending on its validation status.

The function is attached to the `email` input using a listener for the `input` event, which is new to HTML5. This event fires whenever the value of an input or textarea element is updated—sort of similar to the keypress event—but it allows for the user entering blocks of text before firing on a pause or on the use of auto-suggested values:

```
var email = document.getElementById('email');
function checkStatus(e) {
```

```
  var valid = e.currentTarget.checkValidity(),
  validMsg = e.currentTarget.nextSibling,
  status = (valid) ? '✓' : '✗';
  validMsg.textContent = status;
}
email.addEventListener('input', checkStatus, false);
```

You can try this in the example file *checkvalidity.html*, which also runs the script on a tel input that accepts only numbers.

As well as the input event, HTML5 brings us the invalid event. This event is fired on an element with an invalid value when either the form is submitted or the checkValidity() method is run and returns a standard HTMLEvent object. That being the case, I could update the previous code to attach an extra event listener to each field, logging the invalid event whenever it occurs:

```
inputField[i].addEventListener('invalid', logInvalid, false);
```

If you want to get information about why a value doesn't validate, you can use the validity property. This property returns a validityState object with a range of properties related to validity; for example, if the field is required but contains no value, the valueMissing property returns true; or, if there are no validation errors, the valid property returns true.

The following script builds on the previous one by displaying a status message if the checkValidity() method returns false. It uses the validity property to check if a few common statuses are true and outputs a custom message if so, or a message of "Unknown error" in other cases:

```
var email = document.getElementById('email');
function statusMsg(e) {
  var valid = e.currentTarget.checkValidity(),
      validStatus = e.currentTarget.validity,
      validMsg = e.currentTarget.nextSibling,
      status;
  if (valid) {
    status = '✓';
  } else {
    if (validStatus.patternMismatch) {
      status = 'Pattern mismatch';
    } else if (validStatus.typeMismatch) {
      status = 'Type mismatch';
    }
    ...
  }
  validMsg.textContent = status;
}
email.addEventListener('input', statusMsg, false);
```

You can run this script for yourself in the file *validitystate.html*; check the console to see the validityState object, and explore the different true and false values. Figure 8-14 shows an example as logged in Firebug.

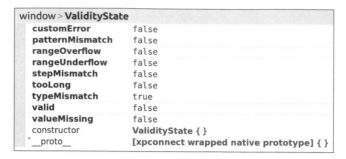

window > **ValidityState**	
customError	false
patternMismatch	false
rangeOverflow	false
rangeUnderflow	false
stepMismatch	false
tooLong	false
typeMismatch	true
valid	false
valueMissing	false
constructor	**ValidityState { }**
__proto__	**[xpconnect wrapped native prototype] { }**

Figure 8-14: The validityState object logged in Firebug, showing the current state of validity for the form field

Browsers that have native validation alerts create their own messages that appear on screen; for example, submitting an empty input that has the required attribute applied displays the message "Please fill in this field" in Firefox. The validationMessage property holds this message when the field is in an invalid state; if the value of the field is valid, the validationMessage property is an empty string.

You can set the message using the setCustomValidity() method, which also allows you to set a custom validation rule. For example, in the following code, I have two tel input types, referred to as *telHome* and *telWork*, and I want to ensure that the two values are different. To do this, I add an input listener on *telWork*, and each time the user types in this field, the rule checks if the value is the same as *telHome*, and if it is, a custom validation message is created:

```
var telHome = document.getElementById('tel-home'),
    telWork = document.getElementById('tel-work');
telWork.addEventListener('input', function (e) {
  if (e.currentTarget.value === telHome.value) {
    telWork.setCustomValidity('Must be different');
  } else {
    telWork.setCustomValidity('');
  }
}, false);
```

Take a look at *customvalidity.html* to see this in action; you can see the result in Figure 8-15.

Home Telephone

123

Work Telephone

123

Must be different

Figure 8-15: A custom error message created with setCustomValidity()

Forms and CSS

A new range of CSS pseudo-classes, known as the *UI element states pseudo-classes*, augments the extra functionality provided to forms by HTML5. These pseudo-classes let you style form elements based on their current interaction or validation state. The names of the pseudo-classes are really quite descriptive, and I imagine their meanings are clear to you, but just in case you've had a hard day and aren't thinking straight, I'll briefly explain them.

Form fields that are required (that is, have the required attribute set to *true*) can be styled with the :required pseudo-class, the opposite of which is :optional. You could, for example, give a dark border to required fields and a lighter border to optional ones:

```
input:required { border-color: black; }
input:optional { border-color: gray; }
```

The :valid and :invalid selectors are applied to elements based on their current validation state; :valid is used to apply styles to a valid form field, and :invalid to an invalid form field. That being the case, you may want to style the text of each input element in a different color based on its state: green for valid and red for invalid:

```
input:valid { color: green; }
input:invalid { color: red; }
```

NOTE *The latest CSS Selectors specification proposes a :user-error pseudo-class, similar to :invalid but applying only when a user has entered data that doesn't match the required pattern in a field. At the time of writing, this pseudo-class has not been implemented in any browsers.*

You can style form elements that have the disabled attribute applied by using the :disabled pseudo-class and, conversely, :enabled for those that have the enabled attribute. Likewise, a form element that has the readonly attribute set to *true* can be styled using :read-only, the opposite of which is :read-write.

radio and checkbox input types have some dedicated pseudo-classes: :indeterminate, which is when the user has neither checked nor unchecked the input, and :checked for when the user has checked the input. Curiously, no matching unchecked state exists; for this, you must use the negation selector:

```
input[type='checkbox']:not(:checked) { ... }
```

For number and range inputs, you can use the :in-range and :out-of-range pseudo-classes, which apply if a value is in or out of the acceptable range—either 0 to 1 or a custom range set with max and min. If using on-screen controls, the user can't exceed these limits, so the :out-of-range selector is unlikely to be used frequently.

Summary

From humble beginnings, forms in HTML5 are now tremendously flexible and powerful, providing natively much of the functionality that we as developers have been adding in with JavaScript over the years. The new input types alone are a welcome addition, especially for those of us who use dynamic soft keyboards, and the new attributes offer fine control over form elements.

But the native validation puts the icing on the cake, replacing the many different JS libraries that have been written to solve the client-side validation problem. And while that's welcome, the Constraint Validation API really gives full power to developers, enabling custom validation across different browsers and platforms in a fully standardized way.

With the extra styling capability provided by new CSS pseudo-classes, HTML5 forms are a prime example of the power of the new web platform.

Further Reading

The ever-helpful MDN provides a concise and complete guide to the new input types at *https://developer.mozilla.org/en-US/docs/HTML/Element/ Input/*. PPK has detailed tables showing support on the desktop at *http:// www.quirksmode.org/html5/inputs.html* and for mobile devices at *http://www .quirksmode.org/html5/inputs_mobile.html*.

Ryan Seddon wrote a polyfill for providing HTML5 form capabilities to browsers that don't support them natively: Find it at *https://github.com/ ryanseddon/H5F/*.

Bruce Lawson's discussion of autofocus accessibility, "The Accessibility of HTML 5 Autofocus," is on his blog at *http://www.brucelawson.co.uk/2009/ the-accessibility-of-html-5-autofocus/*.

HTML5 Rocks has a good overview of the Constraint Validation API at *http://www.html5rocks.com/en/tutorials/forms/constraintvalidation/*.

A useful application for testing regular expressions is Rubular. Don't worry that it's aimed at Ruby; it works just as well for JavaScript and HTML5 forms: *http://rubular.com/*.

And your humble author wrote an introduction to CSS3 pseudo-classes for HTML5 forms at HTML5 Doctor: *http://html5doctor.com/ css3-pseudo-classes-and-html5-forms/*.

9

MULTIMEDIA

Although audio and video have been a popular part of the Web for many years on sites such as YouTube, Dailymotion, and SoundCloud, they've always been second-class citizens, relying on third-party plug-ins (especially Flash) to operate. A reliance on plug-ins isn't a good long-term plan for website owners or browser makers, not least because the user is responsible for keeping them up-to-date. Surely, updating audio and media capabilities along with the browser is best, especially since most browsers have a frequent update cycle nowadays.

Plug-ins can also cause stability issues, as Steve Jobs famously noted when detailing the reasons for not supporting Flash on iOS:

> We also know firsthand that Flash is the number one reason Macs crash. We have been working with Adobe to fix these problems, but they have persisted for several years now. We don't want to reduce the reliability and security of our iPhones, iPods, and iPads by adding Flash.

For these reasons, having audio and video natively in the browser is extremely important, and one of the big pushes in HTML5 has been toward making this happen in the form of a pair of media elements that are widely implemented in browsers today. These elements control playback of audio and video from multiple sources, and in addition to robust HTML implementation, they also have an extensive API and set of events, giving developers granular control over what they can do. Being part of the web platform, they interact well with other content—far beyond what was possible with sandboxed plug-ins—making the new media elements true first-class web citizens.

After exploring the media elements, I'll take a brief look at the future of multimedia on the Web, from audio mixing and effects APIs to the future (or at least a possible future) of real-time voice, video, and data communication—the WebRTC project.

The Media Elements

To play either audio or video files, you need to use the audio or video element, respectively. They are similar, sharing the same attributes and child elements, with the type of media they deliver being the key difference. At their most simple, each element requires only a single attribute, src, which is the path to the media file to be played:

```
<audio src="foo.oga"></audio>
<video src="foo.ogv"></video>
```

What you see depends on the element: with video, you see the video file at its natural dimensions with the first frame showing; with audio, you see nothing. In either case, you can't play the file because there are no on-screen controls. You add them using the controls attribute:

```
<audio src="foo.oga" controls></audio>
<video src="foo.ogv" controls></video>
```

Now you'll see on-screen controls for each of the media elements, as illustrated in Figure 9-1, and you can take a look for yourself in the file *media-elements.html*. I suggest you view this example file in Chrome, Firefox, or Opera, for reasons that will become clear in this chapter.

Using these attributes, a media file plays only at the user's request and only once; if you prefer, you could have the file play as soon as it has loaded by

Figure 9-1: Native controls for the video (top) and audio (bottom) elements on Chrome for Ubuntu

using the `autoplay` attribute and make it loop indefinitely (until the user pauses it or leaves the page) by using the `loop` attribute; both are Boolean, so they require no value:

```
<audio src="foo.oga" autoplay loop></audio>
```

Autoplayed sound has accessibility drawbacks; see the WCAG Audio Control advice, listed in "Further Reading" on page 175, for more information on how best to cater to everyone.

On some mobile devices, media files won't play where they're embedded in the page; instead, they're launched and played in the device's own media player framework. If this happens, the `autoplay` attribute is ignored.

If you do autoplay or loop a file, keep in mind that the sound can be annoying or confusing to some users and consider muting the volume by default using the Boolean `muted` attribute:

```
<video src="foo.ogv" autoplay muted></video>
```

The full media file isn't normally downloaded when the page loads, but only when playback is requested; instead, metadata about the file—length, file size, and so on—is loaded into memory (a key exception to this is when the `autoplay` attribute is applied, which requires the full file to be downloaded). If you prefer to change this behavior, you can use the `preload` attribute, which has three values: `metadata` is the default and behaves as mentioned; auto indicates to the browser that it should download and cache the file because the user will probably play it; and `none` means the file probably won't be used, so don't download anything.

```
<video src="foo.ogv" preload="auto"></video>
```

Note that these are only hints, not commands; the browser makes the final decision about when to download media files based on variables such as the current network and the device that is running the browser. Mobile browsers will likely ignore the `auto` value, as downloading a potentially huge video when the user has metered bandwidth is a real no-no. In many cases, `metadata` is the sole acceptable value.

Extra Attributes for the video Element

Although the `audio` and `video` elements share many attributes, the latter, by virtue of it having more of a presence in page layout, also has several extra attributes. Video files will, by default, be displayed on the page at the dimensions in which they were coded. You can change this using the `height` and `width` attributes:

```
<video src="foo.ogv" height="360" width="240"></video>
```

Note that these attributes set the size of the video element, not the video itself, so if the values you supply aren't in the same ratio as the file, the video won't be stretched to fill the space; it maintains its aspect ratio and position in the center of the element, as you can see in *video-dimensions.html* (and in Figure 9-2). If you prefer to change this behavior, use the object-fit and object-position properties from Chapter 3.

Figure 9-2: The video file won't lose its aspect ratio when the video element is resized.

The video element is blank or uses a platform-specific graphic by default, until the first frame of the video has loaded, at which point that first frame is displayed as a still image. If you prefer a different still or image entirely, you can specify your own with the poster attribute:

```
<video src="foo.ogv" poster="foo.png"></video>
```

Multiple Source Files

In the examples I've shown so far, I'm using the *.ogv* extension for video files and *.oga* for audio files, which are extensions of the *Ogg* format. Ogg is a container format, which means it can hold different video and audio formats within it; for Ogg video, the most common format is *Theora*, and for audio, *Vorbis*.

Both Theora and Vorbis are free formats—that is, no licensing fees are involved in using them. This fact would seem to make them ideal for Web use, and indeed, some sites like Wikimedia do encode their media with them. They're not supported in many browsers, however, for reasons I explain in "Format Wars" on page 166. So what can you do?

Both audio and video elements have provisions for specifying multiple source files. You leave out the src attribute and use source child elements instead. In the following example, I set two different source files for a video element: The first is an *.ogv* file; the second, a *.webm* file; and the third, an *.mp4* file. The browser plays the first video format that it supports.

```
<video>
  <source src="foo.ogv" type="video/ogg"></source>
  <source src="foo.webm" type="video/webm"></source>
  <source src="foo.mp4" type="video/mp4"></source>
</video>
```

The example file *media-elements-sources.html* demonstrates this feature; the file appears to be the same as *media-elements.html*, but unlike that first example, it shouldn't matter which browser you use to open this file. As long as the browser supports HTML5 video, one of the provided source files should play.

Notice that I've included the type attribute, which contains the MIME type of the different formats and lets the browser know which type of file it should play without having to access the file itself. This attribute isn't required, but including it is considered good practice (although some older browsers used to have trouble with the type attribute). As always, test to see if it causes any problems.

The source element has a media attribute, which takes a media query as a value (see Chapter 3), meaning the specified file is used only if the query returns true—handy for supplying different files to different devices. Most likely you won't supply a 1920×1080 video file to a 480×320 screen, or vice versa. The following code example sets a different source file, *foo hd.ogv*, if the screen is at least 1920px wide and has an aspect ratio of 16/9:

```
<video>
  <source src="foo-hd.ogv" media="(device-aspect-ratio: 16/9) and (min-device-
width: 1920px)"></source>
  <source src="foo.ogv"></source>
</video>
```

The real utility of this attribute has been debated; some feel a better solution is to use JavaScript to adapt the quality of the video, depending on device resolution and network status, and a spec is being proposed to handle this. For the near future, however, the media attribute is the best approach to adaptive video.

Fallbacks

You should provide some kind of fallback if a user's browser doesn't support the media elements, so the user doesn't just see empty space on the page. Anything inside the video element is displayed when the video is not present, so the fallback can be as simple as a line of text that explains the problem or perhaps an image showing a key frame as an alternative.

```
<video src="foo.ogv">
  <img src="foo.png">
</video>
```

If you simply must have media available to everyone, you can include a Flash object as fallback; if the user's browser doesn't have native audio or video, the plug-in is used instead. And you can put a fallback to the fallback inside the object element to cover all bases.

```
<video src="foo.ogv" height="240" width="360" poster="foo.png">
  <object width="640" height="360" type="application/x-shockwave-flash" data="foo.swf">
    <param name="movie" value="foo.swf">
    <param name="flashvars" value="controlbar=over&amp;image=foo.png&amp;file=foo.mp4">
    <img src="foo.png" width="360" height="240">
  </object>
</video>
```

This code is quite lengthy, but it does seem to cover all eventualities. Kroc Camen developed it, and I recommend you read his article "Video for Everybody!" to see all of the notes and caveats that I was unable to include here (see "Further Reading" on page 175).

Subtitles and Captions

You can add optional text tracks to run alongside the media file; these could be subtitles or captions for video files, or associated metadata files for either media type. You can have as many tracks as you like—for example, different languages for subtitles or a caption track and a metadata track—and each is added with a track child element.

This element has a few key attributes: kind tells the browser the purpose of your track—*subtitles*, *captions*, and *descriptions* are among the possible values; src describes the path to the file; srclang is the language of the track; label is the description of the track shown to the user if multiple options are available (if the browser UI supports it); and the Boolean default sets the track to use if more than one is available or ensures that a track is shown even if the user hasn't explicitly requested one (only the first instance is recognized).

The following code shows how you might offer subtitles in two different languages—English and Brazilian Portuguese—on the video element:

```
<video src="foo.ogv">
  <track kind="subtitles" src="foo.en.vtt" srclang="en" label="English" default>
  <track kind="subtitles" src="foo.pt.vtt" srclang="pt-br" label="Brazilian Portuguese">
</video>
```

You can see an example of subtitles in the file *video-subtitles.html* and in Figure 9-3. If your browser's native video UI supports it, try changing the language of the subtitles.

Figure 9-3: Subtitles added using the track element

Different browsers accept different types of files for subtitles and captions, but the emerging standard is known as *WebVTT*. This format is simple, displaying captions from a start time to an end time. Here's an example:

```
WEBVTT

1
00:00:00.500 --> 00:00:04.000
Hello to all readers

2
00:00:06.000 --> 00:00:10.000
Thanks for reading this book
```

The first caption appears on screen after half a second and is shown until the fourth second; the second caption appears in the sixth second and is shown until the tenth second. Although extra configuration options are available, the core has been kept very simple.

Encoding

You have many different variables to consider when encoding video for the Web; for example, my experience is that some files encoded for iOS may not play on Android, and vice versa. If you're happy using the command line, then FFmpeg is your best bet; it's a free and open source encoder that's extremely configurable. You need to give it the path to the source video, a series of (optional) encoding parameters, and then a path to the output file. Here's a simple example, converting from AVI to MP4:

```
ffmpeg -i foo.avi foo.mp4
```

If you prefer a GUI, there are many video-encoding tools available, but I rely on two that are easy to use and free. Miro Video Converter is a Mac or Windows program handy for quick conversions; you simply drag a file into the app, choose an output mode from a list that includes MP4, Ogg Theora, and WebM, and the tool outputs the converted file for you. If you prefer to have more options to control your conversions, HandBrake is probably the easiest and most powerful tool, although it outputs only MP4 so you may need to convert to Miro anyway. Both these tools are graphical shells for FFmpeg.

Media Fragments

On occasion you may want to play only a portion of a media file, but you don't want to edit the clip manually. You can do this with JavaScript, as you'll see in the next section, but many browsers also support the Media Fragments URI. This information is appended to the URL of the media file, which sets certain parameters on it. To set a time range, as in this notional example, you would use something like this:

```
<audio src="foo.oga#t=4,8"></audio>
```

The *#t* notation is a shortcut for a time range, with the two comma-separated values after it representing the start time and end time in seconds. In this case, the clip would play for between four and eight seconds. You can leave out either number; leaving out the first means "play from the start until this point," and leaving out the second means "play from this point until the end." Either way you must still include the comma. So to play from 7.5 seconds until the end, you would use this:

```
<video src="foo.oga#t=7.5,"></video>
```

The Media Fragments URI module contains many more options than time range, but this is the only option that currently has widespread adoption in browsers.

The Media API

One of the complaints about using plug-ins to display audio and video is that they are dumb elements on the page; you can't interact unless the plug-in specifically makes itself available. The HTML5 media elements, however, have the big advantage of an extensive API that allows you access to information about the media file and makes interacting simple. You access the API through a set of interfaces: Each media element has shared properties and methods in the HTMLMediaElement interface; audio also has the unique HTMLAudioElement interface; and video has HTMLVideoElement.

The first two methods I'll introduce have obvious functions: They are play() and pause(), and are simply applied to the media element. Given unique controls on a page, you might end up with a script like this to control them:

```
var pause = document.getElementById('pause'),
    play = document.getElementById('play'),
    video = document.getElementById('video');
pause.addEventListener('click', function () {
  video.pause();
}, false;
play.addEventListener('click', function () {
  video.play();
}, false;
```

Separate buttons seem somewhat wasteful, so combining them into a Play/Pause button is more efficient. You can do this by adding an if...else statement to the code, checking to see whether the video is in a paused state using the paused property, which is Boolean. You can see this demoed in the file *media-play-pause.html* and shown in Figure 9-4.

```
var playPause = document.getElementById('play-pause'),
    video = document.getElementById('video');
playPause.addEventListener('click', function () {
  if (video.paused) {
    video.play();
  } else {
    video.pause();
  }
}, false);
```

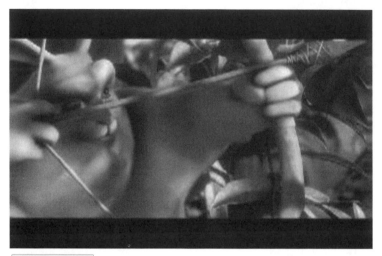

Play/Pause

Figure 9-4: A simple Play/Pause toggle created using the Media Elements API

The attributes of media elements are mirrored in the API so you can update them dynamically: preload can get or set the preload attribute and accepts the same values; autoplay, controls, loop, and muted set the relevant Boolean attributes; and src updates the path to a different media file. Note that if you do change the path to a new file, you have to use the load() method to load the new file into the cache:

```
video.src = 'bar.oga';
video.load();
```

Further information about the media file can be obtained through other properties. The currentSrc property returns the URL string of the file that's currently being played; when you have multiple source elements, this lets you know which element the browser is currently using (depending on formats and media queries). The currentTime property returns a value, in seconds, of the current playback point; you can also use this property to set the time, handy if you want to build your own controls with a seek bar:

```
video.currentTime = 4.5;
```

If the user has interacted with the seek bar and the media is in the process of moving to a new position to resume playback, the seeking property returns true. You can get the duration of the media with the duration property and the time that playback begins with initialTime; both also return a value in seconds.

As an example of what you can use these timing properties for, take a look at the following code. In it, I've defined the video element and a progress element for measuring the progress through the video file. What I want to do is change the value of the progress bar to measure the progress through the video; this rate is determined by dividing the currentTime value by the duration.

To make this work, I rely on the new timeupdate event. I explain this more fully in "Media Events" on page 173; for now, you just need to know that the event is fired when the current time of the media file changes, such as when the file is being played. When it does fire, the progress bar is updated to show the current progression. You can try this for yourself in the file *media-progress.html*, shown in Figure 9-5.

```
var progress = document.querySelector('progress'),
    video = document.querySelector ('video');
video.addEventListener('timeupdate', function () {
  progress.value = video.currentTime / video.duration;;
}, false);
```

Figure 9-5: A progress bar using Media Elements API timing properties

You can get or set the volume with the volume property, the value of which is a number between 0 and 1. This property is useful if combined with a range element to create a custom control, as in the following code example. When the range element changes value, the change event fires and updates the volume property with the current value divided by 100 (to match the scale of the volume). You can try this for yourself in the file *media-volume.html* and see it in Figure 9-6:

```
var video = document.querySelector('video'),
    volume = document.getElementById('range');
volume.addEventListener('change', function (e) {
  video.volume = e.currentTarget.value / 100;
}, false);
```

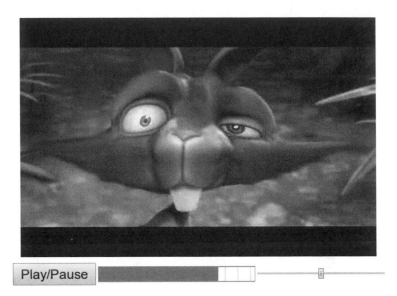

Play/Pause

Figure 9-6: The range element controls the video's volume. With this, the video now has basic controls made using HTML elements and the Media Elements API.

The previous three code examples show how easily you can build custom media controls using HTML5 forms and UI elements; with a little extra work, you can replicate all of the basic media UI functionality and go even further to create completely tailor-made interfaces on your websites.

Network and Ready States

Media files tend to be quite large and don't load all at once. Knowing a couple of things about them is useful: their current loading state and readiness to be played.

You can learn the first part using the networkState property, which has four value states: 0 means there is no data yet, 1 means the network is idle, 2 means the media is loading, and 3 means the media has loaded. You might use this property to add an on-screen indicator while the media is loading:

```
if (video.networkState === 2) { ... }
```

Perhaps more useful though is the readyState property. This property is similar to the previous one in that it has value states, but these report on the readiness of the media to be played—whether it has loaded the meta-data, loaded the file fully, and so on. The five states are:

- 0 when no information about the media is available
- 1 when the metadata of the media has loaded
- 2 when data is available about the current frame or playback position
- 3 when information about the current frame and at least the next one is available
- 4 when sufficient data and an acceptable download rate are available so the media can be played through to the end

For example, you might want to run a function only when metadata has loaded, say, to obtain a video's duration. To do this, you need to check that the readyState is at least 1:

```
if (video.readyState > 0) { ... }
```

Doing this requires constant polling (perhaps using setInterval()), so it's not an optimal solution in all situations. A better solution is to get the browser to report this using an event, which I cover in "Media Events" below.

Extra Properties for Audio and Video

In addition to the shared properties and methods of all media types, both audio and video have a unique interface. The HTMLAudioElement interface has just a single extra method, audio(), which is a constructor used to create a new audio element. You can optionally add in a source URL as an argument:

```
var audio = new Audio('foo.oga');
```

The HTMLVideoElement interface contains a series of properties regarding the video's appearance. You can use the poster property to get or set the poster attribute. The remaining four attributes regard dimensions: height and width are used for the dimensions of the element, whereas videoHeight and videoWidth are the dimensions of the video as it displays within the element.

Media Events

JavaScript events are fired during the course of loading, playing back, and interacting with media files, providing plenty of scope for attaching event handlers. Let's begin with events for the multiple stages of the readyState property: State 1 is represented by loadedmetadata, state 2 by loadeddata, state 3 by canplay, and state 4 by canplaythrough.

For example, the following code logs a message into the console when a video file has reached state 4—that is, sufficient data is available for the media to play through until the end:

```
video.addEventListener('canplaythrough', function () {
  console.log('Can play through.');
}, false);
```

For the playback state, playing is fired when the media is first played and pause when playback is paused. If playback is restarted after a pause, the play event fires, and when the media reaches the end, ended fires. If playback is interrupted for some reason—for example, if the media is playing but the user restarts it manually from the beginning—the abort event is fired.

The volumechange event fires when the volume property value changes or the muted attribute is toggled, seeking when the seek bar is being used, and seeked when the seek operation ends. When the currentTime property updates, the timeupdate event fires.

Advanced Media Interaction

Just the two media elements (plus their associated API) that you've seen so far in this chapter provide many more options for media than developers have ever had in the past, but this is only the beginning. Plans are already underway to provide far more granular control and extensibility to playing media natively in the browser, with advanced audio capabilities and peer-to-peer data connection acting as the vanguard.

Web Audio API

For people who want to go beyond simple playback of audio files, an emerging standard called the Web Audio API aims to provide high-level processing and synthesizing of audio in web applications. The Web Audio API is based on the concept of Audio Routes, a common tool in sound engineering (but way over my head!).

Like the canvas element, the Web Audio API uses a context, which is constructed with the AudioContext() method:

```
var context = new AudioContext();
```

Going further on this subject is far beyond the scope of this book, and my own capabilities, but if you're interested in advanced audio processing, I suggest you read the article "Web Audio API – Getting Started" on the CreativeJS site (see "Further Reading" on page 175).

WebRTC

Back in Chapter 6, we looked at the getUserMedia() method. There, I mentioned that it's part of the wider WebRTC project. WebRTC is an exciting proposal aimed at allowing all web-connected devices to communicate with each other, using audio, video, and data in real-time and using a single standardized protocol.

At the moment, many tools do this, but all of them require plug-ins or extra software, and very few actually use the same protocol and are able to talk to each other, creating a series of "walled gardens" with no way to get data from one to the other. WebRTC aims to remove those walls.

WebRTC has three key APIs: *MediaStream* gives access to data streams such as from a camera or microphone (using getUserMedia()), *PeerConnection* allows voice or video communication between devices, and *DataChannel* is for generic data communication. As I write this, Chrome and Firefox have experimental support for all three, and Opera supports MediaStream through getUserMedia().

As with so much of the media landscape on the Web, however, even the current WebRTC specification has an uncertain future. An alternative specification, CU-RTC-Web, has been proposed by Microsoft based on their experience of owning the Skype platform. Going into detail on either of the two specs is very probably a fool's errand, so I'll leave it at this: Real-time communication will come to the Web, even if the precise shape it takes is not currently known.

Summary

In this chapter, you've learned ways to include media on your page using the audio and video elements and the many attributes that give you control over how the media are displayed. You've also seen the Media API, which allows deep interaction with media elements, and the broad range of events that are fired by media interactions.

I also touched on the future audio APIs—a subject I would like to have gone into more, but the uncertain landscape prevents me from doing so. Finally, I talked about the WebRTC project, an exciting set of APIs that aim to provide amazing new ways for us to swap video, voice, and data between devices without third-party plug-ins, and a project that really deserves a book of its own.

Further Reading

The full text of Steve Jobs's "Thoughts on Flash" is at *http://www.apple.com/ hotnews/thoughts-on-flash/*.

Advice on audio and video accessibility around autoplaying is on the WCAG Audio Control page at *http://www.w3.org/TR/UNDERSTAND ING-WCAG20/visual-audio-contrast-dis-audio.html*.

MDN has tables showing the current state of media format implementation across different browsers at *https://developer.mozilla.org/en-US/docs/ Media_formats_supported_by_the_audio_and_video_elements/*, and Kroc Camen's technique and notes for cross-browser implementation, "Video for Everybody!", is at *http://camendesign.co.uk/code/video_for_everybody/*.

The best introduction to WebVTT and the track element is on Dev.Opera, *http://dev.opera.com/articles/view/an-introduction-to-webvtt-and-track/*, and a useful WebVTT validation tool is on Anne van Kesteren's website, *http://quuz .org/webvtt/*.

I mentioned three encoding tools in this chapter: The FFmpeg command-line tool is at *http://ffmpeg.org/*, Miro Video Converter at *http:// www.mirovideoconverter.com/*, and HandBrake at *http://handbrake.fr/*.

The W3C's Media Fragments specification is at *http://www.w3.org/TR/ media-frags/*.

MDN has the best documentation of the Media API and Events that I've found at *https://developer.mozilla.org/en-US/docs/DOM/HTMLMediaElement/* and *https://developer.mozilla.org/en-US/docs/DOM/Media_events/*, respectively.

CreativeJS has a great introductory article on the Web Audio API at *http://creativejs.com/resources/web-audio-api-getting-started/*.

You can expect to hear a lot more about WebRTC in the future, but Sam Dutton wrote a good introduction at HTML5 Rocks: *http:// www.html5rocks.com/en/tutorials/webrtc/basics/*. Microsoft's introduction to the CU-RTC-Web proposal is on the Interoperability blog at *http:// blogs.msdn.com/b/interoperability/archive/2012/07/28/customizable-ubiquit ous-real-time-communication-over-the-web-cu-rtc-web.aspx*.

10

WEB APPS

So far, most of this book has been about web technologies that can be used anywhere, from open websites to device-specific web apps. In this chapter, I'll take a short detour to talk about the extra steps required to create applications—how you can adapt your site to make it available through an online application store, or even to make it installable on a device.

Before moving on to talk about the mechanics of creating applications, we should start by defining the core types:

- *Native apps* are built using non–web technologies for specific platforms such as OS X, iOS, Windows, and Android.
- *Web apps* use web platform languages and can include hosted websites or ones packaged inside compressed containers and installed on a device.
- *Hybrid apps* use web platform technologies but are wrapped or packaged inside native containers.

In this chapter, I'll look specifically at the latter two types, web apps and hybrid apps, and at how to make them available through some of the many application stores. But even that's not as simple as it sounds: Many rival platforms and stores exist, each has a different development platform and submission process, and there isn't a single standard way of defining an app (although there are a number of proposals to do so).

The good news is that many new app stores recognize the benefit of using web platform technologies to attract developers: huge time and money savings from not having to create an app multiple times in a different programming language for every platform. Many vendors, including Microsoft (Windows 8), Samsung (Smart TV), and Opera (Opera TV Store), use web platform technologies to power their apps. Although not quite a case of write once, run everywhere (you still have to consider each device's unique APIs, and levels of browser support), developing a web app can be much more efficient than developing multi-platform native apps in both Java for Android and Objective-C for iOS.

In addition to discussing the different methods of building apps, I'll also look at ways to make resources available offline and how to store them on a user's device when a network connection isn't available (something that's still pretty common even in today's wireless age). You accomplish this through the application cache (commonly known as *AppCache*), which, although quite powerful, is not without its pitfalls.

Web Apps

I'll begin by looking at web apps, that is, apps built entirely using web platform technologies. Although called web apps, they don't necessarily have to exist on the open Web; they can also be packaged and distributed through online stores for download onto devices. There are, of course, many online stores, but I'll look specifically at two with the lowest barriers to entry: the Chrome Web Store, which has been around for a few years, and the newer Firefox Marketplace. While both are created by browser vendors, the big difference between them is that the Chrome Web Store works only in the Chrome browser, whereas the Firefox Marketplace is aimed at creating an open standard that any browser can use.

Hosted vs. Packaged Apps

Before moving on to look at the different app store requirements, let's take a few minutes to define two subdivisions of web apps: *hosted* and *packaged*. Although most web app stores accept submissions of either, each type of app has certain advantages or disadvantages (largely around restrictions or permissions to core device functions), which are useful to know about in advance to help you choose the right approach to building your app.

Hosted Web Apps

A hosted app is one that holds all files on an external web server, usually accessible via a public URL. Essentially, a hosted app is like a website with a little extra metadata to allow app stores to index it. A hosted app isn't installed onto a device; a shortcut is created on the device that launches a browser or embedded web view when the user decides to open the app.

Hosting a web app has the advantage of allowing you, the developer, to make updates without requiring reauthorization from a store, but the flip side is that the security risk is higher (an evil developer could smuggle in compromising code), so hosted apps generally don't get access to restricted device APIs.

Packaged Web Apps

Unlike hosted apps, a packaged app contains all the assets necessary to run it, compressed (usually zipped) in a single file. All the files are installed on the device, and although the app can connect to external web services, such a connection isn't always required. Packaging an app in this way means the store owner can review and authorize the app's contents and grant extra permissions if the app is found to be secure; in practice, this means the developer can access restricted APIs on the device, such as those used to access the address book or text messaging functions.

Packaged apps open and shut more quickly than hosted ones because all their files are held on the user's device, so they're less dependent on network capabilities. But packaged app developers need to be sure to store data locally and allow it to be synced to the data server while online, which requires more development work. To help with this, you can use local storage (discussed in Chapter 6), but for more extensive offline access options, you'll want to use AppCache, which I cover in "Application Cache" on page 185.

Manifest Files

Regardless of whether an app is hosted or packaged, every app designed for an app marketplace has to contain some data that's formatted or presented in a specific way in order to identify it as an app that belongs in that particular store. Usually this process involves no more than filling in a few required data fields and adding an icon to display on the target device, both of which are contained in a *manifest file*.

The manifest file is a simple XML or JSON text file hosted somewhere in the folder that holds your site assets. It contains key information about the app, including its name and description, although the required information varies slightly between stores, as I explain in the following sections.

The Chrome Web Store

When hosted by the Chrome Web Store, the manifest file must be JSON-formatted, named *manifest.json*, and stored in a folder called *myapp* in the app's root folder. The following annotated code shows a short example of *manifest.json* for the Chrome Web Store, with the bare minimum of required fields.

```
    {
❶      "name": "App Name",
❷      "description": "Short description",
❸      "version": "0.1",
❹      "manifest_version": 2,
❺      "icons": {
           "128": "icon_128.png"
        },
❻      "app": {
           "launch": {
             "web_url": "http://foo.example.com/"
           }
        }
    }
```

The first item ❶ in the manifest is the name of your app. Next ❷ is the description, which should be 132 characters (or fewer) in length and contain no HTML. The version property ❸ is the custom release version of your app, which is handy for bug reporting and informing users of updates. The manifest version ❹ tells the Chrome Web Store that you're using the most up-to-date manifest format (version 1 will be phased out throughout 2013).

The icons object ❺ is a list of image files that are to be displayed at different resolutions, depending on where they will be shown (such as on a device desktop or in a list of apps); here, the file *icon_128.png* will be used whenever a 128×128px icon is displayed. Finally, the app object ❻ contains a web_url subfield, which includes the URL of the page to be displayed when your app launches.

The Firefox Marketplace

The manifest required by the Firefox Marketplace is known as an Open Web App Manifest. As the name implies, Mozilla is hoping this format becomes a general standard for web apps, as a way to simplify the process of submitting a web app to multiple stores in the future. This manifest is usually called *manifest.webapp* and served with the MIME type *application/ x-web-app-manifest+json*. Full instructions can be found in the slides of Robert Nyman's talk "WebAPIs and Apps" listed in "Further Reading" on page 188.

The Open Web App Manifest file is JSON-formatted and, by design, similar to that of the Chrome Web Store. The listing here shows a minimal, annotated example.

```
    {
❶      "name": "App Name",
❷      "description": "Short description",
```

```
❸    "version": "0.1",
❹    "launch_path": "http://foo.example.com/",
❺    "icons": {
       "128": "icon_128.png"
     }
}
```

The name ❶ and version ❸ fields and the icons object ❺ are the same as previously described for the Chrome Web Store. The description field ❷ is the same too, except that its length can be up to 1024 characters. The biggest difference is the launch_path ❹ field, which has the same behavior as app > launch > web_url in the Chrome manifest. No manifest version is required, although one could be added as an extension when submitting the app to the Chrome Web Store (which requires it).

W3C Widgets

The W3C has developed their own standard for packaged web apps, known in their parlance as *widgets*. Widgets work like other packaged web app formats, except that the manifest file (called *config.xml*) is in XML format, and all the files are zipped with the suffix *.wgt*.

As it's in XML, the manifest file is a little different from the ones I've already shown you, although most of the information in it should be familiar:

```
<widget version="0.1">
  <name>App Name</widgetname>
  <description>Short description</description>
  <content src="http://foo.example.com"/>
  <icon src="icon_128.png"/>
</widget>
```

Having been around for a while, widgets are considered quite stable, but they don't have many implementations in the modern device environment. The Opera browser uses a widget as a base for its extensions specification, but the largest current user of the widget is probably the PhoneGap project, which I cover next.

Hybrid Apps

If you want to publish your web apps through the big device app stores—such as the Apple App Store, Google Play, or the Windows Store—you need to create a hybrid app. These apps are similar to packaged apps in that all their resources are contained in a single archive, but they go one step further by adding a native shell, or wrapper, around the files, which ensures that the app can be integrated into the main operating system, providing security and better performance and also allowing access to restricted device APIs. A number of software solutions exist for making hybrid apps, but one of the most common—and certainly the easiest to learn—is PhoneGap.

PhoneGap

Although owned by Adobe, a commercial entity, PhoneGap is free, open source software that allows you to build semi-native mobile applications using web platform technologies. PhoneGap is a distribution of software called Apache Cordova, which used to be called PhoneGap before it was sold to Adobe and things became complicated. The names are often used interchangeably, but I'll stick to calling it PhoneGap for consistency's sake.

PhoneGap works across multiple platforms, chief among them iOS, Android, and Windows Phone, and one of its major selling points is that, as it's a native OS wrapper around web platform code, it allows access to APIs on a device that are not always available through the browser. For this, it uses its own API, which matches standard APIs from each device where present, acts as a bridge when devices have differing implementations of an API, and otherwise creates new methods and objects where necessary.

To set up PhoneGap, you need to download the SDK for each device you want to target and, in some cases (notably for iOS), also get a developer certificate. When you've done all this, you complete the setup for each environment (full instructions are on the PhoneGap website, linked to in "Further Reading" on page 188) and start a new project, which creates a folder structure with a few key files, including the ones necessary for access to the API.

Granting Permissions

Once your setup is complete, you can add all the files to the project that your app needs to run, and then begin to take advantage of the PhoneGap API. Some of the properties in the API require that you add permission requests to a manifest file because (as I mentioned earlier) PhoneGap uses the XML-based widgets specification for requests. For example, to request access to the Notification API, you include the following XML element in the file *config.xml*:

```
<plugin name="Notification" value="org.apache.cordova.Notification"/>
```

Some platforms require no extra permissions, or make some methods available without requiring permissions, whereas others insist on permission requests for all methods. The API documentation has full details.

The PhoneGap API

The PhoneGap API is largely composed of a series of properties and methods on the navigator object. Some of these properties are already available through browsers. When they are, as with the geolocation object you learned about in Chapter 6, PhoneGap's API chooses the native implementation first, falling back to its own implementation on systems where the property is not available.

Other properties require heightened permissions and, as such, are available on some platforms exclusively through PhoneGap. For example, consider the contacts object, which provides access to the user's contact list—not something you want exposed to the Web without special authorization.

The contacts object has two functions: create() and find(). To select items from the contacts list, you use the latter with two required arguments: contactFields (a list of fields to return) and contactSuccess (a function to be run when a successful query takes place).

In the following code, I set up a query to get the display name and birthday of all contacts in the address book; then if this query is successful, it runs an anonymous function. This function loops through all of the results (in the *contacts* object I defined) and adds them to a string called *contactDOB*, which I use here to populate a list.

```
navigator.contacts.find(['displayName','birthday'], function (results) {
  var i, contactDOB;
  for (i=0; i < results.length; i++) {
    contactDOB += '<li>' + results[i].displayName + '(' + results[i].
birthday + ')</li>';
  }
});
```

Future browsers and web-based operating systems (such as Firefox OS) will probably provide direct access to some of these methods in the future, meaning the long-term future of PhoneGap will likely be in polyfilling features on legacy devices. PhoneGap's developers are cognizant of this, as stated clearly in a blog post called "Beliefs, Goals and Philosophy":

> The ultimate purpose of PhoneGap is to cease to exist.

PhoneGap Events

In addition to its device properties API, PhoneGap also has a number of extremely useful events that register changes to the device's status, from its network status and capability to the battery level. These events are critical if you want your app to provide users with the best possible experience, such as ensuring data is saved before a battery runs out or when network connection is lost.

The most important event is deviceready, which fires when PhoneGap has fully loaded and is ready to execute. The deviceready event is functionally identical to the DOMContentLoaded event you saw in Chapter 5 in that it also should be used in every script to ensure that all required libraries have been loaded and are in place before the rest of the scripts are run. As such, all of your functions that require access to the PhoneGap API should be run in the callback function:

```
document.addEventListener('deviceready', function () {
  // All PhoneGap-related functions
}, false);
```

Other events include pause and resume. The former is fired when the current application is closed and moved to a background process, and the latter when it becomes active again. For example, you may want to store data when the application is moved to a background process to make sure users doesn't lose their work:

```
document.addEventListener('pause', function () {
  // Backup data
}, false);
```

Some events fire when an application disconnects or reconnects from a network (offline and online); when the volume or call buttons are pressed (volumedownbutton, volumeupbutton, startcallbutton, and endcallbutton); and when the battery status changes (batterystatus detects changes in status, whereas batterylow and batterycritical fire when the battery is low or in a critical state, as defined by the device).

Titanium

Another popular approach to publishing hybrid mobile apps is Appcelerator Titanium. Rather than acting as a wrapper around a web app like PhoneGap, Titanium is an SDK that lets you develop applications with JavaScript using native UI elements from the target device platform. This approach has the advantage of making your app look and feel more like a native app, but it requires that you write it in a way that isn't compatible with the standard open web platform approach.

For that reason, I won't cover Titanium further in this book, although knowledge of its existence is useful.

TV Apps

So far in this chapter I've covered mostly mobile device development, but a new and thriving area lies in development for Internet-connected smart TVs. The big players in this arena include device manufacturers Samsung, Sony, and Panasonic; plug-in box makers Roku and Boxee; and the browser vendor Opera. Installable apps on smart TVs are generally seen as a good idea, as it's easier to navigate a series of icons than it is to type long URLs when using a remote control.

Early smart TVs had proprietary and conflicting app development platforms, but 2012 saw a sector-wide move toward web platform technologies that made developing for TV much less demanding. Each party to the development maintains their own developer program and documentation, some of which is free. If you're interested in developing in this area, Opera's developer portal has some great articles and tutorials on best practices (see "Further Reading" on page 188).

Webinos

If your goal is to develop for true cross-device communication, you may want to consider the Webinos framework. This open source, browser-based application platform is co-funded by the European Union together with major players such as BMW, Samsung, Sony, and the W3C. It's intended to simplify communication between devices, ranging from in-car systems to mobile devices to your TV.

Because Webinos is browser based, it uses web platform technologies; it's even built on top of Node.js and uses HTML5 WebSockets for communication. The first release was in 2012 and development is ongoing, but its potential is already exciting.

Application Cache

Users have certain expectations of website-delivered apps, notable among them is that the apps should work offline or at least save data if the connection is lost. One way to provide offline assets is to save the data in local storage using the API I talked about in "Web Storage" on page 117, but a better approach might be to use the Application Cache, or AppCache. This is an interface that lists files that should be downloaded by the user agent and stored in the memory cache for use even when a network connection is unavailable.

The first step in making an AppCache is to create a manifest file, a text file with the suffix *.appcache*, which must be served with the *text/cache-manifest* MIME type. Link to this manifest using the manifest attribute of the html element on every page that you want to make available offline:

```
<html manifest="foo.appcache">
```

Some browsers alert the user that your application is asking to store files offline and request permission to do so. Figure 10-1 shows how this looks in Firefox on Android.

You need to consider a number of gotchas with the application cache if you're thinking of using it on your site. These were exhaustively listed in Jake Archibald's article "Application Cache is a Douchebag," published on *A List Apart* (see "Further Reading" on page 188). I touch on a few of these in the following sections.

Figure 10-1: Some browsers, such as Firefox, request permission from the user before allowing AppCache to store files.

Contents of the AppCache File

The *.appcache* file begins with the words CACHE MANIFEST and then follows with a list of all files that should be cached. Each file is on a new line, and you can add single-line comments by entering a hash (#) at the start of each line.

The following listing shows a manifest file that stores three files in the cache. The comment with the version and date isn't required but will come in handy later:

```
CACHE MANIFEST
# Version 0.1, 2013-04-01
index.html
foo.css
foo.js
```

You don't need to explicitly list the pages to which the *.appcache* file is linked, because any page that includes the manifest attribute on the html element will be cached by default. These automatically cached pages are known as *master entries*, whereas files listed in the manifest are known as *explicit entries*. If some files require online access (such as access to a database using JavaScript), you can create a kind of whitelist of files to always be loaded over the network by listing them after the NETWORK: header. These files are known as *network entries*.

In the following example, files listed in the */dynamic* folder will be loaded over the network instead of from the cache:

```
NETWORK:
/dynamic
```

You can also add fallback files in case an attempt to load a resource fails, owing to the loss of a network connection or something else. You do this below the FALLBACK: header, where each new line lists a file or folder with the fallback file after it, separated by a space.

In the following example, if any file from the */templates* folder fails to load the page, *fallback.html* will be displayed from the cache instead:

```
FALLBACK:
/templates/ fallback.html
```

These files are known as *fallback entries* and, along with the three previous entries, complete the categories of file that will be cached.

The Caching Sequence

When the browser loads your page, it first checks for the manifest file. If the manifest exists and hasn't been loaded before, the browser loads the page elements as usual and then fetches copies of any files that are in the manifest but haven't yet been loaded. The browser stores all the listed entries in the cache to be loaded on the next visit.

If the manifest file exists and has been loaded before, the browser loads all the files held in the cache first, followed by any other files that are required to load the page. Next, it checks to see if the manifest file has been updated and, if so, downloads another copy of all the listed files. These files are then saved into the cache and used the next time the page is loaded; they won't be presented to the user immediately.

One important peculiarity is that in order for the browser to check for new versions of files to be loaded, the manifest file itself must be changed. This is where the version number or timestamp comment comes in handy: Changing either (or both) tells the browser that the manifest has been updated, and it will then download the updated files.

The AppCache API

If you need to access the cache through JavaScript, you can use the `window .applicationCache` object. This object contains some properties and methods that you'll find useful if you want to force downloads of updated files after the initial page load or otherwise interact with the manifest.

The `status` property returns the current status of the cache, with a numeric value and named constant for each state as follows:

- 0 (UNCACHED) means that no cache is present.
- 1 (IDLE) means that the cache is not being updated.
- 2 (CHECKING) means that the browser is checking the manifest file for updates.
- 3 (DOWNLOADING) means that new resources are being added.
- 4 (UPDATEREADY) means that a new cache is available.
- 5 (OBSOLETE) means that the current cache is now obsolete.

You can force a check of the manifest file using the `update()` method, which checks to see if the manifest file has been updated. The `update()` method gives the `status` property a value of 2 while it checks the manifest; it gives a value of 3 if updated resources exist and are downloading, and a value of 4 when updated files are ready.

When the `status` value is 4, you can use the `swapCache()` method to load the updated files. At this point, remember the browser has loaded the currently cached version of some files for the user in order to speed up the page load, and any updated files in the cache won't be presented to the user until the page is reloaded. To get around this, you can use an AppCache event, which fires at various points of the cache cycle, most notably when the `status` property updates. For example, when the `status` value becomes 2, the `checking` event fires, and when it becomes 3, the `downloading` event fires.

The following code shows one approach to reloading a page with updated assets. Here, the `updateready` event fires when a new cache has been downloaded and then runs a function that double-checks that the `status` property has a value equivalent to UPDATEREADY (4). If so, `updateready` swaps the cache and then asks the user if it's okay to upload the latest version of the files by reloading the page.

```
var myCache = window.applicationCache;
myCache.addEventListener('updateready', function(e) {
  if (myCache.status === myCache.UPDATEREADY) {
    myCache.swapCache();
    if (confirm('Load new version?')) {
      window.location.reload();
    }
  }
}, false);
```

By requesting permission to reload the page, this script ensures that the user doesn't suddenly lose data or have an action interrupted by a forced reload. This approach is used by many popular web apps, including Google's suite of tools.

Summary

In this chapter, we've taken a (necessarily) brief look at packaging websites to act as apps for release through app marketplaces. I discussed the difference between hosted and packaged apps, the manifest files required for submitting to two web-based marketplaces, and the W3C's own manifest standard. I also covered hybrid apps, which use web technologies in a native wrapper, and discussed how to use the open source PhoneGap to interact with a device more deeply than most browsers can. Finally, I discussed AppCache, a way of storing files on a device to allow offline access. We looked at what it does and how to access it with JavaScript, and briefly covered its limitations.

Further Reading

The Chrome Web Store has in-depth documentation on preparing an app for submission, including details about the manifest file, at *https://developers .google.com/chrome/web-store/docs/get_started_simple/*.

Firefox Marketplace provides details about the manifest file at *https:// developer.mozilla.org/docs/Apps/Manifest/*, and it has a useful manifest validation tool at *https://marketplace.firefox.com/developers/validator/*. Robert Nyman's talk "Web APIs and Apps" is a great primer for building apps for the Firefox Marketplace: *http://www.slideshare.net/robnyman/web-apis-apps-mozilla-london/*.

The latest version of the W3C widgets specification is at *http://w3.org/TR/ widgets/*, and you'll find a useful introduction on Peter-Paul Koch's site— even though it was written a few years ago, and some small details of the spec have changed since then: *http://quirksmode.org/blog/archives/2009/04/ introduction_to.html*.

The PhoneGap project is at *http://phonegap.com/*, and the API documentation is at *http://docs.phonegap.com/*. You can read the PhoneGap article "Beliefs, Goals, and Philosophy" at *http://phonegap.com/2012/05/ 09/phonegap-beliefs-goals-and-philosophy/*.

You can read more about the Titanium project at *http://appcelerator.com/platform/*.

Each smart TV platform has its own developer forum, but a good example for getting started is Samsung's site at *http://www.samsungdforum.com/*.

The Opera TV Store is gaining some traction as a custom-made solution; learn more about it at *http://business.opera.com/partners/tv/store/*. The Dev.Opera site has some great reference articles on designing and developing for TV at *http://dev.opera.com/tv/*.

The Webinos project, which aims to create a standard common device API, is hosted at *http://www.webinos.org/*.

The Mozilla Developer Center has great AppCache documentation at *https://developer.mozilla.org/en-US/docs/HTML/Using_the_application_cache/*, and Mark Christian and Peter Lubbers created a handy page of AppCache facts at *http://appcachefacts.info/*. For all of AppCache's drawbacks and tips and techniques for using it, read Jake Archibald's "Application Cache is a Douchebag" at *A List Apart*: *http://www.alistapart.com/articles/application-cache-is-a-douchebag/*.

11

THE FUTURE

So far in this book I've aimed to discuss only those web features that are pretty stable in at least a few browsers, or that should be stable sometime in the near future. But now that we've arrived at this last chapter, I can really cut loose and talk about some of the more experimental features on the horizon.

Changes are planned everywhere: A new revision of JavaScript, code-named Harmony, is due for release sometime in 2013 and should make its way into browsers over the coming years; many new APIs are being proposed to the W3C, including one for discovering devices on the same network using *Universal Plug and Play (UPnP)* and one for measuring ambient light; work on the draft specification for HTML5.1 is well underway; and many CSS modules are already moving to Level 4. I could talk about any number of changes, but I'll focus on the ones that I think will have the greatest impact on the way we work and that have a good chance of being implemented.

Web Components

I don't think I'm exaggerating when I say that the Web Components specification proposes the most radical changes to HTML since its creation some 20+ years ago. Even the much-hyped HTML5 is a small point-version update that doesn't really add anything genuinely new.

Web Components is a collective title for a group of additions to HTML and the DOM aimed at making rich interfaces for web applications—a kind of reusable widget specification. As I write this, four main components exist: *templates*, *decorators*, *custom elements*, and the *Shadow DOM*. I'll explain what each does in turn, but first let me sum up what they do when combined.

One of the principal problems of building application components in HTML today is that the elements used to build them are part of the DOM and, as such, are open to conflicts from CSS or JavaScript. These could be inheritance conflicts, such as rules applied to parent elements cascading into component elements or, inversely, rules applied to component elements leaking or cascading to elements elsewhere in the DOM.

Another problem results from naming conflicts, where the same class or ID is unknowingly used in different pages of a site, meaning rules intentionally declared on one element are also unintentionally applied to others. This problem is commonly found on large sites that lack a clear naming scheme, and it can be made even worse by conflicts in JavaScript when selectors apply unwanted functional behavior to an element.

The best way to avoid conflicts like these is to separate the component from the rest of the DOM to prevent any inheriting or leaking. This technique is known as *encapsulation* and is fundamental to object-oriented programming languages.

Web Components attempts to bring encapsulation into the HTML DOM by allowing you to create elements that appear only in the rendering of a page, not in the DOM itself. Web Components will offer a way to build widgets that can be reused across many different pages on a site without having to worry about conflicts with existing CSS and JavaScript, since the widget lives in a parallel DOM.

The Web Components spec is still in the draft stage as I write this, so I won't explore the concepts in great detail, but I will cover the basics since it could be so significant.

Templates

Probably the easiest way to grasp Web Components is with an understanding of templates. The idea of developing with reusable blocks of code, or *templates*, has been a staple of web development for quite some time, although we've never seen a native implementation in HTML; server-side languages or JavaScript (such as the Mustache library from Chapter 5) have been required in order to use templates.

Think of a Web Component template as a kind of inert block of DOM. The significance of this is that the contents are parsed, but not rendered, by the browser. This means images and other external elements aren't loaded and included scripts won't run, which can be a real performance boost compared to hiding elements with CSS, where assets are still loaded.

A template is declared with the `template` element, and any child elements form the content of the template. The following code block shows a template element with the id #*foo*, which has two child elements (an h2 and a p). Outside of the template is a div with the id #*bar*, which contains an h1 element.

```
<template id="foo">
  <h2>Gorilla Beringei</h2>
  <p>A species of the genus Gorilla...</p>
</template>
<div id="bar">
  <h1>Eastern Gorilla</h1>
</div>
```

If you were to view this page with your browser's developer tools, you would see the `template` element with no content inside it because, essentially, the contents of this element are invisible to the DOM.

You access the template through script using the `content` object, which returns the child elements of the template as an HTML fragment. For example, you can see that the next code snippet assigns the template to the variable *tpl* and logs its content object to the console:

```
var tpl = document.getElementById('foo');
console.log(tpl.content);
```

Once you have the fragment, you can manipulate it as you see fit. The following code uses `cloneNode()` to create a clone of the content and `appendChild()` to add it inside #*bar*:

```
var bar = document.getElementById('bar'),
    clone = tpl.content.cloneNode(true);
bar.appendChild(clone);
```

At this point, you would see this markup if you inspected the DOM:

```
<template id="foo"></template>
<div id="bar">
  <h1>Eastern Gorilla</h1>
</div>
```

But the page would be rendered as if it were using this markup:

```
<div id="bar">
  <h1>Eastern Gorilla</h1>
  <h2>Gorilla Beringei</h2>
  <p>A species of the genus Gorilla...</p>
</div>
```

You can see it for yourself in the example file *templates.html*; the output is shown in Figure 11-1 (see Appendix A for information on current browser support). Note that in order for the contents of the template element to show in the DOM, I had to enable the **Show Shadow DOM** option in my developer tools; if that option wasn't enabled, the element would appear to be empty.

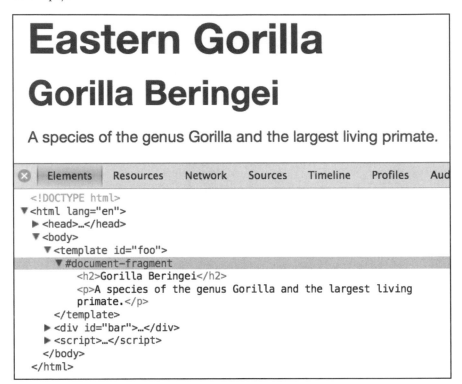

Figure 11-1: The code inspector shows the contents of the template element, which exists outside the regular DOM.

Code that was inert inside the template element becomes active once it's inserted into another DOM element, at which point any external resources will load, scripts will be parsed, and so on.

Decorators

Decorators extend the utility of templates by allowing you to add custom markup through CSS. Decorators use the decorator element, which must have a unique id assigned. Inside the decorator element, you'll find a template element with some custom markup and the content element, which is where the element that the rule is applied to is rendered. Not clear? It took me a while to get it too.

Let's break this down into stages. The following code shows an example of a decorator. I gave it the unique id *#foo* (for a change). Inside is a template that contains a div, with the content element and an h2 inside that.

```
<decorator id="foo">
  <template>
    <div>
      <content></content>
      <h2>A great ape!</h2>
    </div>
  </template>
</decorator>
```

Now imagine that in the main document I have an h1 element with the id *#bar*, as in the following code:

```
<h1 id="bar">Gorilla</h1>
```

I apply the decorator using CSS and the new decorator property, which has as its value a url() function containing the decorator's id.

```
h1#bar { decorator: url(#foo); }
```

Once I've done this, the markup in the template *#foo* is added to the markup of the element *#bar*, with *#bar* itself replacing the content element of *#foo*. However, this takes effect only at the point of rendering and doesn't alter the DOM. Although an inspection of the DOM shows only the element *#bar*, the element will be rendered as though the markup were this:

```
<div>
  <h1 id="bar">Gorilla</h1>
  <h2>A great ape!</h2>
</div>
```

You can do more with templates and decorators, but to show you more, I first need to make a brief digression to talk about *scoped styles*.

Scoped Styles

One of CSS's greatest strengths is its use of *inheritance*—that is, the way that values can cascade through selectors to apply to multiple elements. That strength can also be a drawback, however, if you're working on large sites with many stylesheets, where experiencing the naming and inheritance conflicts that I mentioned at the start of this section is not uncommon.

Scoped styles are a way to avoid these conflicts. They're applied in the document using the style element with the attribute scoped, and any rules contained therein are inherited only by the children of the element they're used in, and won't be applied anywhere else in the document.

You can see this in action in the following code: A scoped `style` tag is used inside a `div` element, and the rules applied to the `h1` apply only to the `h1` within that element (the one with the `id` of *#foo*), and not the one outside the `div` (with the `id` *#bar*). The scope of the rule applies only to the children of the `div`.

```
<div>
  <style scoped>
    h1 {
      background-color: #333;
      color: #FFF;
    }
  </style>
  <h1 id="foo">Scoped</h1>
</div>
<h1 id="bar">Not Scoped</h1>
```

Take a look at the example file *scoped-style .html*. Here, the `h1` with the `id` *#bar* follows the one with the `id` *#foo* in DOM order, so you would expect the rules inside the `style` element to apply to both. In fact, the `scoped` attribute means the rules apply only inside the parent `div`. You can see the result in Figure 11-2 and in *scoped-style.html*.

Scoped
Not Scoped

Figure 11-2: The first h1 has rules applied to it that do not affect the subsequent h1 because the rules are scoped to a different node branch.

Scoped Styles and Templates

Having the ability to scope styles in this way is ideal for encapsulation, and it combines especially well with templates and decorators. Case in point, if I return to an earlier example using the markup from the first code block in "Decorators" on page 194, I could create a set of rules to be applied to the original `h1` element only when the decorator is applied by using a scoped `style` tag inside the `template` element:

```
<decorator id="foo">
  <template>
    <div>
      <style scoped>
      h1 { color: red; }
      </style>
      <content></content>
      <h2>A great ape!</h2>
    </div>
  </template>
</decorator>
```

In this case, the `h1` element is colored red only when the decorator is applied. Even better, that color won't apply to any subsequent `h1` element in the document because of its limited scope—a perfect example of encapsulation.

Custom Elements

Although decorators are handy for adding extra presentational markup to an element, when you want to make more substantial changes, use a *custom element*. The key difference between custom elements and decorators is that the latter are transitory; they can be applied or removed by changing an attribute or selector. Custom elements, on the other hand, are fixed; they are applied when the DOM is parsed and can be changed or removed only with scripting.

A custom element is like an extended template that replaces or enhances a standard element. You create a custom element with the element element (this paragraph is going for a new record in the number of occurrences of the word "element"), which has some new attributes that I'll discuss shortly. Inside this element, you can add a template element with new markup, as well as scoped styles and even a script.

If this sounds a bit confusing, consider this illustration. The following code snippet shows a simple example: an element containing a template, which, in turn, contains a div, which itself contains the content element I introduced in "Decorators" on page 194. The element has two attributes: extends, which takes as a value the name of the element that it will extend (in this case, a button element), and name, a user-defined unique identifier value (which must start with x- to avoid conflicting with existing elements).

```
<element extends="button" name="x-foobutton">
  <template>
    <div id="foo">
      <content></content>
    </div>
  </template>
</element>
```

Once the custom element has been defined, you can apply it to an existing element with the is attribute. The is attribute is applied to the element to be extended and takes as a value the unique identifier from the name attribute (*x-foobutton*) defined on the custom element. Actually, this is simpler than it may sound:

```
<button is="x-foobutton">Go</button>
```

The resulting effect is the same as that of a decorator: The markup of the custom element extends the markup of the element it's applied to but only in the rendered view. Although viewing the DOM shows only the button element, it renders like this:

```
<div id="foo">
  <button>Go</button>
</div>
```

This example is simple, but you can see how the extensibility of this technique would make it easy to build completely tailor-made widgets that could be reused across many documents. As a result, many of the cumbersome widgets we build today (such as carousels, accordions, and date pickers) could be applied to existing elements without filling the DOM with unnecessary markup, with the added benefit of implementing encapsulation to avoid conflicts.

I mentioned earlier that the core difference between a custom element and a decorator is in the permanence of the markup. One advantage of this is that scripts can be included in a custom element that will always be present (a benefit you can't rely on for the more impermanent decorators). All this means you could even define an imperative API for each custom element, thereby taking interactivity to a whole new level.

The Shadow DOM

The final piece of the Web Components specification is the *Shadow DOM*. This is not only a cool-sounding name for a supervillain, but it's also a way to create and access, with script, the elements that exist in the parallel DOM I've shown you in this chapter. Just as decorators use CSS to alter elements and custom elements use HTML, Shadow DOM uses script to achieve the same ends.

The Shadow DOM describes the ability of a browser to create a new, fully encapsulated node tree inside the existing DOM. The browser does this by creating a *shadow root* inside an element, which can be traversed and manipulated like a regular node tree. (A shadow tree won't show up in the DOM, but it will be rendered.)

Now for an example. The following code snippet contains some simple markup: a div called *#foo*, which contains a single h1 element. This is the base markup in the DOM, inside which I'll add a new shadow root.

```
<div id="foo">
  <h1>Hello, world!</h1>
</div>
```

Now I'll add a new shadow root inside the div, and then create and append a new element to the new root. I explain this code point by point in the discussion that follows.

```
  var foo = document.getElementById('foo'),
❶     newRoot = foo.createShadowRoot(),
❷     newH2 = document.createElement('h2');
  newH2.textContent = 'Hello, shadow world!');
❸ newRoot.appendChild(newH1);
```

The first thing to note ❶ is the creation of a new shadow root inside *#foo*, using the createShadowRoot() method. In the following two lines ❷, I create a new h2 element with the text content '*Hello, shadow world!*'. And finally ❸, I append the new h2 element into my new shadow root.

When this code executes, users see an h2 element with the text '*Hello, shadow world!*', but if they viewed the DOM, users would see the original content, '*Hello, world!*'. The h1 element has been completely replaced by the new shadow node tree. The DOM remains unaffected.

Figure 11-3 shows how this renders in the Chrome developer tools, with the contents of the shadow root displayed in a new node tree below the identifier *#shadow-root*.

Figure 11-3: The shadow root is clearly marked in the DOM tree.

If you don't want to replace the content in the element in which you've created a new root, you can once again use the content element (again introduced in "Decorators" on page 194) to include the original elements. I illustrate this in the following code, where I create the content element and then append it to the new shadow root. As a result, the user sees the new shadow h2 first, followed by the original h1, although only the h1 appears in the DOM.

```
var content = document.createElement(content);
newRoot.appendChild(content);
```

You can also use templates with shadow node trees. For example, here's how to append an HTML fragment of the template *#foo* content into the Shadow DOM:

```
var foo = document.getElementById('foo');
newRoot.appendChild(foo.content);
```

The Shadow DOM goes even further than this simple example and is a very powerful and flexible tool. I can't spend any more time on it here, but see "Further Reading" on page 209 for some links to more detailed articles.

Putting It All Together

I've only brushed the surface of the Web Components specification, but I hope I've offered enough to get you excited by the possibilities. Web Components promises to offer fully reusable code components to enhance existing elements. These components will be fully encapsulated from the rest of the document and rendered by the browser but not accessible through the DOM, although a parallel shadow DOM will allow complete manipulation of and access to the elements inside each component.

If the Web Components specification is implemented, it will revolutionize the way we build applications and websites. And if that doesn't get you excited, you may be in the wrong business!

The Future of CSS

CSS3 has already revolutionized the Web in some ways, with its introduction of behavioral aspects such as transitions and animations and by seriously addressing the problem of layout mechanisms. But those features barely scratch the surface of what's to come. Lots of big tech companies are betting their futures on the Web, and their involvement in shaping the future of web standards brings with it some incredible innovation.

For example, Adobe's wholesale embrace of open standards (a pleasant surprise!) is making it a major player in browser development, and its experience with graphics and publishing is being applied to CSS. The first fruits of this labor are CSS *Regions* and *Exclusions*, which open up the possibility of major changes to the way we'll lay out pages in the future, as dynamic web pages finally begin to catch up with what desktop publishing has been doing for years.

But the web development community is having the biggest effect on the development of CSS. Developer-built JavaScript libraries such as jQuery and Modernizr are directly influencing the language, as you've seen with `querySelector()` and `querySelectorAll()` (back in Chapter 5), and that influence will be felt further with the introduction of *feature queries*.

Additionally, the rise in popularity of CSS preprocessors such as Sass and LESS means that front-end developers are becoming accustomed to using programming principles, such as variables and functions. The demand for these to be introduced into the language is manifesting itself through *cascading variables*.

Regions

Back in Chapter 4, I discussed CSS columns, where inline content is divided into columns and flows through the first column and then the second, the third, and so on. Imagine that those columns are not immediately adjacent to each other; the first is on the left of the page, the second is on the right, and the third is at the bottom, but the content still flows sequentially through them. That's the gist of a new CSS concept called *Regions*.

Regions work like this: An element is declared as a source, and the content of that source is flowed into another element, or series of elements, known as a *region chain*. What that means in practice is you can have content flowing across multiple elements in a sequence that doesn't flow in natural DOM order.

Here's a simple illustration that starts with three div elements: a #*foo* and two *.bar*s. The first, #*foo*, is filled with content, and the others are empty:

```
<div id="foo">
  <p>...</p>
</div>
<div class="bar"></div>
<div class="bar"></div>
```

The next step is to get the content of #*foo* and put it into a *named flow*, kind of like storing it in a variable (or the clipboard on your computer). In CSS Regions, you create this named flow by declaring the flow-into property on the source element (#*foo*). The value of the property is a unique name of your choosing, so I'll name mine *myFlow*. Having named my flow (or clipboard, if you're still following the metaphor), I can flow it into other elements, which become known as the titular *regions*:

```
#foo { flow into: myFlow; }
```

In Internet Explorer 10, the source element must be an iframe, *and the content inside the body of the linked document will become the content of the flow.*

When this property is applied, the source element and all its children are no longer rendered on screen, although they are still visible and accessible in the DOM.

Next I must declare a region chain that the content will be flowed into. Each element that forms part of the region chain should have the flow-from property declared on it, the value of which is the previously defined named flow. The following code shows how to flow the content of the flow *myFlow* into all regions called *.bar*:

```
.bar { flow-from: myFlow; }
```

The content in *myFlow* flows through the region chain in DOM order; it starts by flowing into the first instance of *.bar*, and then any overflow flows into the second instance of *.bar*, and so on, until the end of the content. Try this out with the file *regions.html*, as shown in Figure 11-4.

As I mentioned at the beginning of this section, CSS Regions work like multiple columns, without the columns needing to be immediately adjacent. This new element creates some amazing opportunities for making dynamic, interesting page layouts, inspired by years of experience with the possibilities of print media.

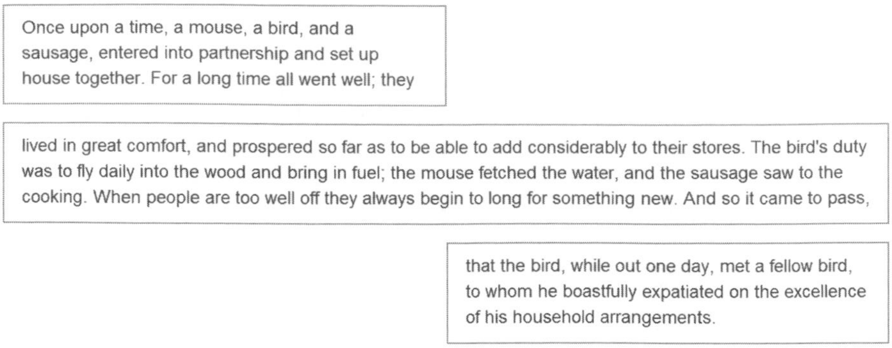

Once upon a time, a mouse, a bird, and a sausage, entered into partnership and set up house together. For a long time all went well; they

lived in great comfort, and prospered so far as to be able to add considerably to their stores. The bird's duty was to fly daily into the wood and bring in fuel; the mouse fetched the water, and the sausage saw to the cooking. When people are too well off they always begin to long for something new. And so it came to pass,

that the bird, while out one day, met a fellow bird, to whom he boastfully expatiated on the excellence of his household arrangements.

Figure 11-4: Using CSS Regions, you can flow content across multiple elements that don't need to be adjacent.

Exclusions

CSS Exclusions can be thought of as a kind of positioned floats—indeed, an earlier concept described them as exactly that. In CSS2.1 you can float elements only to the left, where other content flows around their right side, or vice versa. But the idea of CSS Exclusions is that you can flow content around an element no matter where it's positioned on the page.

To illustrate, consider the following markup with a container element *#foo*, some text content in a p, and a child element *#bar*:

```
<div id="foo">
  <p>...</p>
  <div id="bar"></div>
</div>
```

I want to position *#bar* absolutely over the content in *#foo*, which will require style rules somewhat like this:

```
#foo { position: relative; }
#bar {
  left: 20px;
  position: absolute;
}
```

As written here, *#bar* sits in a layer stacked above the text content, obscuring what's behind it, as you can see in Figure 11-5. But I want to make *#bar* part of the same layer and to float the text content around it. In the parlance of Exclusions, I want *#bar* to become an *exclusion element*.

I can accomplish this with the wrap-flow property, which makes the element it's applied to an exclusion element. Any sibling content flows around it according to the keyword value of the property.

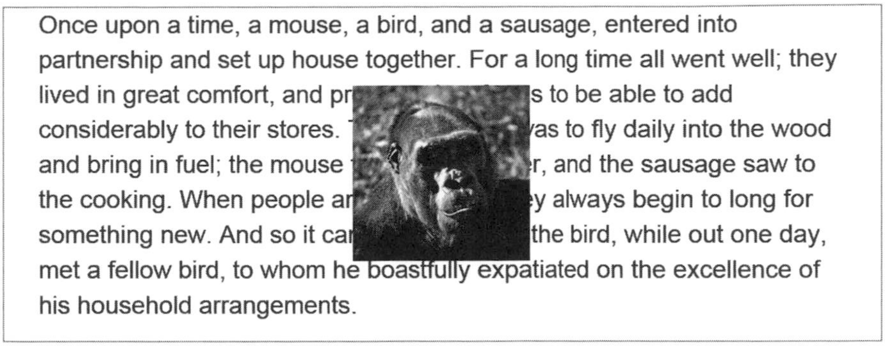

Once upon a time, a mouse, a bird, and a sausage, entered into partnership and set up house together. For a long time all went well; they lived in great comfort, and prs to be able to add considerably to their stores. as to fly daily into the wood and bring in fuel; the mouse r, and the sausage saw to the cooking. When people ary always begin to long for something new. And so it cathe bird, while out one day, met a fellow bird, to whom he boastfully expatiated on the excellence of his household arrangements.

Figure 11-5: An element that's absolutely positioned doesn't affect the flow of the content beneath it. (This gorilla photo is by Chris Willis and can be found at http://www.fotopedia .com/items/flickr-3059127796/. It used under a Creative Commons license.)

The following example uses the keyword value both to make content flow around both sides of the exclusion element:

```
#bar { wrap-flow: both; }
```

You can see the difference this makes in Figure 11-6. The elements are in the same positions as before, but because *#bar* has now been declared an exclusion element, the content in *#foo* flows around it on both sides.

Once upon a time, a mouse, a bird, and a sausage, entered into partnership and set up house together. For a long time all went well; they lived in great comfort, and  prospered so far as to be able to add considerably to their stores. The bird's duty was to fly daily into the wood and bring in fuel; the mouse fetched the water, and the sausage saw to the cooking. When people are too well off they always begin to long for something new. And so it came to pass, that the bird, while out one day, met a fellow bird, to whom he boastfully expatiated on the excellence of his household arrangements.

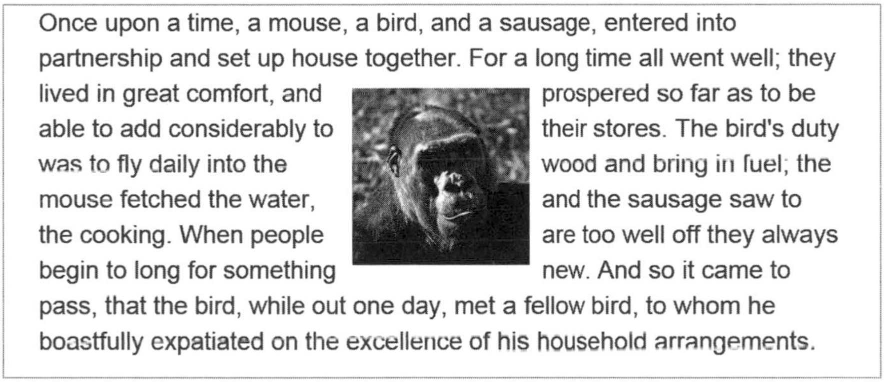

Figure 11-6: Applying the wrap-flow property makes the positioned element become part of the document flow, and the content flows around it on both sides.

Alternative values for wrap-flow include:

- start to flow the content on the left side (in left-to-right languages) of the exclusion element, but not the right
- end to do the opposite
- maximum and minimum to flow content only on the side with the most or least space (respectively) between it and its containing element
- clear to flow content only above and below the exclusion element

Figure 11-7 shows a few of the different values at work. The first example has a value of start, so the content flows to the left of the exclusion element. The next has the end value, so the content flows on the opposite side. And in the final example, the clear value makes content flow on neither side of the element.

To permit more control over the flow of inline elements around the exclusion, you have the wrap-through property. This property takes one of two keyword values: flow and none. The former, the default, makes inline content flow around the exclusion element; the latter doesn't. This is useful if you want to enable content flow on a per-element basis.

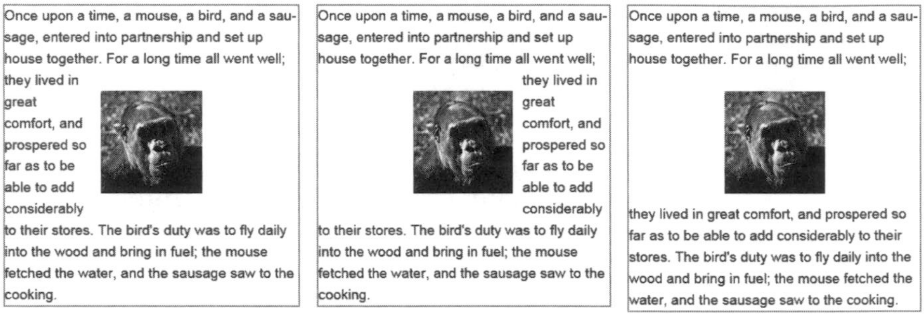

Figure 11-7: Content flows on different sides of the exclusion element as various values are applied to wrap-flow.

Exclusions and Grids

For me, one of the most exciting things about CSS Exclusions is the way they interact with the Grid Layout module that I introduced in Chapter 4. Any grid item can be made into an exclusion element, which really expands grid layout possibilities. As a simple example, consider a grid with three columns and two rows:

```
E {
  display: grid;
  grid-columns: 1fr 1fr 1fr;
  grid-rows: 100px 1fr;
}
```

On that grid, I'll place two items that have overlapping cells (they'll overlap in row two, column two):

```
F, G { grid-column-span: 2; }
F {
  grid-column: 2;
  grid-row-span: 2;
}
G { grid-row: 2; }
```

ALLEYN'S SCHOOL LIBRARY

Under the usual rules of grid placement, element *G* would stack over the top of element *F*, as it appears later in the DOM order. But by making element *G* the exclusion element, the inline content of element *F* will flow around it:

```
G {
  grid-row: 2;
  wrap-flow: both;
}
```

As you can see in the example file *grid-exclusion.html* (and in Figure 11-8), *F* now takes on a kind of inverted upside-down L shape as it flows around element *G*. This kind of layout is quite common in print so being able to reproduce it in web pages is really quite exciting. By making possible the kind of art direction that books and magazines have taken for granted for hundreds of years, CSS Exclusions ushers in a whole new era of laying out pages on the Web.

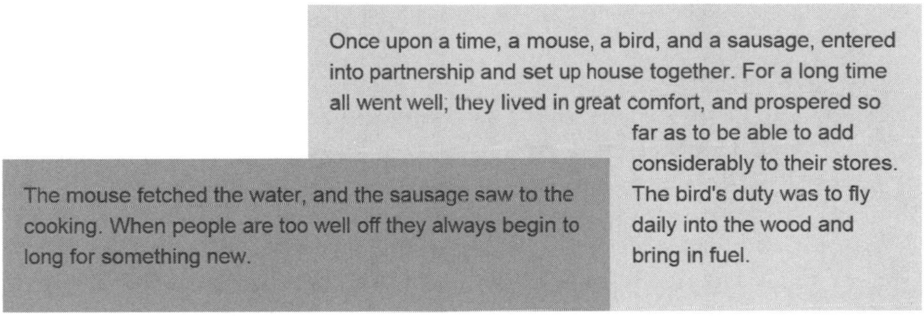

Once upon a time, a mouse, a bird, and a sausage, entered into partnership and set up house together. For a long time all went well; they lived in great comfort, and prospered so far as to be able to add considerably to their stores. The bird's duty was to fly daily into the wood and bring in fuel.

The mouse fetched the water, and the sausage saw to the cooking. When people are too well off they always begin to long for something new.

Figure 11-8: CSS Exclusions work nicely with CSS grids to create layout patterns that have previously not been possible.

Shaped Exclusions

The CSS Exclusions used in the examples in this section so far are based on standard block elements, so they appear boxy. The plan in the future is that you won't be limited to rectangular exclusions because a pair of new properties will allow you to draw geometrical exclusion shapes.

The shape-inside and shape-outside properties will accept as a value either a simple geometric shape such as a circle or ellipse, or a series of coordinates that will create a completely customized polygonal shape. Content could then be flowed around either the inside or outside of this shape (or both), opening up possibilities for the types of rich layout long possible in print but now improved with the dynamism of web content.

Even Further Future Layouts

As I write this in early 2013, a series of new rules and properties that affect layout are at various degrees of implementation—from barely there to only a proposal. My hope is that they will all be adopted and implemented because they solve different problems. With the CSS specification in a constant state of flux, however, nothing can be taken for granted; these rules and properties may be implemented, partially implemented with a different syntax, or not implemented at all.

Still, I think looking at them is worthwhile for two reasons: First, so you can see the thinking that goes on in trying to find solutions to the problems of web layout; and second, if they are implemented, you may need to use them.

Box Alignment

The idea behind the Box Alignment module is to create a syntax that's common across many different modules, for aligning elements within their parent. Box Alignment takes the Flexbox syntax as its inspiration, using `justify-` properties for inline/main axis alignment and `align-` properties for stacking/cross-axis alignment. For example, to align an element along its main axis, you'd use the `justify-self` property; and to align the child elements of an element along the cross axis, you'd use `align-content`.

Line Grid

In addition to the well-known grid formed with rows and columns, typographers also use what's often known as a *line grid*, or a *vertical rhythm*, a secondary grid created from the lines of text and headings on a page. When using a line grid, you try to make the vertical dimensions and alignment of objects harmonious with the text for better readability.

The Line Grid module creates a virtual vertical grid based on the `font-size` and `line-height` of text elements and lets you better align objects within that grid. It allows you to snap block elements to fixed points in that grid, overriding the default layout position created by the browser's engine.

Paged Media

Scrolling is the de facto way to work with content that overflows its container, especially the screen, but scrolling isn't always easy with devices such as television remote controls and liquid paper ebook readers, for example. A better approach for these devices might be to use paginated overflow instead.

You can do this easily with features proposed in the Paged Media module, which introduces the `overflow-style` property. A value of `paged-x` or `paged-y` automatically creates pages horizontally or vertically (respectively), while `-controls` (such as `paged-x-controls`) adds on-screen controls generated by the browser for interfaces that require them.

A further proposal, Pagination Templates, extends this even further, creating content regions that are fixed to each page for a consistent experience, allowing rich interactive magazine-style layouts.

Feature Queries

In Chapter 5 I discussed the JavaScript library Modernizr, which is used for detecting the existence of certain features in a visitor's browser, and briefly mentioned its native adaptation into CSS through the @supports at-rule. I want to return to that now and explore it in a little more detail, as it's extremely useful and fast making its way into browsers.

The @supports at-rule behaves like a media query: You create a logical query that, if it returns true, will apply the rules contained within the subsequent brackets. But instead of media features, the test conditions are CSS property-value pairs, known as *feature queries*. For example, to test whether a user's browser supports the column-count property so you can serve appropriate styles, you could construct a query like this:

```
@supports (column-count: 1) { ... }
```

As with media queries, you can build more advanced queries using logical operators. For example, the following query uses the and operator to serve styles to browsers that support both the column-count and box-sizing properties:

```
@supports (column-count: 1) and (box-sizing: border-box) { ... }
```

You can also use the or operator to build queries that detect defined features, which is extremely useful when dealing with vendor-prefixed properties. Here, both the hyphens or -moz-hyphens properties are tested against, and if either is supported, the rules are applied:

```
@supports (-moz-hyphens: auto) or (hyphens: auto) { ... }
```

The not operator allows you to serve styles to browsers that don't support a given property. (Note that unlike the other operators, this one must be inside parentheses.)

```
@supports (not (-webkit-hyphens: auto)) { ... }
```

Feature queries include an API that is as simple to use as the at-rule. For example, you can use the CSS.supports() method to detect a single feature by passing a property-value pair as two arguments. Here, it tests for the flex value on the display property:

```
var supports = CSS.supports('display','flex');
```

And you can pass in full queries as a single argument, quoted as a string:

```
var supports = CSS.supports('(column-count: 1) and (display: flex)');
```

The Modernizr project has already begun implementing this in its library; if native CSS.supports() implementation is present, the script will use that, and if not, it will fall back to Modernizr's own tests.

Cascading Variables

Variables have proven their utility over the years in just about every programming language, but they have never been implemented in CSS, despite regular calls for implementation from the community. But with the surge in popularity of CSS preprocessors, a generation of coders is learning to love variables in their stylesheets, and calls to include them natively in the language can no longer be ignored.

As currently proposed, CSS variables have limited scope. A true variable permits any type of value and could be used at any point in the code—say, to assign a selector to a variable. The proposed CSS variables can be assigned only a valid CSS value and can be used only as the value of a property. For this reason, they're distinguished with the name *Cascading Variables*.

Each Cascading Variable is declared using a *custom property*: a user-defined property name beginning with var- to which a value is assigned. Here, the color value *#F00* is assigned to the custom property *var-foo*:

```
:root { var-foo: #F00; }
```

Notice that I've declared this custom property using the :root selector. (I explain why shortly.)

To use the value of the custom property, you call it using the var() function, with the user-defined name (the bit after var-) in parentheses. The value of the custom property is used as the value of the property it's called on. For example, in the following listing, the h1 element calls the *var-foo* property using the var(foo) function twice: once on the border-bottom property and once on color. The color value *#F00* will be applied appropriately to each property.

```
h1 {
  border-bottom: 1px solid var(foo);
  color: var(foo);
}
```

Cascading Variables are *scoped*, meaning they apply only to the element on which they are declared and to any child element. My use of the :root selector to declare a custom property in the example in this section means the variable has *global scope*: It can be applied on any element on the page. Had I used a different selector, the value of the variable declared in the custom property would apply only to children of the matching element(s).

For example, in the following code the custom property *var-foo*, with a value of *#F00*, is declared on the :root element, but I'll also add a different value and selector below it. In this case, the value of the variable would be *#F00* for the whole document, but it will now be *#00F* for the *.bar* element and its children.

```
:root { var-foo: #F00; }
.bar { var-foo: #00F; }
```

NOTE *In the longer term, the preprocessor favorite* mixins *will also be implemented in CSS. A mixin is like an extended variable, allowing blocks of code to be reused across multiple selectors. There's even been talk of implementing full variables, allowing replacement of property names and selectors.*

Summary

In this chapter, we've looked at some of the more experimental features of the web platform. These are all still in the testing phase and are liable to change, but they're so powerful and potentially important to the platform's future that I couldn't really finish this book without mentioning them.

First up was Web Components, the biggest change to HTML since its invention. Web Components is a suite of features. It makes a parallel DOM that allows reusable code blocks to enhance and extend the standard HTML elements with full encapsulation, protecting them from conflicts with other CSS rules and JavaScript functions.

Next we looked at the future of CSS, which is also undergoing huge changes thanks to the involvement of big tech companies. CSS Regions and Exclusions promise to provide the tools required to create dynamic custom layouts that rival (and exceed?) anything possible in print media.

Finally, I covered new CSS features that are being developed based on innovation from the web development community. These include feature queries that bring native Modernizr-like feature detection to CSS and Cascading Variables that begin the adoption of the best preprocessor features into the language itself.

Further Reading

Web Components are quite new as of this writing, so not many resources are around. The developer-friendly introduction written by the spec authors should be your first stop. Next might be Eric Bidelman's presentation. Both resources are helpful in learning the core concepts. You can find them at *http://dvcs.w3.org/hg/webcomponents/raw-file/tip/explainer/index.html* and *http://html5-demos.appspot.com/static/webcomponents/index.html* (you may need to use Google Chrome to view this correctly).

The Shadow DOM is the best-implemented piece of Web Components and, as such, has more online documentation. Both Sitepoint and HTML5 Rocks have clearly written explanations of the topic, which you'll find at *http://www.sitepoint.com/the-basics-of-the-shadow-dom/* and *http://www.html5rocks.com/en/tutorials/webcomponents/shadowdom/*.

If your browser doesn't support custom elements, consider X-Tags, an experimental library created by Mozilla that replicates the behavior of custom elements and has an extensive registry of prebuilt components: *http://x-tags.org/*.

Internet Explorer 10 was the first browser to implement CSS Regions, so their documentation is useful for covering the basics. See *http://msdn.microsoft.com/en-us/library/ie/hh673537%28v=vs.85%29.aspx/*.

CSS Exclusions are also in IE10, so their documentation should be the first point of call again. Once you've finished there, check out some of the demos from Adobe. See *http://msdn.microsoft.com/en-us/library/ie/hh673558%28v=vs.85%29.aspx/* and *http://adobe.github.com/web-platform/samples/css-exclusions/*.

MDN has the best documentation of feature queries, although the API is currently undocumented. See *https://developer.mozilla.org/en-US/docs/CSS/@supports/*.

As I write this, the only place to learn about Cascading Variables is in the draft specification at *http://dev.w3.org/csswg/css-variables/*.

If the Box Alignment proposal is still ongoing as you read this, you can follow its progress at *http://dev.w3.org/csswg/css3-align/* and find the Line Grid proposed spec at *http://dev.w3.org/csswg/css-line-grid/*.

Håkon Wium Lie and Chris Mills wrote a very nice introduction to CSS pagination in their article "Opera Reader: Paging the Web": *http://people.opera.com/howcome/2011/reader/index.html*. For more on Pagination Templates, see the *Adobe Web Platform* blog at *http://blogs.adobe.com/webplatform/2012/05/31/pagination-templates-in-css/*.

A

BROWSER SUPPORT AS OF MARCH 2013

 Documenting feature implementation in browsers means aiming at a moving target, so the best I can do is take a snapshot. When considering whether to use one of the features in this book, always check the following sites for the most up-to-date information:

- HTML5 Please, *http://html5please.com/*
- The CSS3 Test, *http://css3test.com/*
- The HTML5 Test, *http://html5test.com/*
- Can I Use…, *http://caniuse.com/*

When I started this book midway through 2012, I took a gamble on which features I thought would be best to cover, including not only those that had already been well implemented but also some that I thought stood a good chance of being implemented when the book went to print (or soon after). As I write this in early 2013, it seems that the pace of wider adoption has been slower than I anticipated for some of the features contained in Internet Explorer 10 (such as Grid Layout, Regions, and Exclusions), but everything else is proceeding apace.

The Browsers in Question

Far too many browsers exist for me to provide a decent overview of feature support on each. Instead, in this appendix, I'll stick to the key modern desktop browsers—Chrome, Firefox, Internet Explorer 10, and Safari— and their mobile equivalents, as I've done throughout this book.

As this book was going to press, Opera announced that it would be phasing out its own Presto rendering engine and that future versions of the browser would instead use Chromium, the branch of WebKit that Chrome is also based on. But that doesn't mean Presto will be going away in the short term—it's already embedded on many devices that don't tend to update, such as TVs and games consoles. In the long term, feature support should be considered the same as Chrome, but I've kept it distinct here for legacy support.

When discussing mobile browsers, I usually mean both smartphone and tablet and, more often than not, that means Safari mobile and the Android browser (although both are based on WebKit, there's quite a deal of variety between them). Firefox, Internet Explorer, and Opera use the same rendering engine across different platforms (although see the previous paragraph about Opera), so I'll only mention the mobile version of those browsers where any differences exist (which is not often).

When I refer to Android, I mean the stock browser that comes with most versions of the Android OS up to 4.2 (the most recent as I write this). Newer releases will likely include the new mobile version of Chrome, which, like Firefox and Opera, can be considered more or less equivalent to its desktop sibling.

As I've mentioned before, there really is no substitute for testing on actual devices. If possible, you should create a device library or join one in your area; if that's completely out of the question, ask other developers for their experiences.

Enabling Experimental Features

Many browsers, especially Chrome and Firefox, are being much more cautious than they used to be with regard to implementing experimental features. Where previously they would implement features with a vendor prefix and roll them out to all users, now they usually require that you explicitly enable certain features with a configuration flag.

In Firefox, you do this by entering **about:config** in the URL bar, at which point you'll see a message that warns you of the consequences of dabbling in the browser's inner workings. If this doesn't deter you, you can find the feature you want and enable it before restarting your browser in order to gain access to the now-enabled feature.

In Chrome, the process is much the same except that you enter `chrome://flags`, no warning message appears, and the features are usually enabled by toggling a link marked **Enable**.

Chapter 1: The Web Platform

Every major modern desktop browser comes with a set of developer tools that includes a console (only Internet Explorer 7 and below don't have one). The situation on mobile devices and tablets is a bit more complicated: Most browsers don't have developer tools by default, but they can be connected to their desktop equivalents for debugging, as explained in "Test and Test and Test Some More" on page 19.

Chapter 2: Structure and Semantics

The newer HTML5 structuring elements appear in Internet Explorer 9 and above and in all other major modern browsers. Discussion around some of these elements is still ongoing as I write this. Some browsers are beginning to support a `main` element despite opposition from spec editor Ian Hickson, whereas other elements such as `hgroup` are at risk of being dropped.

Using the attribute-based accessibility and semantic extensions WAI-ARIA, microformats, RDFa, and microdata in any browser is completely safe. The microdata API is implemented in Firefox and Opera.

Data attributes are also supported in all browsers, although the API using `dataset` is not present in Internet Explorer or Android 2.3 and below. The jQuery method works cross browser.

Chapter 3: Device-Responsive CSS

As I write this, media queries are available in Internet Explorer 9 and above and in all other major modern browsers. The media features related to device dimensions are the most widely implemented. The `resolution` media feature is in Internet Explorer 10, Firefox, and Opera and was implemented in the WebKit core at the end of 2012, so it's making its way into WebKit-based browsers.

The `dppx` unit should be in all modern browsers bar Internet Explorer by the time you read this, and `devicePixelRatio` is in WebKit browsers, Opera, and Firefox (including mobile versions).

The `@viewport` at-rule is in Opera, Internet Explorer 10, and WebKit, using the vendor prefix of each. The `matchMedia` API is in Internet Explorer 10 and all other modern browsers but not in Android 2.3 and below.

The CSS property `box-sizing` is in all browsers, although it requires a vendor prefix in Firefox and versions 3.0 and below of Android. Only Firefox supports the `padding-box` value. The `calc()` value function is in IE9 and above, Firefox, desktop WebKit browsers, and from version 6.0 of mobile Safari. It's not in Android or Opera and requires the `-webkit-` prefix in other mobile WebKit browsers.

The viewport-relative length units—vh, vw, etc.—are in IE9 (with a few bugs) and IE10, Firefox, and most WebKit browsers except Android, but not present in Opera. The rem unit is in IE9 and above and all other major browsers.

The object-fit and object-position properties are implemented in Opera only and marked as "at risk" in the spec, so face an uncertain future, especially now that Opera is moving to use WebKit.

Chapter 4: New Approaches to CSS Layouts

The multi-column layout properties are implemented in IE10 and all other modern browsers. The use of vendor prefixes is required in WebKit-based browsers and Firefox, and Firefox also lacks support for the column-span property. Only Opera and IE10 support the break-before and break-after properties.

Flexbox is supported in all major browsers and requires a vendor prefix in WebKit-based user agents. IOS6.1 and below use a hybrid of the current syntax and an older one: The justify-content property isn't implemented, and it instead has the old box-pack property. I hope this will no longer be the case when you read this appendix.

IE10 also uses an outdated syntax, fully vendor prefixed. I recommend you read the documentation in the "Internet Explorer 10 Guide for Developers" for detailed information: *http://msdn.microsoft.com/library/ie/hh673531%28v=vs.85%29.aspx/.*

Firefox supports only single-line Flexbox, so the flex-wrap property and flex-flow shorthand property are ignored.

As explained in Chapter 4, IE10 is the only browser to support Grid Layout, using an older version of the syntax with the -ms- prefix. Work is underway on implementing this in WebKit, which should use the spec-compliant syntax. The grid-template property is not currently implemented in any browser.

Chapter 5: Modern JavaScript

The async attribute is in IE10 and most other browsers other than Android versions 2.3 and below and Opera. The defer attribute is the same but also has support at least back to IE8.

The addEventListener() method is in IE9 and above and all other major browsers, as is the DOMContentLoaded event.

Despite the uncertainty around existing patents, touch events are in Chrome, Firefox, Safari for iOS, and Android. IE10 has support for pointer events, such as MSPointerDown, which are vendor prefixed.

The querySelector() and querySelectorAll() methods are fully implemented in all modern browsers, from IE8 and higher. The getElementsByClassName() method is almost as well implemented, lacking support only in IE8. The classList object is in IE10 and above, and most other browsers except for Android version 2.3 and below.

Chapter 6: Device APIs

The Geolocation API is in IE9 and all other major browsers. Device orientation is present in mobile WebKit browsers, Chrome, and Firefox mobile. Do bear in mind, however, that device APIs depend on certain functions being available on the phone; just because the Device Orientation API is implemented in a browser, it doesn't necessarily follow that the device has an accelerometer.

Opera has implemented the Full Screen API, as have desktop WebKit browsers, Chrome for Android, and Firefox. The WebKit and Firefox implementations have some subtle differences, but rather than trying to explain those here, I'll refer you to the MDN article "Using Fullscreen Mode" at *https://developer.mozilla.org/docs/DOM/Using_fullscreen_mode/*. Firefox and WebKit browsers support the `:-moz-full-screen` and `:-webkit-full-screen` pseudo-classes, respectively.

The Vibration, Battery Status, and Network Information APIs are available in Firefox mobile only. Despite support for each apparently landing in WebKit throughout 2012, I can't find any working implementations.

The `getUserMedia()` method is implemented in Opera, and in Firefox and Chrome with vendor prefixes (`mozGetUserMedia`, `webkitGetUserMedia`). Firefox currently requires that you opt in to use `getUserMedia()` with the **media.navigator.enabled** flag because of its experimental nature.

Web Storage is in IE8 and above and all other major browsers.

The Drag and Drop API is partially supported in IE8 and IE9, and fully implemented in IE10 and other major desktop browsers. Owing to its nature, it isn't supported in mobile browsers.

The File API is fully implemented in Firefox, Chrome, Safari (iOS and desktop), and Opera, and partially supported in IE10 and Android. The FileReader API is fully implemented in IE10 and all other desktop browsers, plus WebKit mobile browsers including Android from version 3.0.

Chapter 7: Images and Graphics

Some form of SVG support is present in IE9 and above, Android 3.0 and above, and all other major browsers. SVG filters are slightly more limited, being unavailable in IE9 and Android, although using SVG filters on HTML elements works reliably only in Firefox. The new CSS `filter()` function is currently implemented in nightly Chrome builds, but it is disabled by default. The use of fragment identifiers in SVG is possible only in IE10 and Firefox.

Support for the canvas element is in IE9 and above and all other major browsers. Firefox, Chrome, Safari (desktop), and Opera all have implementations of WebGL, although it's disabled by default in some browsers, notably Safari and Chrome for Android.

Chapter 8: New Forms

Levels of support for the various form elements, especially those with on-screen controls, vary wildly among browsers and are changing all the time.

Rather than try to capture that here, I'll refer you to the HTML5 Test, which has the most comprehensive and up-to-date coverage. Using the new `input` types is generally considered safe, as the browser will fall back to the `text` type if a different value is not recognized.

The Constraint Validation API is present in IE10 and all other major browsers. Safari supports the API but has no on-screen error notifications.

Chapter 9: Multimedia

The `video` and `audio` elements, along with their related APIs, are in IE9 and above and all other major browsers, although with the caveat about supported file types discussed in Chapter 9. The `track` element is supported in the desktop versions of IE10, Safari 6 and above, Chrome, and Opera; Chrome for Android is the only mobile browser to offer support. Media Fragments are implemented in Firefox and WebKit browsers.

The Web Audio API is experimentally implemented in Chrome and Safari (iOS and desktop) using the `webkitAudioContext()` constructor. Of WebRTC, only the `getUserMedia()` method is currently supported, which was mentioned in Chapter 6.

Chapter 10: Web Apps

Support for AppCache is present in IE10 and all other major browsers.

Chapter 11: The Future

Chrome is the only browser to have any support for the new Web Components features; it has implemented the Shadow DOM (with the vendor-prefixed `webkitShadowRoot()` constructor) and templates. Both must be explicitly enabled. Work on custom elements is underway.

As far as I know, no other browser vendors have committed to implementing Web Components yet, although I understand that Firefox will in the future. Firefox already has support for scoped styles, as does Chrome.

CSS Regions are implemented in IE10 and Chrome, although, once again, the latter currently requires that you enable it using a flag. Both require vendor prefixes on the properties, and IE10 allows only content inside an `iframe` as the source.

Exclusions are available exclusively in IE10, using the `-ms-` prefix.

The feature queries `@supports` at-rule is available in Firefox and Opera, and Firefox also recognizes the `CSS.supports()` method. Work is underway to bring them to WebKit browsers and may already be in place as you read this.

Cascading Variables are implemented in Chrome only and must be explicitly enabled.

B

FURTHER READING

This appendix is simply a collection of all of the links contained in the "Further Reading" section of each chapter, brought together in one place for your convenience. My plan is to host this list on the companion website, *http://modernwebbook.com/*, and update it with new and interesting links as I find them (and perhaps prune out-of-date ones).

Introduction

Statistics used in this chapter were taken from many sources, notably Vision Mobile's "The Mobile Industry in Numbers" at *http://www.visionmobile.com/blog/2012/10/infographic-the-mobile-industry-in-numbers/* and Cisco's "The Internet of Things" at *http://blogs.cisco.com/news/the-internet-of-things-infographic/*.

You can find a good primer on the IoT in The Next Web's article "Why 2013 Will Be the Year of the Internet of Things": *http://thenextweb .com/insider/2012/12/09/the-future-of-the-internet-of-things/*.

David Storey wrote a great post about the non-smartphone mobile web, "See your site like the rest of the world does. On the Nokia X2-01," at *http:// generatedcontent.org/post/31441135779/mobileweb-row/*.

The best article I've read on designing for mobile devices, and from which I quote in this chapter, is Jonathan Stark's "The 10 Principles of Mobile Interface Design": *http://www.netmagazine.com/features/ 10-principles-mobile-interface-design/*. Jason Grigsby's excellent article "Responsive Design for Apps" is a good primer for designing for multiple screen dimensions and capabilities: *http://blog.cloudfour.com/ responsive-design-for-apps-part-1/*.

UX Magazine's article by Brennen Brown, "Five Lessons from a Year of Tablet UX Research," has some great findings on how people use tablets: *http://uxmag.com/articles/five-lessons-from-a-year-of-tablet-ux-research/*.

A good starting point for Anna Debenham's research on games console browsers is an *A List Apart* article "Testing Websites in Game Console Browsers": *http://www.alistapart.com/articles/testing-websites-in-game-con sole-browsers/*.

Jason Grigsby (again) gave an excellent talk, "The Immobile Web," on developing for TV. The video is at *http://vimeo.com/44444464/*, and the accompanying slides are at *http://www.slideshare.net/grigs/the-immobile-web/*.

For the full research on multi-device usage, see Google's blog post "Navigating the New Multi-screen World" at *http://googlemobileads.blogspot .co.uk/2012/08/navigating-new-multi-screen-world.html*.

Making your websites Future Friendly is always good: See *http:// futurefriend.ly/*.

Chapter 1: The Web Platform

In case you missed it, the list of technologies that make the web platform is at *http://platform.html5.org/*. Bruce Lawson proposed NEWT on his blog: *http://www.brucelawson.co.uk/2010/meet-newt-new-exciting-web-technologies/*.

The W3C's HTML5 spec is at *http://www.w3.org/TR/html5/*, and the WHATWG's living spec is at *http://whatwg.org/html*. More usefully, they also have an *Edition for Web Developers*, which leaves out some of the more arcane language and is, therefore, more readable: *http://developers.whatwg.org/*.

The complete HTML5 Boilerplate is at *http://html5boilerplate.com/*. Remember, just use the bits you need; don't copy the whole thing verbatim.

For finding out about feature implementation levels, I recommend Alexis Deveria's site Can I Use... at *http://caniuse.com/*, the community site HTML5 Please at *http://html5please.com/*, and The HTML5 Test at *http:// html5test.com/*.

The LabUp! website is a resource for finding or getting involved with open device testing labs: *http://lab-up.org/*. The chief tester at the BBC, David Blooman, wrote a long and detailed article, "Testing for Dummies," about how a global organization performs multi-device testing: *http://mobiletestingfordummies.tumblr.com/post/20056227958/testing*.

Patrick Meenan's slides for his talk "Taming the Mobile Beast" contain a wealth of links and information on testing mobile devices: *http://www.slideshare.net/patrickmeenan/velocity-2012-taming-the-mobile-beast/*, and Anna Debenham's article for *A List Apart*, "Testing Websites in Game Console Browsers," is about . . . well, the title's quite self-explanatory: *http://www.alistapart.com/articles/testing-websites-in-game-console-browsers/*.

Opera has written detailed instructions about remote debugging at *http://www.opera.com/dragonfly/documentation/remote/*. weinre is available to download from *http://people.apache.org/~pmuellr/weinre/docs/latest/*. You can get more information on Adobe Edge Inspect at *http://html.adobe.com/edge/inspect/*.

Chapter 2: Structure and Semantics

HTML5 Doctor is the best source information for most HTML5 topics, including the clearest definition of the new outline algorithm I've read so far, in this article by Mike Robinson: *http://html5doctor.com/outlines/*. You can download the element flowchart shown in Figure 2-1 from *http://html5doctor.com/resources/#flowchart/*. See also Derek Johnson's article in *Smashing Magazine*: *http://coding.smashingmagazine.com/2011/08/16/html5-and-the-document-outlining-algorithm/*.

For much more detail on the HTML5 structural elements problem, I strongly suggest you read Luke Stevens's book *The Truth About HTML5*; find it at *http://www.truthabouthtml5.com/*. If you want to read the full HTML5 specification and make up your own mind, I advise going for the developer's version at *http://developers.whatwg.org/sections.html*.

Read the full WAI-ARIA specification at *http://www.w3.org/TR/wai-aria/*. The *Paciello Group Blog* is worth reading for information about accessibility in HTML5, and this post on landmark roles is directly relevant: *http://www.paciellogroup.com/blog/2010/10/using-wai-aria-landmark-roles/*.

Divya Manian's article on semantics was published by *Smashing Magazine* at *http://coding.smashingmagazine.com/2011/11/11/our-pointless-pursuit-of-semantic-value/*. For more on aboutness and the importance of semantics, I highly recommend the book *Ambient Findability: What We Find Changes Who We Become* by Peter Morville (O'Reilly, 2005). The website *http://webdatacommons.org/* provides information and statistics about sites that use structured data.

Read all about microformats at *http://microformats.org/*. A revision of the syntax, microformats 2.0, was started in 2010 and is still underway; learn more about that at *http://microformats.org/wiki/microformats-2*.

If you want to learn more about the RDFa format, the W3C published an excellent primer: *http://www.w3.org/TR/xhtml-rdfa-primer/*.

The best resource for learning about microdata comes from the HTML5 Doctor again: *http://html5doctor.com/microdata/*. If you're feeling masochistic and prefer to read the spec in detail, you'll find it at *http://www.w3.org/TR/microdata/*.

You can get more information on Schema.org at—wait for it!—*http://schema.org/*, and Google's documentation of rich snippets is at *http://support.google.com/webmasters/bin/answer.py?hl=en&answer=99170*. You'll find the testing tool at *http://www.google.com/webmasters/tools/richsnippets/*.

John Resig wrote a concise introduction to data attributes on his blog, *http://ejohn.org/blog/html-5-data-attributes/*, and the `data()` method is fully documented on the jQuery website at *http://api.jquery.com/data/*.

Chapter 3: Device-Responsive CSS

First port of call for learning more about media queries should be Zoe Mickley Gillenwater's post "Essential Considerations for Crafting Quality Media Queries": *http://zomigi.com/blog/essential-considerations-for-crafting-quality-media-queries/*.

The authority on mobile devices is PPK, and if you want to find out more about physical and virtual pixels, I suggest you start with his article "A Pixel Is Not a Pixel Is Not a Pixel": *http://www.quirksmode.org/blog/archives/2010/04/a_pixel_is_not.html*. Wikipedia has a list of common device resolutions and pixel density: *http://en.wikipedia.org/wiki/List_of_displays_by_pixel_density*.

Patrick Lauke wrote an article about user-controlled DPR, "devicePixelRatio in Opera Mobile": *http://my.opera.com/ODIN/blog/2012/07/05/devicepixelratio-in-opera-mobile*. Matt Wilcox's article "The Responsive Design Process" has a good glossary of key terms as well as plenty of practical advice on the design side: *http://mattwilcox.net/archive/entry/id/1078/*.

Read more about the way that different browsers round decimal places in John Albin Wilkins's post "Responsive Design's Dirty Little Secret": *http://www.palantir.net/blog/responsive-design-s-dirty-little-secret/*.

Paul Irish's blog post "box-sizing: border-box FTW" sets out his reasons for applying this property globally: *http://paulirish.com/2012/box-sizing-border-box-ftw/*.

Luke Wroblewski's book *Mobile First* is published by A Book Apart: *http://www.abookapart.com/products/mobile-first/*.

To learn more about content breakpoints, read a pair of articles from Australian web design studio Jordesign (*http://www.jordesign.com/blog/responsive-breakpoints-from-the-content-out/*) and developer Thierry Koblentz (*http://coding.smashingmagazine.com/2012/03/22/device-agnostic-approach-to-responsive-web-design/*).

The history of the current favorite responsive images proposal, and latest news on the state of its adoption, can be found on the website of the Responsive Images Community Group: *http://www.w3.org/community/respimg/*.

Find Matt Wilcox's Adaptive Images tool at *http://adaptive-images.com/*.

Chapter 4: New Approaches to CSS Layouts

The ever-dependable MozDev has a really clear introduction to multiple columns, "Using CSS multi-column layouts," at *https://developer.mozilla.org/en-US/docs/CSS/Using_CSS_multi-column_layouts/*.

The Flexbox syntax has changed so often that almost every current online resource is out-of-date! That said, I recommend Stephen Hay's article "Learn You a Flexbox for Great Good!" at *http://www.the-haystack.com/2012/01/04/learn-you-a-flexbox/*, even though it refers to an outdated syntax, as Stephen's knowledge of CSS layouts is second to none.

The best explanation of the Grid Layout module, at least in regard to the IE10 implementation, is contained in the "Internet Explorer 10 Guide for Developers": *http://msdn.microsoft.com/en-us/library/ie/hh673533%28v=vs.85%29.aspx/*.

Read Mark Boulton's open letter on the subject of grid terminology at *http://www.markboulton.co.uk/journal/comments/open-letter-to-w3c-css-working-group-re-css-grids*.

Chapter 5: Modern JavaScript

The illustration in Figure 5-1 is adapted from Peter Beverloo's blog: *http://peter.sh/experiments/asynchronous-and-deferred-javascript-execution-explained/*.

Christian Heilmann wrote an in-depth introduction to JavaScript events for *Smashing Magazine*: *http://coding.smashingmagazine.com/2012/08/17/javascript-events-responding-user/*. The PointerEvents library is hosted on GitHub at *https://github.com/toolkitchen/PointerEvents/*.

The jQuery website, *http://jquery.com/*, has instructions for getting started, while the excellent documentation is at *http://docs.jquery.com/Main_Page*. Statistics about jQuery usage are from the blog post "jQuery Now Runs on Every Second Website" at *http://w3techs.com/blog/entry/jquery_now_runs_on_every_second_website/*.

All mobile libraries are fully documented: jQuery Mobile at *http://jquerymobile.com/*, Zepto.js at *http://zeptojs.com/*, and jQTouch at *http://jqtouch.com/*.

YepNope.js is available from *http://yepnopejs.com/*, and you'll find a good introductory tutorial at *http://net.tutsplus.com/tutorials/javascript-ajax/easy-script-loading-with-yepnope-js/*.

Modernizr's website, *http://modernizr.com/*, has full documentation plus a configurable build system and also plays host to "The All-In-One Entirely-Not-Alphabetical No-Bullshit Guide to HTML5 Fallbacks" (their title, not mine) at *https://github.com/Modernizr/Modernizr/wiki/HTML5-Cross-browser-Polyfills/*.

Christopher Coenraets wrote an excellent introductory tutorial to Mustache, although bear in mind that the syntax has changed a little: *http://coenraets.org/blog/2011/12/tutorial-html-templates-with-mustache-js/*. The full documentation of Mustache.js is at *https://github.com/janl/mustache.js/*.

Many different experimenting and debugging tools are available, and both *http://jsbin.com/* and *http://jsfiddle.net/* are excellent.

Chapter 6: Device APIs

Dive Into HTML5 has an in-depth explanation of the Geolocation API at *http://diveintohtml5.info/geolocation.html*, whereas the MozDev article "Orientation and Motion Data Explained" gives a good overview of three-dimensional orientation and movement: *https://developer.mozilla.org/en-US/docs/DOM/Orientation_and_motion_data_explained/*.

The Fullscreen API is explained in the Sitepoint article "How to Use the HTML5 Full-Screen API" by Craig Buckler, although the API changed slightly as I was writing this, so some object names or properties may have been updated. You can find the article at *http://www.sitepoint.com/html5-full-screen-api/*.

The Battery Status API is well explained by David Walsh at *http://davidwalsh.name/battery-api/*, and a discussion of the previous and newly updated Network Information API is at *http://nostrongbeliefs.com/a-quick-look-network-information-api/*.

HTML5 Rocks gives the best explanation of getUserMedia() in their article "Capturing Audio & Video in HTML5": *http://www.html5rocks.com/en/tutorials/getusermedia/intro/*. The full aims of the WebRTC project are listed at *http://www.webrtc.org/*.

MozDev (again) gives a concise introduction to the Web Storage API: *https://developer.mozilla.org/en-US/docs/DOM/Storage/*.

The most accessible guide to the Drag and Drop API that I found was written by the HTML5 Doctors at *http://html5doctor.com/native-drag-and-drop/*, while the five-part "Working with Files in JavaScript" by Nicholas Zakas is an excellent resource for the File API: *http://www.nczonline.net/blog/2012/05/08/working-with-files-in-javascript-part-1/*.

The APIs that form the Firefox OS project are listed at *https://wiki.mozilla.org/WebAPI/*, and the slides from the presentation "WebAPIs and Apps" by Robert Nyman provide a great overview of the APIs: *http://www.slideshare.net/robnyman/web-apis-apps-mozilla-london/*. "Are We Mobile Yet?" gives an at-a-glance guide to levels of API implementation: *http://arewemobileyet.com/*.

Chapter 7: Images and Graphics

You can find a great introduction to SVG at the SVG Basics website: *http://www.svgbasics.com/*, and the W3C's own SVG Primer is a useful way to dig deeper: *http://www.w3.org/Graphics/SVG/IG/resources/svgprimer.html*. MDN has a quite complete list of elements and attributes: *https://developer.mozilla.org/en-US/docs/SVG/*.

The technique for stacking SVG icons was developed by Erik Dahlström and is described on the blog of Simurai: *http://simurai.com/post/20251013889/svg-stacks/*. Mozilla's Robert O'Callahan warns of the possible changes to the stacking technique: *http://robert.ocallahan.org/2012/10/impending-doom-for-svg-stacks-sort-of.html*. I detailed the svgView() method on my blog, *Broken Links*: *http://www.broken-links.com/2012/08/14/better-svg-sprites-with-fragment-identifiers/*.

The IE Testdrive site has a good hands-on tool for experimenting with SVG Filter Effects: *http://ie.microsoft.com/testdrive/graphics/hands-on-css3/hands-on_svg-filter-effects.htm*.

Dirk Schulze wrote a good, concise introduction to the features planned for SVG2: *http://dschulze.com/blog/articles/8/new-features-in-svg2/*.

You can find a good range of canvas tutorials, from beginner to expert level, at *http://www.html5canvastutorials.com/*, and an excellent cheat sheet with all of the core properties and methods on Jacob Seidelin's blog at *http://blog.nihilogic.dk/2009/02/html5-canvas-cheat-sheet.html* (last updated in 2009 but still relevant).

HTML5 Rocks has a tutorial on making more advanced image manipulation effects at *http://www.html5rocks.com/en/tutorials/canvas/imagefilters/*.

In his blog post "Building a Live Green Screen with getUserMedia() and MediaStreams," Tim Taubert explains the basics of live video image manipulalation: *http://timtaubert.de/blog/2012/10/building-a-live-green-screen-with-getusermedia-and-mediastreams/*.

The *Learning WebGL* blog has lessons for complete beginners on working in a three-dimensional context in canvas at *http://learningwebgl.com/lessons/*, and WebGL.com has frequent roundups of demos, tutorials, and developer meet-ups: *http://www.webgl.com/*.

Chapter 8: New Forms

The ever-helpful MDN provides a concise and complete guide to the new input types at *https://developer.mozilla.org/en-US/docs/HTML/Element/Input/*. PPK has detailed tables showing support on the desktop at *http://www.quirksmode.org/html5/inputs.html* and for mobile devices at *http://www.quirksmode.org/html5/inputs_mobile.html*.

Ryan Seddon wrote a polyfill for providing HTML5 form capabilities to browsers that don't support them natively: Find it at *https://github.com/ryanseddon/H5F/*.

Bruce Lawson's discussion of autofocus accessibility, "The Accessibility of HTML 5 Autofocus," is on his blog at *http://www.brucelawson.co.uk/2009/the-accessibility-of-html-5-autofocus/*.

HTML5 Rocks has a good overview of the Constraint Validation API at *http://www.html5rocks.com/en/tutorials/forms/constraintvalidation/*.

A useful application for testing regular expressions is Rubular. Don't worry that it's aimed at Ruby; it works just as well for JavaScript and HTML5 forms: *http://rubular.com/*.

And your humble author wrote an introduction to CSS3 pseudo-classes for HTML5 forms at HTML5 Doctor: *http://html5doctor.com/css3-pseudo-classes-and-html5-forms/*.

Chapter 9: Multimedia

The full text of Steve Jobs's "Thoughts on Flash" is at *http://www.apple.com/hotnews/thoughts-on-flash/*.

Advice on audio and video accessibility around autoplaying is on the WCAG Audio Control page at *http://www.w3.org/TR/UNDERSTANDING-WCAG20/visual-audio-contrast-dis-audio.html*.

MDN has tables showing the current state of media format implementation across different browsers at *https://developer.mozilla.org/en-US/docs/Media_formats_supported_by_the_audio_and_video_elements/*, and Kroc Camen's technique and notes for cross-browser implementation, "Video for Everybody!", is at *http://camendesign.co.uk/code/video_for_everybody/*.

The best introduction to WebVTT and the track element is on Dev .Opera, *http://dev.opera.com/articles/view/an-introduction-to-webvtt-and-track/*, and a useful WebVTT validation tool is on Anne van Kesteren's website, *http://quuz.org/webvtt/*.

I mentioned three encoding tools in this chapter: The FFmpeg command-line tool is at *http://ffmpeg.org/*, Miro Video Converter at *http://www.mirovideoconverter.com/*, and HandBrake at *http://handbrake.fr/*.

The W3C's Media Fragments specification is at *http://www.w3.org/TR/media-frags/*.

MDN has the best documentation of the Media API and Events that I've found at *https://developer.mozilla.org/en-US/docs/DOM/HTMLMediaElement/* and *https://developer.mozilla.org/en-US/docs/DOM/Media_events/*, respectively.

CreativeJS has a great introductory article on the Web Audio API at *http://creativejs.com/resources/web-audio-api-getting-started/*.

You can expect to hear a lot more about WebRTC in the future, but Sam Dutton wrote a good introduction at HTML5 Rocks: *http://www.html5rocks.com/en/tutorials/webrtc/basics/*. Microsoft's introduction to the CU-RTC-Web proposal is on the Interoperability blog at *http://blogs.msdn.com/b/interoperability/archive/2012/07/28/customizable-ubiquitous-real-time-communication-over-the-web-cu-rtc-web.aspx*.

Chapter 10: Web Apps

The Chrome Web Store has in-depth documentation on preparing an app for submission, including details about the manifest file, at *https://developers .google.com/chrome/web-store/docs/get_started_simple/*.

Firefox Marketplace provides details about the manifest file at *https:// developer.mozilla.org/docs/Apps/Manifest/*, and it has a useful manifest validation tool at *https://marketplace.firefox.com/developers/validator/*. Robert Nyman's talk "Web APIs and Apps" is a great primer for building apps for the Firefox Marketplace: *http://www.slideshare.net/robnyman/web-apis-apps-mozilla-london/*.

The latest version of the W3C widgets specification is at *http://w3.org/TR/ widgets/*, and you'll find a useful introduction on Peter-Paul Koch's site— even though it was written a few years ago, and some small details of the spec have changed since then: *http://quirksmode.org/blog/archives/2009/04/ introduction_to.html*.

The PhoneGap project is at *http://phonegap.com/*, and the API documentation is at *http://docs.phonegap.com/*. You can read the PhoneGap article "Beliefs, Goals, and Philosophy" at *http://phonegap.com/2012/05/ 09/phonegap-beliefs-goals-and-philosophy/*.

You can read more about the Titanium project at *http://appcelerator.com/ platform/*.

Each smart TV platform has its own developer forum, but a good example for getting started is Samsung's site at *http://www.samsungdforum.com/*.

The Opera TV Store is gaining some traction as a custom-made solution; learn more about it at *http://business.opera.com/partners/tv/store/*. The Dev.Opera site has some great reference articles on designing and developing for TV at *http://dev.opera.com/tv/*.

The Webinos project, which aims to create a standard common device API, is hosted at *http://www.webinos.org/*.

The Mozilla Developer Center has great AppCache documentation at *https://developer.mozilla.org/en-US/docs/HTML/Using_the_application _cache/*, and Mark Christian and Peter Lubbers created a handy page of AppCache facts at *http://appcachefacts.info/*. For all of AppCache's drawbacks and tips and techniques for using it, read Jake Archibald's "Application Cache is a Douchebag" at *A List Apart*: *http://www.alistapart.com/ articles/application-cache-is-a-douchebag/*.

Chapter 11: The Future

Web Components are quite new as of this writing, so not many resources are around. The developer-friendly introduction written by the spec authors should be your first stop. Next might be Eric Bidelman's presentation. Both resources are helpful in learning the core concepts. You can find them at *http://dvcs.w3.org/hg/webcomponents/raw-file/tip/explainer/index.html* and *http:// html5-demos.appspot.com/static/webcomponents/index.html* (you may need to use Google Chrome to view this correctly).

The Shadow DOM is the best-implemented piece of Web Components and, as such, has more online documentation. Both Sitepoint and HTML5 Rocks have clearly written explanations of the topic, which you'll find at *http://www.sitepoint.com/the-basics-of-the-shadow-dom/* and *http://www.html5rocks.com/en/tutorials/webcomponents/shadowdom/*.

If your browser doesn't support custom elements, consider X-Tags, an experimental library created by Mozilla that replicates the behavior of custom elements and has an extensive registry of prebuilt components: *http://x-tags.org/*.

Internet Explorer 10 was the first browser to implement CSS Regions, so their documentation is useful for covering the basics. See *http://msdn.microsoft.com/en-us/library/ie/hh673537%28v=vs.85%29.aspx/*.

CSS Exclusions are also in IE10, so their documentation should be the first point of call again. Once you've finished there, check out some of the demos from Adobe. See *http://msdn.microsoft.com/en-us/library/ie/hh673558%28v=vs.85%29.aspx/* and *http://adobe.github.com/web-platform/samples/css-exclusions/*.

MDN has the best documentation of feature queries, although the API is currently undocumented. See *https://developer.mozilla.org/en-US/docs/CSS/@supports/*.

As I write this, the only place to learn about Cascading Variables is in the draft specification at *http://dev.w3.org/csswg/css-variables/*.

If the Box Alignment proposal is still ongoing as you read this, you can follow its progress at *http://dev.w3.org/csswg/css3-align/* and find the Line Grid proposed spec at *http://dev.w3.org/csswg/css-line-grid/*.

Håkon Wium Lie and Chris Mills wrote a very nice introduction to CSS pagination in their article "Opera Reader: Paging the Web": *http://people.opera.com/howcome/2011/reader/index.html*. For more on Pagination Templates, see the *Adobe Web Platform* blog at *http://blogs.adobe.com/webplatform/2012/05/31/pagination-templates-in-css/*.

INDEX

audio format, variation in browser
support, 166
audio() method, 173
AudioContext() method, 174
auto value
for column-fill property, 67
for height property, 60
for preload attribute, 163
autocomplete attribute for form, 145
autofocus attribute for form, 144
autoplay attribute, for media
elements, 163
avoid-column value, for break-before
property, 69
axes
in Flexbox, 73
in Orientation API, 110

B

B2B (business-to-business) sites, 2
balance value, for column-fill property, 67
bandwidth attribute, of connection
object, 115
banner role, 27
baseline value, for align-items
property, 74
Battery Status API, 114–115
information sources, 124, 222
battery, vibrating impact on, 113
beta property, for orientation, 111
Beverloo, Peter, 106, 221
Bidelman, Eric, 209, 225
bitmap images, 46
vs. vector graphics, 126
Blackberry, 19
blockquote element, 24
Blooman, Patrick, 20, 219
Blueprint.css file, 18
Boolean attributes, 16
Bootstrap framework, 18
border-box value, for box-sizing
property, 54
both keyword, for wrap-flow property, 203
bottom value, for object-position
property, 61
Boulton, Mark, 85, 87, 221
Box Alignment module, information
sources, 210, 226
box-sizing property, 54–55, 207
break-after property, 68–69
break-before property, 68–69

break-inside property, 68–69
breakpoints, 53
content, 57–59, 64, 220
breaks for columns, 68–70
broadband connections, 8
Brown, Brennen, 10, 218
browsers, 12
alert on size, 52
default behavior, 90
desktop, 3
developer tools in, 12
experimental features, enabling,
212–213
implementation of client-side
validation, 154
rendering modes, 14–15
support, 18–19, 211–216
"business card" syntax, 29
business-to-business (B2B) sites, 2

C

caching sequence, 186–187
calc() function, 55–56
Camen, Kroc, 167, 175, 224
camera, 116–117
accessing data stream from, 175
canvas
information sources, 140, 223
vs. SVG files, 138–139
canvas element, 125, 135–138
captions, for media files, 167–168
cascading variables, 200, 208–209,
210, 226
CDATA section in SVG file, 129
center value
for align-items property, 74
for grid alignment properties, 83
for justify-content property, 73
for object-position property, 61
chaining methods in jQuery, 99
change event handler, in Network
Information API, 116
charging attribute, of navigator.battery
object, 114
chargingchange event, in Battery Status
API, 115
chargingTime attribute, of navigator.battery
object, 114
chargingtimechange event, in Battery
Status API, 115
charset attribute, for meta tag, 15
checkValidity() method, 156

M

main axis, in Flexbox, 73
main role, 27
Manian, Divya, 28, 38, 219
manifest attribute, of html element, 185
manifest files
 information sources, 188, 225
 for web apps, 179–181
manifest.webapp file, 180
master entries, 186
matchMedia() method, 52
max attribute
 for date or time, 149
 for meter element, 152
 for number input type, 148
max- prefix, for media features, 42–43
maximum keyword, for wrap-flow
 property, 203
max-width property, 60
MDN (Mozilla Developer Network)
 on feature queries, 210
 on forms, 160
 on Full Screen API, 215
 on Media API and Events, 176
 on media formats, 175
measurement unit
 fraction unit (fr), 79–80
 for viewport dimensions, 41
media. *See* multimedia
Media API, 169–173
media attribute, of source element,
 63, 165
media elements, fallbacks, 165–167
media events, 173–174
media features, 40
 device adaptation, 48–50
 dimensions as basis, 41–44
 input mechanism, 50–51
 max- and min- prefixes for, 42–43
 -webkit-device-pixel-ratio, 47
Media Fragments URI, 168–169
media queries, 17, 40–51
 browser support, 213
 combining and negating, 44–45
 comma-separated list of, 48
 information sources, 63, 220
 in JavaScript, 51–53
 in mobile-first methodology, 58
 resolution query, 47
 for screen resolution, 46–48
Media Queries Level 4 spec, script
 feature, 51

media stream, element for display, 116
MediaQueryList object, 52
MediaStream API, 175
Meenan, Patrick, 20, 219
meta tag, 15
metadata, in Dublin Core, 127
metadata value, for preload attribute, 163
meter element, 114, 152–153
metered attribute, of connection
 object, 115
microdata, 31–34
 information sources, 38, 220
 rich snippets, 34
 Schema.org, 33–34
Microdata API, 32
microformats, 29–30
 information sources, 38, 219
microphone, 116–117
 access to data stream from, 175
Microsoft, 1
 and MP4 format, 166
 Surface, 6
milestones, in JS Bin, 105
Mills, Chris, 210, 226
MIME type, 165
min attribute
 for date or time, 149
 for meter element, 152
 for number input type, 148
min- prefix, for media features, 42–43
minimum keyword, for wrap-flow
 property, 203
Miro Video Converter, 168
mixins, 209
mobile devices, 3–4
 information sources, 63–64, 220
 media playback on, 163
mobile first methodology, 57–59
Mobile First (Wroblewski), 58, 64, 220
mobile libraries, information sources,
 106, 221
Modernizr, 101–102, 200
 information sources, 106, 222
Modernizr.load() method, 101
modules, in CSS, 17
monochrome query, for ebook reader, 51
month, for date input, 149
Morville, Peter, *Ambient Findability*,
 38, 219
MouseEvent interface, 96
MozDev, 124, 222
 on columns, 87, 221
Mozilla Developer Center, 189, 225

Sitepoint, 210, 226
sites. *See* websites
smart TVs
information sources, 189, 225
Internet-connected, 184
smartphones, 3–4
PPI count, 45
use stereotypes, 8
snapshots, in JS Bin, 105
soft keyboard, for form input, 143
software development kits (SDK), 19
Souder, Steve, 40
source element, 62, 64, 220
SourceGraphic keyword, 132
space-around value, for justify-content
property, 73
space-between value, for justify-content
property, 73
spans for columns, 68–70
speed, 8–9
spellcheck attribute for form, 145
sprites for icons, 129
square bracket ([ ]) notation, for
storing item, 117
src attribute, of track element, 167
srclang attribute, of track element, 167
srcset attribute, 62, 63
stacking, in grid layout, 83–84
standalone attribute, in XML
declaration, 127
standards mode, 15
Stark, Jonathan, 4, 10, 218
start keyword
for grid alignment properties, 83
for wrap-flow property, 203–204
statistics, information sources, 10, 217
status property, of window.applicationCache
object, 187
stdDeviation attribute, for feGaussianBlur
element, 132
step attribute, for date or time, 149
stepDown() method
for date or time, 150
for number input type, 148
stepUp() method
for date or time, 150
for number input type, 148
stereotypes, context, 8
Stevens, Luke, *The Truth About HTML 5*,
25, 38, 219
storage event, 118
Storey, David, 10, 218

stretch value
for align-items property, 74
for grid alignment properties, 83
stroke() method, 136
structure
browser support, 213
importance of, 21
structured data, 29
style tag, declaring type for, 15–16
styles, scoped, 195–196
stylesheets
media queries to apply to
viewport, 58
use of external based on media, 40
subsequent screening, 7
subtitles, for media files, 167–168
@supports at-rule, 102, 207
svg element, 127
SVG (Scalable Vector Graphics)
files, 125
vs. canvas, 138–139
convergence with CSS, 134–135
drawback, 135
embedded, 130–132
filters, 132–134
information sources,
139–140, 223
linked files, 128–130
format, 125, 126–135
anatomy of image, 127–128
linked files, 128–130
sprites, 129–130
SVG2, 134
swapCache() method, of window
.applicationCache object, 187
sympathetic keyboard layout, 143

T

tablets, 5, 50
tags, lowercase or uppercase
characters for, 16
:target pseudo-class, 130
Taubert, Tim, 138, 140, 223
tel input type, for forms, 143
template element, 193
templates
client-side system, 102
for grid, 85–86
and scoped styles, 196
for script tags, 104
for web components, 192–194

X

x-axis, 110
    rotation around, 111
XML file
    manifest file as, 179
    SVG file format as, 127
    Widget manifest file as, 181
X-Tags, 210, 226

Y

y-axis, 110
    rotation around, 111
YepNope, 100–101
    information sources, 106, 221
    properties used in Modernizr, 102

Z

z-axis, 110
    rotation around, 111
z-index property, 84
Zakas, Nicholas, 124, 222
Zepto, 100
    information sources, 106, 221
zoom level, user control over, 49
zoomed-out view, 48

The Electronic Frontier Foundation (EFF) is the leading organization defending civil liberties in the digital world. We defend free speech on the Internet, fight illegal surveillance, promote the rights of innovators to develop new digital technologies, and work to ensure that the rights and freedoms we enjoy are enhanced — rather than eroded — as our use of technology grows.

EFF.ORG

ELECTRONIC FRONTIER FOUNDATION

Protecting Rights and Promoting Freedom on the Electronic Frontier

The Modern Web is set in New Baskerville, TheSansMono Condensed, Futura, and Dogma.

This book was printed and bound at Edwards Brothers Malloy in Ann Arbor, Michigan. The paper is 60# Williamsburg Smooth, which is certified by the Sustainable Forestry Initiative (SFI). The book uses a RepKover binding, in which the pages are bound together with a cold-set, flexible glue and the first and last pages of the resulting book block are attached to the cover with tape. The cover is not actually glued to the book's spine, and when open, the book lies flat and the spine doesn't crack.

UPDATES

Visit *http://nostarch.com/modernweb/* for updates, errata, and other information.